Endorsements

180 Your Life is like finding a compass for the uncharted territories that come from losing a loved one. As a widow, I worked through the pages of this guide, and I applied the practical life principles you will find at the end of each chapter. *It was transformative!* If you have experienced loss, then grab this book and allow the pages to chart your course to healing and restoration.

—Julie Stewart Griffis
widowed 10 months, Mother of 3

180 Your Life offers practical steps to get us moving physically, emotionally, and spiritually. This book helps us discover that God can handle our anger and disappointment, and that when we trust Him, He comes through again and again. I know that many who are grieving will benefit from Mishael's wisdom. I know that those who lovingly walk alongside the grieving will also learn so much.

—Susanne Fatigati
widowed 23 years, Pastor of Care Ministry, Buckhead Church
in Atlanta, Georgia

As a Pastor, I find this book to be the best resource on grieving and overcoming emotional and spiritual pain. Mishael provides tools for healing as well as a practical plan to effectively move forward. This book is a must-read for anyone experiencing the deep pain of loss. I recommend *180 Your Life* as the best curriculum for any small group dealing with grief and healing.

—Dan Plourde
Senior Pastor, Calvary Chapel Jupiter Beach, Florida

As a ministry leader, it truly excites me to be able now to give my grieving people this empathetic compass as a year-long guide after trauma. Mishael Porembski speaks like a seasoned sister, who has been where no one would choose to go and charted a powerful path through the treacherous terrain of devastating loss. As practical as it is poetic, this curriculum not only inspires, but insists on hope. It's a compassionate but firm hand that strengthens every part of the grief-stricken life, including finances, fitness, and friendships. It's real. It's raw. And it's brilliant in a way that begs the question, "Why hasn't anyone thought of this before?"

180 Your Life is an authentic perspective of how challenging dealing with the sudden and unexpected loss of a spouse can be. Mishael takes the reader on her own personal journey to the depths of depression and then shares her inspirational story of how she was able to regain her passion for life and even find more purpose than before the tragedy. This is a must-read book for anyone dealing with losing a spouse as well as those who are close to someone who has recently gone through such grief.

Time does not heal all wounds. It just gives you a few more seconds before the loss begins again each day. How is it possible to rebuild from so much grief? Mishael Porembski survived this harsh, tilted world and will show you the way out. Her book is a blueprint for something you need as badly as rebuilding — a cry of joy and not pain.

The greatest stories are shaped by our most challenging moments. Mishael is an example of great triumph after tragedy. You will be inspired by her resilience and reminded of our call to love and care for widows and the bereaved in our community. I believe in Mishael and her important message.

Mishael has opened her heart, her soul, her grief, in order to serve you and me. She describes her "epic, emotional disaster" with humility and humor. If you are experiencing your own trauma, or know someone who is, this book is a must-read. It is a beautifully practical work of love, and is filled with helpful insights and information.

—Robert Fountain
Founder and Senior Pastor of Calvary Chapel Miami Beach, Chaplain with the Miami Division of the FBI and the Miami Beach Police Department

Most women I know have been touched by devastating loss in one way or another. We all need an arsenal of tools for recovery. Mishael's book focuses on the most positive and efficient path to wellness and conveys the courage and strength to survive and thrive!

—Ingrid Noerenberg
Single Mom of 3 teenagers

180 Your Life's year-long grief empowerment plan provides a practical, healthy roadmap to recovery from trauma or loss. Mishael presents the wisdom needed to restore a healthier order to this sacred time of grief. I strongly recommend this beautiful work. It's an incredible read.

—Amy Billingsley, MS, LPC
Covenant Counseling and Consulting

Mishael Porembski allows us into her journey through one of the greatest tragedies in life—that of losing a spouse. I longed for someone to understand the depth of my pain, and to give me hope for the days ahead. Mishael provides the guidance and direction needed to survive grief and to ultimately turn tragedy into triumph.

—Lori McNamara
widowed 15 months, Founder of 320 Ministries International

I joined Team Lady 180 seeking friendship with women who understood my grief. Being a part of such a supportive group was life-changing for me. *180 Your Life* is the blueprint of positive steps that really worked to strengthen the widows of our team and help us craft a fun and adventurous "New Normal."

—Natalie Simmons
Army widow 12 years, Mother of 3 sons, and one of the original members of Team Lady 180

180 YOUR LIFE
From Tragedy to
TRIUMPH

A Woman's Grief Guide

MISHAEL POREMBSKI,
Bethany Rutledge,
Ilana Katz, MS, RD, CCSD,
Bridget Heneghan, PhD

Cover photo by photographer Justyna Kawiak, (Justynakawiak.me).

Mishael Porembski's author photo by Atlanta-based photographer, Matt Sims of City Light Productions (GoCityLight.com)

Photos of Team Lady 180 and flamenco photo of Mishael by Asheville-based photographer Gina Palermo of Promotion Online (PromotionOnline.biz)

Front cover compass graphic by Loveleen Kaur of Kaazuclip (Creativemarket.com/Kaazuclip) Front and back cover flower graphic by Loveleen Kaur of Kaazuclip (Creativemarket.com/Kaazuclip)

Front and back cover design by Michele Slobin at Gryphon Design Strategy (gryphondesignstrategy.com)

www.xulonpress.com

Disclaimer

This book contains the opinions and ideas of its authors. It is solely for informational and educational purposes and should not be regarded as a substitute for professional medical treatment. The nature of your body's health condition is complex and unique. Therefore, you should consult a health professional before you begin any new exercise, nutrition, or supplemental program, or if you have questions about your health.

Neither the authors nor the publisher shall be liable or responsible for any loss or damage allegedly arising from any information or suggestion in this book.

Any similarity between the names and stories of individuals described in this book to individuals known by the readers is purely coincidental.

The statements in this book about consumable products or food have not been evaluated by the Food and Drug Administration. The authors or publisher are not responsible for your specific health or allergy needs that may require medical supervision.

Any recipes in this book are to be followed exactly as written. The authors or publisher are not responsible for any adverse reaction to the consumption of food or products that have been suggested in this book.

While the authors have made every effort to provide accurate telephone numbers and Internet addresses at the time of publication, neither the publisher nor the authors assume any responsibility for the errors or the changes that may occur after publication.

Other books in this series:

180 Your Life from Tragedy to Triumph: A Woman's Grief Guide

180 Your Life from Tragedy to Triumph: A Facilitator's Guide

180 Your Life from Tragedy to Triumph: A Personal Study Guide & Journal

Learn more at 180YourLife.com

Dedication

To my father, Jan, you are the most excellent father and grandfather that a daughter and granddaughters could ever ask for. You never put limits on us, teaching your girls to fly ever stronger and higher. You are my mentor, my friend, my coach, my example, and my hero.

To my mother, Thea, though you await us in heaven, your joy and adventurous spirit live on within us. I am so thankful that I had you as an example for a mom. We love you always.

To my late husband, Jason, I will always love you and am deeply thankful for you. See you at the finish. As we said in our wedding years ago, "Many waters cannot quench love, nor can rivers drown it..." (Song of Solomon 8:7 NLT).

To my daughters, Arie and Sophia, your unwavering love, profound faith, and sheer joy drove me to discover a way to join in your celebration of life and to revel in your laughter together enjoying this Grand Adventure. You are my heart-song, my Magnum Opus, my inspiration, and my daily effervescence. To be such a powerful source of hope at such a young age, my Daughters, is truly a gift from God. May you always rely on His faithfulness and so let His dawn of love and hope shine ever brighter through your lives. I love you dearly and am so proud of the powerful young women you already are.

Acknowledgements

T his book is the result of many hands working together to craft beauty from ashes. Many gifts of time and expertise have been given in honor of Jason to tell this story. Friends, colleagues, neighbors, widows, single moms, and family members all "cleaning the bricks" of our family's broken dreams and repurposing the pain into a bridge of hope for others. Thank you to each person we know that has supported us on this journey of renewal.

To my father, Jan Porembski, now at eighty-one years of age: Thank you for using every inch of your life with purpose, even after a stroke. You are the continual nudge behind this book saying, "You can do it. Don't give up." Thank you, Daddy, for being a very present grandfather figure to my children after our loss. You are a towering example of an honorable man, an inspiring mentor, and the power of loving fatherhood. My girls and I are forever shaped by you, our loving Papa.

To my editor, contributing writer, and neighbor, Bridget Heneghan, PhD, whom we simply call Bridget. As neighbors, you and your family walked alongside my family as we healed. Then my idea grew into a book…this book. Not only are you a highly accomplished author and editor, you are a faithful friend, a giving soul, and a hilarious person to be around. Bridget, you took my words and ideas, expertly cleaned them, and built them together with the touch of a master craftswoman. You helped forge words into purpose and believed in this project with your time and talent for years, even when I had nothing to give you but gratitude. What a truly empowering gift you have given us. I can never thank you enough.

To Dawn Davidson, a wildly talented graphic artist and long-time friend: I am so honored that as an adult who lost her father during childhood, you befriended me after the loss of my husband. Your example gave me real hope that my children would not only survive, but beautifully thrive after loss. I am astounded at the visual beauty you bring to these pages from your own deep understanding of loss. Thank you, Dawn, for sharing your brilliant graphic talent to help others visualize the transformational hope that can be found in the journey of grief.

To Jyn Hall and her husband Steve Keck: I am so thankful for our long-term friendship, which started as couple-friends with Jason and me. Thank you, Jyn and Steve, for fearlessly wading into my trauma after Jason died, sleeping at my house, watching movies, ordering pizza, and infusing laughter and understanding into the epicenter of my Ground Zero. Thank you, Jyn, for being there for the birth of my second daughter, Sophia, and now for using your expertise as a producer to oversee the companion teaching videos for this book. (*180YourLife.com*).

To Frank Bocchino: Thank you so much for lending your expertise in screenwriting to help me communicate a clear, effective message. I am so very thankful for your encouragement, writing expertise, and kind friendship.

To Kate Atwood, founder of Kate's Club: I sincerely thank you and your phenomenal staff, including Lane Pease, Emily Brenner Hawkins, Debra Brook, and the rest of your excellent staff, for bringing real hope and healing into our lives after loss. Kate's Club (KatesClub.org) has brought the wonder of childhood and the companionship of understanding friends into our family's grief journey. Thank you, Kate, for helping us heal and for empowering my children and myself to love life again.

To Julia Edmunds Booher and Michele Casey of Athleta apparel: Thank you for being the first business to believe in our mission of empowering bereaved women and for sponsoring our first triathlon team of widows.

To Carolyn Moore and Mary Hines-Bone of Modern Widows Club (ModernWidowsClub.org). I believe it takes a village to heal a heart. I love being connected to powerful women who are working to do good in their community. Modern Widows Club is a complementary resource to my ladies of Team Lady 180, and I am so thankful for the sister-circle of widowhood that joins us together.

To Donald Newman of Xulon Press: A huge thanks to Don and your team at Xulon who are skilled professionals and also available to talk, inspire, and counsel me on next steps as an author. I am so grateful that you believed in my vision from the start. I feel privileged to have found a publishing house whose chief concern was helping me craft a message of hope.

To Dr. Larry Keefauver, the developmental editor of the workbook questions and leadership guide, and consultant on this book: I am so grateful for your time, dedication, expert insight, and wise counsel during this writing process. I am a better writer for having known you, and I hope to work with you again and again.

To Michele Slobin, my sister-from-another-mother since I was a girl: Thank you, Michele, for supporting me as a dear friend on this grief journey and for using your extensive design expertise to create the cover and the creative content of the two websites, TeamLady180.com and 180YourLife.com. (GryphonDesignStudios.com).

To Gina Palermo: Thank you, Gina, my dear friend, for empowering our journey with your long-time friendship, love, and expert talents of professional photography, content development, and media consultation in support of Team Lady 180 and this book. (PromotionOnline.biz).

To Mike Wein, Vice President of the National USAT board and my mentor: Thank you, Mike, for empowering me to find my voice, supporting this project, and asking the insightful questions that helped me discover my specific edge in helping others. (SpecificEdge.com).

To James Herron: Thank you for your quick response to my father's stroke, helping save his life. Your timely aid gave the priceless and precious gift of time to my girls and me with my dad, their grandfather. It is because my father had to come to live with us after his stroke, and so encouraged me every day since to write, that this book exists.

To James D'Elena and his generous team at Flood Student Ministries: Thank you for being the hands and feet of Jesus in our lives. Thank you for helping my family in a practical way through your "Widows' Watch" initiative. My daughters and I are so very thankful for the help of your students, leaders, and staff in helping me as a widowed mom with essential repairs around my home. (FloodStudentMissions.org).

To Jeff Shinabarger, founder of Plywood People: I offer my sincere thanks to you and your excellent team at Plywood People (PlywoodPeople.com), who have given me wise counsel, and insight to help empower the bereaved toward healthy grief recovery.

To the amazing business support team of Hank Venter and Laura Lee Blake: Thank you for your insight, wisdom, and encouragement in such practical ways to make this project a reality.

To Christina & Rob Loud: Thank you so much for your amazing friendship and expert business support. Your support behind the scenes makes all the difference.

To Bethany Rutledge: thank you for your time, dedication, insight, and heart to help others become strong and healthy through training. I am so grateful to know you as an excellent coach, and also that you have added your expertise to these pages.

To Jim and Vicki Boylan, founders of Atlanta Tri Club: Thank you for partnering with Team Lady 180 to provide training discounts and scholarships to widowed and single-parent families in need. Thank you for also providing scholarships for my children to train for triathlons. We love your heart to empower grieving families.

To Tara McLain: Thank you for donating your time to be the first trainer of Team Lady 180. We so appreciate your dedication and your heart to empower grieving families. We love you, Coach Tara!

To Alison Chandler: Thank you for donating your graphic talents to create the logo for Team Lady 180. I am so honored to work with a fellow widow who is so inspirational, generous, and talented. Thank you! (AlisonChandler.com).

To Rabbi Kevin Solomon: Thank you for your sage advice, kind support of our family, and for being a source of wisdom and understanding in Jewish belief and culture in these pages.

A special thanks to those who have allowed me to share their stories, to those whose full names are used, and for their comments to this book: All of you are such an inspiration to me.

Lori Apon: I really appreciate your mentorship and wise widowhood. You will always be "Queen Widowed Mom" to me.

Scott Rigsby: Thank you for your friendship, insight, and living inspiration. I am so honored to know you and call you friend.

Latonya Pringle: Thank you for trusting me and being one of the original eight members of Team Lady 180 only one year out from losing your husband. I am so honored that you started your journey with us, amazed by your growth, and so thankful that we are friends.

Natalie Simons: Thank you for also being one of the original eight members of Team Lady 180 and for your continual support. I am always awed by your wisdom and joyful spirit. I am so thankful that you ground me because you have been on this widowed journey longer than I.

Kimberly Guinn: Thank you for being my friend and for being such an inspirational widow. I am so proud of your IRONMAN 70.3, only 12 months after you tragically lost your husband, and for your indomitable spirit. I am honored that you shared your story in this book.

Michelle Menifee: I am so honored that you are part of Team Lady 180 so soon after losing your amazing husband. I love watching your growth in love, faith, and hope in the face of tragedy. Thank you for your contributions to this book.

To the host of friends and family, both locally and virtually: your continued support of my daughters and me has been an incredibly tangible testimony of God's love in our lives. We could not have healed as healthfully without you.

To Glenna and Jim McKivergan (from Dr. Bridget McKivergan Heneghan): you deserve an entire paragraph for your wonderful, never-ending support. You have shown me all the sides of strength. I am so grateful for your presence in my life.

To the incomparable, indomitable, tenacious, and hilarious posse of wonder widows and, now, super single moms that make up two Team Lady 180 groups: Your support and friendship, humor, and drive have infused purpose and joy into our loss. I am so thankful for my team of gal pals that make our life a wild, wonderful, and soulful ride.

To Dr. Nik DelFavero, and the amazing team at 1st Choice Sports Rehab Center, LLC: Thank you for your amazing support of this book and your excellent care that enabled me to swim again.

To the amazing attorneys of Duane Morris LLP, Tony Sanacory, Chris Winter, and Kelly Whiteheart: Thank you for your time, support, and dedication as attorneys who are willing to help create and sustain my nonprofit, 180 Your Grief, Inc., the parent company of Team Lady 180. Thank you for your dedication to innovation and empowerment for grieving families by contributing your legal expertise. I have never known better or more generous lawyers.

To Ben Walker: thank you for being such a wonderful support to our family. We love you, "Colonel."

To Ginger Garrett: a very accomplished author in her own right. Thank you for taking time to simply be my friend during my first months and years after I lost my husband. I will never forget that day as I spoke of my overwhelming grief while at your kitchen table. I will always remember when you looked into my eyes and said, "When do you stop asking the question 'Why' and get to the business of 'How?'" I never forgot your gentle challenge to focus on *how* I wanted to live today and *how* I wanted my family to move forward in healing. Ginger, you inspired me to try my first triathlon, which became a powerful theme in our family and with the bereaved women of Team Lady 180. This book, my friend, is the answer to your question. This book is my "How."

Table of Contents

Preface
Why You Should Read This Book

*How do you craft your new normal when life has been shattered
by hardship?*

*Grief is transformative. How it changes you, though, is your decision.
When you learn how to harness the power of grief, allowing the
pain to add purpose to your life, the result is a life you could never
have imagined.*

*This is the book I wish I could have read as I navigated my new life as
a pregnant widow, giving birth two months after my husband's death,
and then grieving the loss of my mother three months later. I didn't
want platitudes or casseroles. I longed for real hope.*

*The Eight Steps, from empowering your ground zero of grief, forging
your team, training your mind, body, and spirit, crossing your finish
line, living your legacy, and unveiling your triumph, provide a
practical roadmap to transfigure your grief journey from tragedy
to triumph.*

- Mishael Porembski

Introduction

G rief can be messy. Navigating the splintered remains after a traumatic loss is overwhelming. It's like wading through the wreckage of a flood disaster site, or picking through the decimated remains of your home after a Category Five hurricane, or living in the hollowed-out shell of an apartment building in a war zone. Trauma can bring with it a raw, naked, painful, isolating, and nightmarish existence. None of it is pretty or clean. None of it goes away by itself.

My own story is complicated, tangled—and more than a little frightening for me to tell. After my husband died, I learned which stories to pack away neatly into the dark recesses of our attic and which to display proudly on our mantel. It would be so easy, Dear Reader, to share a cup of tea with you and show you my mantel, with all my lovely family photos, remembering our accounts of hope and inspiration.

That would be the safe thing to do.
While some of those stories are important,
I know something else is also needed.

When I was in my own Ground Zero of grief, what I desperately craved was the transparency of those who were further along on the same journey. I needed to know that my family and I would really survive such a deep laceration of the soul. I craved a practical, healthy process of recovery, and a friendship with those who understood the loss my children and I were so desperately trying to live with. My daughters and I needed a supportive community of those who knew how to successfully slog into severely broken dreams and emerge transformed on the other side.

Just a few weeks after my husband, Jason, died, a person I call a "Pay It Forward Widow" came to my house. Both Sandy and her ten-year-old daughter were poised, light-hearted, and beautiful. In another room, her child played with my toddler, Arie (then almost three years old), while I talked with my new sister in widowhood. After a few minutes of chatting, I cut to the chase.

"How did your husband die?" I quietly asked her.

"He shot himself," she softly replied.

I sat back, stunned. As odd as this may sound, that moment gave me genuine hope. Why? Because I knew she understood me and the intense pain of surviving suicide. Not only that, the way she was living her life was strong, elegant, and empowered. Her daughter appeared well-adjusted and engaged as she played with my toddler. This child and her mother were living examples of triumph after loss.

By sharing her transparent truth with me, Sandy helped to set me free from the fear that my life, as well as the life of my family, was figuratively over. It wasn't over. We were deeply wounded, but there was vibrant hope to be had. I am so thankful for Sandy and for other men and women like her, who boldly and generously shared their messy, intimate stories with me. In them, I found companionship and empowerment for my own journey as a woman, a mother, and now, a widow.

So, for this adventure that we are about to take together, I must go into our attic and unpack our raw stories for you, the ones that have been neatly tucked away. The purpose behind being transparent through these stories is to give practical hope to those who are grieving and insight to those who walk alongside the grieving, to help them understand the scope of that loss in a more compassionate and effective way.

Some accounts don't bring out the best in those I know, myself included. The desire of my heart is never to hurt those I love and cherish, but that might happen anyway. My children are incredibly important to me, as are my extended family and friendships. Losing a loved one is so excruciating that words fall flat when trying to describe the pain, but the loss is only the very beginning of an arduous process. It was an uphill battle to reestablish peace, in both my home and my soul. To those who are close to us, I ask that you please forgive me if

I offend you in any way and understand my intention as I purpose to use what was painful and make it a helpful recovery tool for others.

When I became a widow, a terrible tsunami of grief washed over my soul. I will warn you; I was enraged with God. I was angry, overwhelmed, and deeply wounded. I wouldn't leave my faith, and I knew instinctively that my spirit needed healing, but my trust in God was shattered. In the midst of my heartache, I chafed at the thought of God as a "Heavenly Husband." I stared blankly at those who said God loved me. I secretly wondered if God and my faith in Him were practical enough to truly help me out of the deep, dark place I now found myself in. I wanted real answers to real pain.

Some people of faith have an ability to be at peace with God right at the epicenter of their Ground Zero of Grief. They can tap immediately into that peace that passes all understanding. These people have always fascinated me. I wish I were one of them. Personally, I did not come to peace with God for a long time, and this book will reflect that process, which I hope will benefit you. My desire is that as you read what I have learned over the past eight years, these lessons will spark healing in your body, mind, and spirit, and even more—a triumph and transformation in your life.

Soon after my husband died, I read a quote from *A Grace Disguised: How the Soul Grows through Loss,* by Jerry L. Sittser. The author tells an allegorical story in which a man does not want the night to come, so he chases the setting sun. Therefore, this man will always be running. The man in the story exhausts himself trying to cling to a light and a life that has dimmed. He wants to preserve his former life and resist the change that loss requires. Sittser writes, "The quickest way for anyone to reach the sun and the light of day is not to run west, chasing after the setting sun, but to head east, plunging into the darkness until one comes to the sunrise."[1]

That story set my course as a widow, and it will start our journey together as well. This book is the real account of my decision to turn into the "night" of my grief and walk doggedly through the pain and questions my husband's death ignited in my life. I chose to face my pain, because I believed that the sun would eventually rise again. As I kept moving forward in the darkness, I trusted that the dawn was coming, and it has. It was an entirely different day, but a good, beautiful day nonetheless. Hope, like the sun, does not disappoint us.

I did not walk perfectly. I did not accept theological answers to my grief just because I knew I should. Instead, I swept away my framed preconceptions, like an enraged woman would swipe all the family pictures off her table, leaving a shattered mess. My faith was stripped bare, to its imperfect core. The process was wildly uncomfortable, but its stunning result has been a truer encounter with God. However, that didn't happen quickly. Not by a long shot.

My experience has been that dynamic healing happens from a holistic approach. I felt stronger when I learned to exercise and nourish my body properly, which calmed my nerves and helped me sleep. More rested, I was better able to make wise decisions for my family and myself. Forging a community that understood our loss helped my family find practical support. Choosing prayer and faith—even enraged prayer and faith, changed me, and eventually helped heal my spirit.

I have divided the process into Eight Steps, beginning with Ground Zero and the decisions that must be made within that maelstrom of emotions, and ending with the "New Normal" of a life transformed into triumph. Each step has helped bring health and peace to my daily life, and has pulled me out of the confusion and into more mindful choices. *Transforming tragedy into triumph* requires that we create a support system of practical help and wise counsel to see us through our everyday trials. It calls for mental, physical, and spiritual exercise to create peaceful environments for our families, to nourish our bodies for optimal health, and to draw supernatural strength to meet life's challenges. This process needs concrete successes, such as crossing the finish line of a race, to propel us forward on our adventure. It demands that we thoughtfully craft our lives in order to empower others, which becomes our legacy.

I consider the grief process to be a journey—and one that doesn't end, but rather works in cycles. That's why the book doesn't end with a finish line. Even crossing the finish line is just part of a never-ending process that calls for constant renewal and constant movement—just like the journey to the sunrise, which bestows its beauty like a revelation each and every day.

My own journey has been at times sporadic or roundabout, so you will find that my stories are not presented chronologically, but rather as they can best illustrate the life lessons I most needed at specific times.

It took me many years to find my way to a better life, and part of my purpose in this book is to offer you a more efficient path to recovery.

To that end, I conclude each chapter with boiled-down versions of both hopeful wisdom and practical tips that are designed to help you on your journey. I also offer a more in-depth study guide and video class featuring the contributing writers, experts, and various persons mentioned in this book. I encourage you to use these resources individually, with a friend, or with a support group. You can find these resources online at 180YourLife.com. These guides are also designed to empower you to leverage your pain into a purposeful teaching tool, and in that process, help others as well.

A "Speak Life" section will end each of the eight steps on our journey. These short sections are meant to literally speak life into your circumstances. There is great power in the spoken word. I will get into the story of Ezekiel in the "Team" section, regarding his vision of speaking life into the dried bones of the battlefield, and so calling forth a mighty army. I encourage you to say this short section out loud, speaking life into your own circumstances and your heart, and asking God to breathe new life into you.

As a Christian on my own transformational journey through grief, I sought wisdom from far and wide, including the Bible and the Jewish roots of my faith. For example, there were times that my Jewish friends added insight into grief processing from their own traditions. I found that information inspiring, and so have included those insights.

Typically, in Jewish tradition, when someone dies, the body is buried within three days. Then family members engage in several stages of mourning. Each stage has its own characteristics and varies in length based on the relation of the mourner to the deceased. However, each stage is accompanied by the Mourner's Kaddish, which is a hymn of praise to God that inspires and encourages those who are grieving. Depending on the relation, this recitation can continue through the twelfth month.

In most American Jewish communities, at the one-year anniversary of the loved one's passing, a special "Unveiling" of the tombstone occurs (Matzevah). At this ceremony, the headstone is installed at the burial site, and this second memorial serves as a celebration of the one who passed and a way to empower the living to turn towards life. Because I found this ritual so helpful personally, I have crafted this book around that timeline. It is broken into twenty-four chapters, or two per month, totaling twelve months of life-affirming activities, including an unveiling ceremony at the end of this course: in essence, a kind of grief liturgy of our own.[2]

Of course, I am not suggesting that you only have one year to grieve your loss. Grief is the flipside of love, and love is eternal. I have been told that you should not make any major life decisions within the first year after a tragedy. The one decision you must repeatedly make, however, is towards life. This is the time, then, to reset your vision, take control, build a fun support community, and actively embrace your new life.

This lifestyle is the lasting legacy I choose out of our family's loss. This is the way I honor the life of Jason, my husband and father of my children. He was a chiropractic doctor focused on healing during his life, so it is a fitting tribute that the journey after his passing should help others heal as well. Though my story is messy, it is my hopeful gift from my family to yours.

If you are interested in taking this raw adventure with me, then, let's turn together from running after the setting sun, and plunge deep into the night, trekking together toward the light of dawn.

Empower your
Ground Zero

Step 1:
Empower Your Ground Zero

Forget the former things; do not dwell on the past.
See, I am doing a new thing! Now it springs up; do you not perceive it?
I am making a way in the wilderness and streams in the wasteland.
(Isaiah 43:18-19)

Streams in the Desert

In the Okavango Delta of the Kalahari Desert in southern Africa, waters from the short rainy season meander along nearly flat streams and riverbeds. These waters flood the desert and miraculously transfigure 4,000 square miles of arid plains into a vast paradise. The desert magnificently becomes a verdant grassland on which millions of animals depend for food and survival.

Not long ago, I was watching a BBC documentary about this phenomenon called "The Great Flood,"[3] and thinking of Isaiah 43:19, "I am making a way in the wilderness and streams in the desert." I had always believed that verse to be symbolic—a poetic claim that good will eventually come of bad. As I watched, I realized that God refreshes our bodies as well as our spirits. This example showed me that He creates physical as well as spiritual gifts, played out on both a grand and humble scale.

I was astounded as I watched the basin of the Okavango, shaped like a huge hand, flood the scorched land around it, and the resulting life that came bursting forth. When the cracked desert transformed into a lush grassland, the parched life of the wasteland faded into the past. There was a whole new way of life taking place. The animals eagerly abandoned their relentless search for water in the dusty African veldt. Instead, they splashed, ate, and leapt with joy.

The most interesting segment of the documentary highlighted the journey of the elephants, considered the most resourceful animals of the Kalahari Desert. Led by a wise, older matriarch, these elephant families walk for months in search of fresh water. As the desert becomes its most desolate, with fires consuming what little grasses are left, the elephants press deeper into the heart of the parched land. They know the water is coming.

The matriarch leads her family along ancient paths to the annual floodwaters. On their trek, these purposeful pachyderms make passages in the wilderness that buffalos and zebras follow. Herds of animals trust the ability of the elephants to find the flood land. On their way to the floodwaters, the elephants trek through desert woodlands and snap off dry tree branches and bark, eating them for their miniscule living-water content. Elephants must drink water every three days, so when they arrive at a muddy waterhole in the desert, they skim the surface with their trunks for a sip of clean water. Even the mud has a use, acting as a sunscreen and insect repellant. The elephants don't stay at the muddy hole, however. Instead, knowing fresh water is coming, they press onward.

Their arrival has to be perfectly timed. Remarkably, the elephant families arrive in the heart of the desert just as the floodwaters overflow the banks of the Okavango basin. Refreshing 4,000 square miles with life-giving water is a process. First, the dry riverbeds fill, and then pools are formed, which draw many animals. The pools overflow into streams throughout the land. Finally, when the streams overflow, the fields are flooded for thousands of miles around, providing nutrient-rich grasses that feed millions of creatures.

The person who has suffered in the desert best understands thirst. C. S. Lewis writes, "As the desert first teaches men to love water, or as absence first reveals affection," so also does our loss most insistently focus our attention on what we most need.[4] Jesus addresses this thirst for the woman at the well, saying, "Whoever drinks the water I give them will never thirst. Indeed, the water I give them will become in them a spring of water welling up to eternal life" (John 4:14).

For me, the drought came on suddenly. It was as if an asteroid had burnt the landscape and left me without sustenance. My desert spread to the horizon, and I wandered in it for several years searching for relief. It wasn't until I stopped trying to escape the wasteland that I could finally pause, lift my head, and look around. Only then was I able to see, in the sand of the desert, the footprints and paths, the fellow creatures, the occasional oases, and finally, the signs of growth.

What if, like those wise elephants, we press into the desert of our grief as a strong family unit, traveling ancient paths to the source of Living Water? In doing so, we know that though we feel parched and our wise decisions splinter and crunch like dried branches and bark in our mouths, we will still press forward in purpose and hope. We will believe, like the elephants, this desert of grief will miraculously transform into a lush grassland teeming with life. We will persevere on the path toward the miraculous Okavango, like the hand of God, knowing it will overflow at its appointed time to refresh our souls.

Will you choose to start the journey
trusting that one day the dry, parched places of your life
will dramatically become green and teeming with life again?

Chapter 1:

Ground Zero

Every act of creation is also an act of destruction.
- Einstein

If that is true, then every act of destruction is also an act of creation.
- Mishael Porembski

I opened my front door to a tall, blond, fair-skinned man, handsomely dressed in dark slacks, white shirt, and an intricately patterned tie. Jason was answering an advertisement for a housemate I had posted at the local college. He was getting his doctorate degree in chiropractic medicine at Life University. He was smiling, handsome in a Pastor-Joel-Osteen kind of way. I usually go for the dark and swarthy type. If I had met a guy who looked like a pirate with a goatee, all the better. Jason was nothing like that. He looked like a strapping accountant from Germany. I figured, "I'll never fall in love with you," so I eventually agreed to let him rent a room in my house.

It was easy enough at first. He was a clean housemate. He cooked and even fixed the toilet. As time went on, I started to see past his Western European coloring and clean-cut exterior. He became my best friend. It was fun to hang out with him. He had a great sense of humor, and we were always laughing. I was falling in love, which was awful. He was the best housemate I'd ever had, and I didn't want to mess up our situation by dating him.

Even though it was a difficult choice, we eventually decided that it would be best if he moved out so we could date in a way that resonated with our Christian faith. Eighteen months later, Jason carried me over the threshold back into our home, now as my husband.

Unbeknownst to him, I had decided I wanted to marry him one day when we were on a roller coaster. Jason had brought me to one of the mega-coasters at Six Flags over Georgia. He was like a kid in a candy store. He was determined to ride in the very front seat of the coaster, unshielded from every twist and turn this terror-on-rails had to offer. I was horrified, but wanting to please him, I reluctantly agreed to sit beside him.

As I white-knuckled the safety bar in a frozen silent scream, we plummeted from ungodly heights to the depths below and then swooped up to wild twists and turns. It was then that I noticed something about him. He laughed into every turn. He put his hand over my white knuckles, looked into my eyes, and laughed as we rode this coaster. His smile was infectious, and eventually, I was nervously laughing, too. It was then that I decided that I would be his. I loved a man who could laugh into the twists and turns of life.

In 2003, I became pregnant with our first daughter, Arie. On a new adventure, we moved to Costa Rica. Jason opened a chiropractic clinic there, and I gave birth at Hospital Clínica Católica in San José, Costa Rica. However, Costa Rica didn't agree with my husband, so we ended up moving back to the US and settling near his family.

Then, in January of 2007, I was four months pregnant with our second daughter when we moved to Cumming, Georgia, so he could open a chiropractic office there. It had been a stressful time for us. We were moving hundreds of miles from family, starting a new business, had an active toddler, and I was pregnant. To add to the stress, our business ventures had severely strapped our finances, and a dear relative of Jason's died within that year. Life was very busy.

Jason had begun taking long naps during the day and acting short-tempered, which was unusual behavior for him. Thinking this was because of the pressure he felt opening a new business, I tried to help with his work and plan fun family outings to relieve the pressure. Looking back, I now know he was much more stressed than I realized.

March 28, 2007, was a crisp, sunny day. Jason looked handsome in his immaculate suit, dressed for an important business meeting with a chiropractic-consulting firm in Chattanooga. Just before he left, he looked deep into my eyes, told me he loved me, and pulled me into a tender kiss goodbye. We agreed we would see each other later that night. He left the house before I did.

I decided to spend the day at the Georgia Aquarium with Arie, who was three months away from her third birthday. I was excited because she had just successfully potty trained, and I was thrilled to be off of diaper duty—for a short time, at least. I drove to the Marta station, thinking Arie would enjoy riding the train into downtown Atlanta.

Throughout the day I tried calling my husband. We always liked touching base when we were apart. My calls kept going straight to voicemail, which was a bit unusual. I thought maybe he needed some time to think during his drive to Chattanooga.

When I arrived home that evening, his car was not in the driveway. I walked in the front door and saw an envelope simply marked "Wife" on the entryway table. "Wife? That sounds rather clinical," I thought. I opened it. The note said that he needed time by himself and that he would be back in about three days.

A feeling like a high voltage electric shock went through my body. I realized I didn't know where he was and I couldn't reach him. I started shaking all over, and felt in my bones that this was very bad. I tried calling him. He had turned off his phone, so I left multiple messages. Really scared now, I called his family, asking if they knew where he was. They didn't. There was a sinking feeling in the pit of my stomach. This behavior was totally out of character for him. *Where was my husband?*

Calling some friends, weeping, I drove with my daughter over to their house to spend the night. The three days that he mentioned in his note turned into five. Over the course of those days, I called everyone we knew and looked anywhere I thought he might be. I called the police—a drastic step, since doing so made my fears official. Because he had left a note stating he would be gone for three days, the police told me that as an adult he would not be considered a missing person until twenty-four hours past the time he said he would be back.

Burning Questions

On the fifth day, Monday, I received a note from Jason that spanned two postcards and said, "I will be home by the time you get this, but I wanted you to know how much I love you." He went on to say that he was sorry for the pain he had caused me, that he was ill-equipped for camping, and that he couldn't wait to see me and our daughter again.

I was relieved to get the postcards and anxious for him to come home. One sentence kept nagging at me as I took a shower that night and got ready for bed: "I will be home by the time you get this, *but* I wanted to let you know how much I love you."

My mind was like a roulette wheel. It was so hard to keep it from spinning and repeatedly settling on certain details. If he was supposed to be home by the time I got the postcards, then where was he? We usually got our mail at around 5:00 p.m. It was already 7:30 p.m. Why wasn't he home yet? Could "home" have a different meaning in his note? In church, we call heaven our home. No, I didn't want to think about that, so I just forced myself to wait.

He did not come home that night. In the morning, I tried calling his cell phone again. I had already called so often that I had maxed out his voice mailbox. My calls had been going straight to his voicemail. This time, though, I didn't get the canned greeting. I got ringing. I was so flustered that I quickly hung up.

What would I say to him when he picked up? I wanted to kiss him and punch him in the arm for the gamut of emotions I had gone through since he left. Mostly, I just wanted him back.

Then my cell phone rang. It was Tuesday morning, April 3, 2007, around 9:00 a.m. Jason had been gone six days. I took a deep breath and answered. We would sort it out.

I didn't expect the voice at the other end. "This is the Union County sheriff's office. Do you know Jason Ramke?"

My stomach seemed to drop into my feet.

"Yes, I do," I said, stunned. *Where was my husband?*

"How do you know him?" the sheriff asked.

"I am his wife. Do you know where he is? Is he all right?"

A pause.

"Yes, ma'am. I do know where he is. He died yesterday."

The distant voice told me that my husband had died of an apparent suicide by carbon monoxide poisoning in his car at a campground in the North Georgia mountains.

I just kept saying, "No. No. No. No."

I had instinctively moved away from my daughter and leaned on the doorway of our spare bedroom, near the front door of our house.

As the police officer on the phone went into the details of the carbon monoxide poisoning, I felt the room start to whirl. *This can't be happening. How can I wake up from this?*

I felt like I was going to faint. I sensed all the blood draining from my body. Just to be sure I wouldn't hurt my unborn child, I knelt on the Persian rug near our front door while the sheriff on the phone continued to explain the specifics to me. As I lay curled up on the floor with a phone to my ear, the doorbell rang. Arie, my toddler, opened the front door. I remember seeing two policemen in uniform looming over me.

Arie told them, "My mommy needs a doctor."

My mother-in-law was in town, and she quickly swept Arie away to the playset in the backyard. The policemen helped me up to the nursing chair I had set up in anticipation for the new baby. We had bought it at a yard sale, and I had recovered the old, faded pattern with happy yellow fabric with colorful polka dots.

Life didn't just stop, though I thought it most certainly would. Phone calls were made, and friends and family started to flood our house. I've heard this phase of shock called "The Cushion of Grief." There is a great deal of activity that momentarily masks the massive amputation of the soul that has suddenly taken place. Not until later, when things have quieted down, do you realize the full scope and breadth of the devastation.

Within the hour, ministers from my large church appeared in my living room to offer comfort and to plan a memorial service. This happened to be Holy Week, the week before Easter Sunday. I was told the only time to have the memorial service for Jason at our church would be in the next two days, on the Thursday before Good Friday. I had forty-eight hours to navigate family members, find a span of life pictures, locate music he liked, and write a eulogy. Forty-eight hours to put a period on the love of my life.

All the while, dear friends and family moved in a steady stream through my front door, offering hugs and condolences. Arie was hungry and wanted to play. The ministers from my church were there with clipboards trying to gently guide me through the process of planning the memorial service, which, frankly, I didn't want to do. The funeral home called. Did I want to bury or cremate? Did I want a viewing at the funeral home or just have friends coming to my house? What would I like done with his personal effects?

Pain and Parenthood

In the midst of this mayhem, Arie snagged my attention with those seven words that no parent of a toddler can fail to attend to, whether they are next in line at Disney World or on the deck of an iceberg-struck ocean liner: "I have to go to the bathroom."

She had just potty trained a few days before, and I couldn't mess with her routine now. I had no desire to add poopy diapers to this toxic mix. So, I excused myself from the crowd, got up from the couch, and joined her in our small restroom.

After she did her business and we had washed our hands, I said to her, "I have something to tell you."

She sat on the little stool in front of me while I put down the toilet seat lid and sat in front of her. Her clear, blue, trusting eyes looked up at mine from under a mop of tousled sandy blond hair.

Taking a deep breath, I said, "Something has happened to Daddy and his body stopped working. That means that his spirit has gone to heaven to be with God, and we won't see Daddy on earth anymore."

We just stared at each other for a moment.

She simply asked, "Why?"

I took another deep breath. How do I term this?

"Daddy made a mistake, and it caused his body to stop working. His body died. When that happens, when the body doesn't work anymore, our spirits go to be with God in heaven." Arie was silent for a moment.

"I want to snuggle," she said definitively.

We both walked out into the living room where the maelstrom still raged. Arie and I lay down on the couch, I wrapped Jason's bathrobe around my daughter, and we held each other.

Even in the midst of such sadness, I could feel a wave of peace as my daughter and I were connected in the middle of this chaos. For a moment, the room melted away. As I closed my eyes and felt my child snuggle close to me, together we rested.

Moments of Grace

There were many moments of grace even in the storm. The *arroz con pollo* my uncle was cooking on the stove was one of my favorite dishes, and it reminded me of the love of my Peruvian family. The presence of friends, the women who stepped up to help provide food, and the men who mowed my large lawn were all gifts of grace. Beyond that, I quickly learned that people don't really know what to say in the face of such a train wreck of the soul. I didn't know what to say either.

Raw grief is such an affront to all that seems right. It's so messy and even distasteful. It's waves of sobbing mixed with moments of rage. It feels out of control, so we want to rein it in before it leads to despair. At that moment, I didn't want anyone to try to make my loss *okay*. I didn't want to hear about how "all things work together for good." The Bible talks about grieving with those who grieve. That is a scary emotional place to go, but it's also one of the deepest gifts you can give a loved one who is grieving.

One of the people I worked with at NBC Network News, Michael, visited me on that first day. We had been on many national news stories together, traveling the southeastern United States for over eight years. He had become my Jewish brother, and I always enjoyed our talks. He had known me when I was single, and our families knew one another as I married and then had a baby. When Michael heard that Jason had died, he dropped everything and came right over.

He gave me a long hug and then sat next to me for the rest of the day. He sat in silence. He offered no platitudes. He didn't try to make it okay. He hugged me when I needed hugging and got me food when I was hungry. He simply gave his presence. I later discovered it's part of a Jewish tradition of sitting Shiva, which comes from the biblical story of Job.[5] When Job lost his home and children, his friends came to grieve with him. For the first seven days, they just sat silently with him in the dust of his devastation. There was nothing to say to make it better.

Michael didn't sit with me for seven days, but he sat for seven hours. He was simply present. He listened when I was ready to talk, and that was all. It was enough. I learned a deep lesson that day from my Jewish brother about how to grieve with those who are grieving: to simply be present, to listen, and to be ready to meet the needs of those who are hurting, on their terms. These were the highlights of the first day.

The Firestorm

The next day was preparation day. More family and friends arrived. People were taking over and helping me host. More food was prepared, and others organized activities in my home. There were family members arriving who hadn't seen one another in over twenty years, by their own choice, which added an extra element of stress to the environment. There was an abundance of motion and emotion.

I had chosen to have Jason's body cremated, so there wasn't a viewing. I thought seeing his lifeless body might be too much for me in my pregnant state. Already emotionally devastated, I didn't want to go into pre-term labor. I decided to have a wake at my home because I couldn't bring myself to go into a funeral parlor. Everyone came to my house and brought more food. Towards the end of the evening, I ended up in Arie's back bedroom chatting with a few close friends. Meanwhile, in the front of the house, some folks were having what might be termed an Irish wake. When I went to the kitchen, I noticed that people were in a very good mood, and the drinks were flowing.

This became the first time I really felt Jason's absence, not just of his person, but of his role in our family. I missed the way his personality would balance and complement mine, and I missed the team we had become. Because there is alcoholism in our family history, the socially lubricated scene was uncomfortable for me. I understand that people needed to grieve in their own way, and these folks were not destructive or belligerent at all. I didn't want drinking, even light drinking, in my house when I felt so vulnerable. I was already emotionally fragile and didn't want any kind of substance temptation in the face of such horrific loss. I needed to be on my A-game for my toddler and child-to-come, so I quietly called for an end to the evening, saying that it was time to turn in, and people soon dispersed.

In the stillness of the next morning, looking in my kitchen cabinets for breakfast food to feed my daughter, I discovered a stash of spirits, possibly ready for another night of "libation grief processing." I poured the alcohol down the drain and put the bottles on the curb, which was soon picked up by the trash service. I then calmly but firmly communicated what would and would not work for me, my daughter, and my baby-on-the-way. Our wishes were respected.

Within a day of discovering Jason's death, I found myself faced with carving out a new role for myself as the head of my little family. I strived to gently but firmly stand up for what I felt was best for me and my children. "Strive" being the operative word. I had to draw new lines that honored the peace my immediate family needed, myself included, insisting that the new boundaries be respected. I was now the sole guardian of my household and my health.

Dear Reader, I'm trying to touch on this terribly difficult time in the most productive way. In short, it was an epic, emotional disaster. It felt like one of those natural catastrophes where the National Guard gets called in and relief teams are arriving in waves and the President is declaring a State of Emergency. I was emotionally decimated, and so were those around me. I didn't behave perfectly, not even close. We were all heart-shattered and did the best we could.

Emotional Drunk Driving

I've discovered that first shock of grief can lead to a state of "emotional drunk driving"—we have little control over our moods, and the emotions can take us where they will. On the day of my husband's memorial service, we were all emotionally swerving from one side of the road to the other.

I woke up at 4 o'clock the next morning. I finally wrote the eulogy and put together a photomontage for the service. With only forty-eight hours to coordinate a memorial service, I had managed to pick out songs the first day, but had put off the other details. Somehow, I felt that writing a eulogy would make all of this too real. However, that morning at 4 a.m., the words came pouring out of me. The photo selections came together soon after. We had to leave at 10:00 for the 11:00 a.m. service.

A surviving spouse and the surviving family are not just dealing with the death of a loved one. The emotional trauma of loss can ripple out to living relationships. In the midst of the storm, you need to find the courage to make wise choices, even while grieving, in order to establish boundaries that honor your lifestyle, your health, and your home.

Lots of widow friends seem surprised that the grief at Ground Zero can be such a rocky ride for all involved. Realize that those who are grieving, especially in a traumatic loss, are all in excruciating, seemingly unending pain. Add to that, grief makes a terrible bedfellow, so everyone is probably severely sleep deprived. It's a recipe for the perfect storm. Raw grief does not always bring out the best in us. It can make us react in ways we never thought possible.

If grief and the surrounding relationships are getting too intense, step back, take the time you need to calm down, try to see things from another's perspective, and give grace when you can. Honor your boundaries when you have to. I can tell you now that taking a break during the intense storm can be as simple as going on a walk, taking time to pray (even if you are really angry), reading promises in the Bible, or going to the park for a while. If you can, make a conscious effort to nourish your body with healthy choices. I wish I could say I knew all this in my Ground Zero, but I didn't. Though, from experience, I can share these healthy steps I've since learned with you now.

Journey to the Sunrise

Discover that grieving families need time to heal. Grief is incredibly painful. In the face of loss, some families may argue or pull back from relationships for a time.
Realize that grief does not always bring out the best in us. It can make us react in ways we never thought possible.
Understand that we can give grace and honor healthy boundaries for ourselves and our children.

Steps on the Path

- *After you have outlined your boundaries, make the setting safe.*
- *Recognize the potential dangers and work to mitigate them.*
- *Clear enough space so that you can perform the necessary everyday activities.*
- *Find ways to infuse fun activities into your family life, even if you don't feel like it.*
- *Bring friends in to help you if necessary.*
- *Focus on the moments of grace in the midst of the storm.*

People don't really know what to say in the face of such a train wreck of the soul, so allow them to lend helping hands and comfort in the little ways designed to help you navigate those first few days.

Chapter 2:

The Howl

The memorial service was held in an intimate, curtain-enclosed rotunda of our large church. The DVD with the photomontage of Jason and our family was playing on a TV at the front entry, so people could see it when they arrived. Arie, then almost three years old, was in childcare because I thought that this memorial service might be too much for her to process. I placed framed pictures of Jason and our family by the guestbook.

The black maternity dress I wore was one that Jason had bought me. The pearls I wore at my neck were a "push present" he had given me when Arie was born. Each detail of my clothes and movement felt like another bee sting. Even if I could distract myself from dwelling on it, some memory of Jason and our life together would imbed itself painfully in my mind.

Before the ceremony began, close friends and family waited in the choir room. I had not known that this would be our holding area. As soon as I walked in, I was assaulted by memories of our fun times there together. Jason and I had loved singing in the church choir, and we had spent many hours together practicing in this room. Jason would always make sure that I had a little plate of food and something to drink. I could picture him singing with such joy, looking over and smiling at me from the tenor section.

On that day, there were snacks on the countertops along the walls, just like we used to have at our choir practices. Someone brought me a plate of grapes and crackers. The food tasted like sand in my mouth, sand with a metallic aftertaste.

I was sitting on a small, overstuffed sofa with my family. Friends and more family came over to say hello and offer me their condolences. I could hear people chatting quietly and the plastic caps of small water bottles being twisted off. I mostly looked down at my hands and the paper I had printed Jason's eulogy on. I alternated between irritation at the milling bodies around me and true comfort from the closeness of my friends and family.

I breathed a sigh of relief when my soul sister, Kiki, who had flown in from Dallas, showed up in her black leather blazer and jeans. In any other setting, she would be my partner in crime, the Thelma to my Louise. She felt like a lifeline of strength. She was a reminder of who I had been and who I might be again.

Someone from the church came in and whispered to me that the service would be starting soon. It was time to go out and take my seat in the front row. Holding my aunt's hand, I looked at her and started to quietly cry. I didn't want this to be my life. I thought, *This cannot be real.* About a week ago, Jason and I had been together in this very church building. How could so much change so quickly?

As I leaned my head on her shoulder, letting the tears stream down my cheeks, she whispered in my ear, "You have to be strong now. Don't cry. You have to be strong for your daughter."

I don't know why, but that was *it.* The water bottles crackling, the murmurs of muffled conversation, the grapes on my plate like *he* used to give me in *this very room,* all the words meant to encourage me, made me want to jump out of my skin. I was furious.

I couldn't be calm. I was enraged. None of this was right!

Some cultures have a tradition of keening or grief wails when death occurs. They let loose with long, loud howls of mourning. It seems to me a logical step in the grief process, especially at first. I wanted to express how unfair all of this was, how great my pain was, how overwhelmingly *wrong* my husband's death had been, and rebuke anyone who tried to make it seem anything less than a horrible, violent injustice. As the soft music played over the speakers and people were seated and waiting for the service to start, something deep and primal rose up inside of me.

As my aunt patted my hair and told me to be strong, a deep growl started in my gut, swelled and grew, rumbling up to my chest, roaring out my mouth as the deepest, loudest, longest, guttural yell. It crashed against the walls of the choir room and echoed down the church halls to the curtained rotunda that shrouded the memorial service.

This tortured roar just came out of me as if to say, *Stop ALL of it!* There is nothing anyone can say to make this okay. Something horrible and horrendous has happened. Someone acknowledge this! This is too deep for words. *You* can mourn quietly, but *I* will wail! In my grief, I can *not* be polite, and I can *not* color inside your lines.

Everyone was instantly silent. The choir room cleared in moments. When I was done, my aunt sat stunned.

Sitting up, head held high, I looked at her, took up my eulogy notes, and said, "I'm ready now. Let's go."

With that, I walked with my family into the memorial service, to be among the gathering of people who had come to stand sentry and remember Jason.

The Eulogy

The fateful moment came for me to speak at my husband's memorial service. It was one day before Good Friday and three days before Easter. What I said was to honor Jason, but it was also to declare the course I was choosing for my family. Whether or not I understood God's plan, I was not going to leave my faith.

1 Corinthians 13:4-13 says, "Love is patient, love is kind. It does not envy, it does not boast, it is not proud. It does not dishonor others, it is not self-seeking, it is not easily angered, it keeps no record of wrongs. Love does not delight in evil but rejoices with the truth. It always protects, always trusts, always hopes, always perseveres. Love never fails. But where there are prophecies, they will cease; where there are tongues, they will be stilled; where there is knowledge, it will pass away. For we know in part and we prophesy in part, but when completeness comes, what is in part disappears. When I was a child, I talked like a child, I thought like a child, I reasoned like a child. When I became a man, I put the ways of childhood behind me. For now we see only a reflection as in a mirror; then we shall see face to face. Now I know in part; then I shall know fully, even as I am fully known. And now these three remain: faith, hope and love. But the greatest of these is love."

These verses were read at our wedding. They reflect the priceless gifts Jason gave me and which still live on. He made my life beautiful beyond what I could have imagined. His gentle, patient ways and unconditional love filled my heart with joy and security. He gave me two beautiful children—living legacies of his life. He daily walked out patience, love, reconciliation, and a forgiving spirit. His strength in caring for others was gentle and profound.

He wrapped me in unconditional acceptance and treated me and our daughter like princesses. He doted on us, giving everything he could to make us happy. His touch was my lifeblood and his laughter my music. His tender affection filled my heart with joy. His faith was practical and simple. He trusted God with a child's whole heart and embraced the loved ones in his path. I was and still am in awe of him.

So many people don't get these gifts in an entire lifetime, and I had him for a total of nine treasured years. He is still my treasure man.

"Love Unconditionally, Laugh Often, and Leave a Lasting Legacy."

We chose this saying as the mission statement of our marriage. My sweet husband's passing leaves me, and all of us, in indescribable pain and with a chasm of loss that is both enormous and confusing. I have been racking my mind with what-ifs. I feel that this is not what he wants us to do. He would want us to honor his life by remembering and practicing the very gifts that he gave us. We should walk out forgiveness toward each other, release past hurts, and refuse to let pride, pain, or anger rob us from savoring the present-day treasures of family and friends. Accept one another unconditionally, and give your heart away for the sheer joy of loving someone.

49

As we celebrate Jason's life, I believe that his desire would be for us to know that it was for this moment that Jesus had to come, live, die, and rise again. So that when we face death, we can know beyond a shadow of a doubt that we are not alone. We can rest in the fact that there is eternal forgiveness and consequently a very real relationship with God. Because of His sacrifice on the cross and resurrection, we have the sure hope that can carry us through deep pain. We know death is not the end of the story, but that we will spend eternity with God in heaven and see our loved ones again.

Jesus said that He is the Resurrection and the Life and then went on to demonstrate that power. He rose from the dead and forever changed history and our personal lives if we choose to open our hearts to His love.

Jason had a very real, personal relationship with Jesus. Because of this relationship, while I am in deep pain over the abrupt ending of his life on earth, I have the knowledge, peace, and assurance that I will see my man again in heaven. Not because I hope so or will it to be so, but because the power of Jesus' gift of forgiveness, death on the cross, and resurrection assures me that what He says is true and backed with God's power.

While this time is filled with deep longing and loss, I choose to believe that God is still present and able to give the peace that passes all understanding. This is not a final farewell but a momentary rest, which will one day culminate in a heavenly reunion and celebration. It is for this reason that the gift of Easter is the sustaining grace and power that makes life livable for me even in the most crushing of circumstances.

Jason would want us to celebrate him and his legacy by exploring God, practicing unconditional love, giving grace with each other's weaknesses, and reaching out to one another in kindness.

This is my man's legacy. Though his body is not walking the earth, I know that his immortal spirit is at peace and in the presence of Jesus. Though I miss him desperately, this assurance and peace will help me to walk out God's plan for us, day by day, moment by moment.

I love you, my sweet, sweet treasure man. Rest well, my Love.

Grief Crazy

It's impossible to accurately describe the emotions and thoughts that were running through my head in the days following my husband's death. I have called it a "firestorm" and "emotional drunk driving," but that doesn't begin to represent the bizarre, disconnected, agonizing experience itself. Crying helplessly at random times, sometimes ten hours a day. Whenever I entered a room full of people, I immediately sketched out an escape plan in case the tears attacked.

My young daughter was quietly terrified that she would lose me, too, so she didn't leave my side for the next ninety days. I didn't do *anything* by myself. You name it; my little girl was there for it.

She told me, "I don't want you to disappear, too, Mommy."

Frankly, while it did drive me a little batty from time to time, I was also glad she wanted to be near me, because I felt like a shell of a person.

Trying to escape grief makes you do crazy things. For example, the day I learned about my husband's death, I began planning a yard sale. All I knew was that I wanted out of my house. It was packed full of memories. How could I stay there? It felt like I was being suffocated by the silence Jason's absence left. After all my family and friends went home, how would I survive there? How would I survive his empty chair at my kitchen table at every meal? Dear God, how would I survive sleeping alone in our bed? My home felt like an instant landmine of painful memories. I saw him everywhere. How could I stay, and yet how could I ever leave?

So, while we were planning the memorial service, I had a friend photographing the rooms in my home, especially Arie's bedroom, so I could recreate it in the basement of my dear friend's house. Amy had already said we were welcome to move into the basement. How could I raise a grieving toddler *and* have a baby while I was massively grieving myself? Instead, I was ready to sell my stuff off and move within a week or two.

While I was coordinating this yard sale, Amy's mom Mimi, who had become a widow seven years prior, gently shared a wise word with me.

She said, "Mishael, I know you're hurting, but let me encourage you not to do anything out of fear. Move toward something, but don't run away in fear."

That statement stopped me in my tracks. Mimi was right. I was already running. I didn't know what this new life was going to look like or how I would survive it, but I realized that I could not run away in fear.

Part of establishing camp in the aftermath of loss is deciding to stay still. I strongly suggest that you don't run. Don't make drastic changes to your setting if you can avoid doing so. I know it's hard, but give it at least six months before you make any major choices. Let your brain and body calm down so you can make wise decisions.

Don't do anything out of fear.
Move toward something; don't run away from anything.
Running just lodges that sense of fear more deeply in your heart.
This running will eventually wear you out. Hold your ground
until the fog of grief lifts.

Not that I was particularly good at this advice early on. A week later, after my house had cleared of most of my visitors, one early morning I drowsily reached my arm across the bed for my husband, only to have a harsh reminder of his absence.

My eyes opened, and I thought, "Just wait a second here, God. Do you mean to tell me that I'm not going to *be* with a husband for a very long time?"

The silence spoke for itself. In my daze of grief, I decided that I could remedy the missing-husband problem in short order. I could bring in a new husband to take care of all the frustration, obliterate the social taboos, the "single" status, and protect my family from the monsters and the melodrama.

Of course, I was seven months pregnant, having skated passed the cute phase right into the whale portion of the program. Timing was not on my side. But that was a minor detail in my campaign to plug the gaping, jagged hole in our lives. I put on my cutest pregnancy frock and set my sights on the next man to enter the room. I can only imagine the scene I cut. Swollen-eyed and swollen-bellied, puffy but well-primped, cocking my hidden hips in imitation of a Marilyn Monroe or Sophia Vergara, my three-year-old clinging like a lamprey to my leg, I tentatively flirted with a family friend who had come to help out around the house.

Luckily, my friend didn't even notice my temporary insanity. It was wishful thinking on my part to believe that quickly finding a perfect husband could whisk me off to a new, pain-free life. I realized it was like trying to put a Band-Aid on an amputation. Even if I did find another man, my heart was too severely hurt to have a healthy relationship at that time. I missed Jason so much that I was far from ready to be in another relationship.

There was no quick fix to this. I had no choice but to be on this grief journey. I didn't know it at the time, but I can testify from more than eight years later that there is a transformative power in grief. If you let grief do its good work in you, your life will never be the same. You can change in amazing ways and your life can still be incredibly beautiful after loss. I know that in Ground Zero, it feels like having a good life again is impossible. Take the time to let your life transform instead of trying to find a quick fix. Trust that there is a higher purpose even though the pain is excruciating.

Collateral Damage

Before ten days were over, the cavalcade of casseroles petered out, the sympathy bouquets wilted, and offers of friendly support dwindled, to be replaced by perfunctory check-ins, mute helplessness, and sometimes silence or impatience. Nobody knows what to say when you are at the scene of an emotional disaster. Platitudes fall flat in the face of pure anguish, and the bystanders are left feeling awkward and ill-prepared. It feels safest for them to cook a casserole and be on their way.

Long before the internal firestorm has passed, friends and family will return to their everyday lives. Their departure will reveal an even bigger crater than you had realized. Gone are the lunch invitations with other couples after church. Enter the long lonely weekends when all your friends are busy with their lives. The weekend becomes a huge reminder of all the things that you're missing and will not get back.

There was a sense of pressure on me, like a gorilla was sitting on my chest all the time, literally making me work to breathe. My heart physically ached. I was exhausted from weeping. Sometimes I wondered how I would get through the next few minutes, let alone my life. Angry with God, I was unwilling to trust Him, but clinging to Him nonetheless. I felt hurt, lost, and damaged.

When he lost his spouse, C. S. Lewis wrote, "No one ever told me that grief felt so like fear."[6] It felt like terror, like getting a million paper cuts and then swimming in salt water. Any kind of movement was incredibly painful. Normal activities became innumerable deaths of remembering the exquisite beauty that had once lived so casually in my home. Now there was a gaping, ghastly hole in its place. Going to the grocery store, where he'd slow dance with me in the aisles to the music on the overhead speakers, was now a landmine. Right after the loss, I avoided the grocery store as much as possible. Of course, that didn't work for long. I remember quietly trying to fight back tears in the spaghetti aisle, just getting the same sauce we used to buy.

Jason used to run around like a kid and slide down the slides with my daughter at the playground. There was the mall where we would window shop, walking with our arms around each other's waists. We'd sit and eat a cookie while watching Arie climb on the indoor playground. After everything changed, I didn't want any part of those activities. It was painful being reminded of our life together at almost every turn. So, I started avoiding the gym, the church, some of our shared friends, and places we'd take walks. The list was endless.

Survival Strategies for Ground Zero

You have to think outside the box in creating your "new normal." Nobody wants to sit around and be sad all the time, and friends can quickly become uncomfortable if those are your weekend plans. People may feel awkward trying to reenter normal activities with a grieving family after loss. You can take the pressure to perform off yourself and go to a family-friendly venue together. It's a great first step, a great way to start to empower yourself as a solo parent, and a great way to let your kids laugh and release some energy.

I have created a week-by-week, month-by-month, comprehensive, practical grief empowerment guide entitled **"Casserole Killer: A Practical Guide to Empowering the First Few Weeks and Months of Your Grief Journey or the Grief Journey of Someone You Know."** It's a step-by-step list of the general logistics necessary for managing the loss of a loved one and empowering the supportive community to aid in productive ways. You can access this comprehensive guide in **Appendix 1** at the back of this book.

Buy Family Memberships to Area Attractions. At one point, I had annual memberships to the Georgia Aquarium, the Atlanta Botanical Gardens, Imagine It: The Children's Museum, Stone Mountain Park, Lake Lanier, and Zoo Atlanta. (By the way, an annual membership lasts a lot longer than flowers, and is a great grief gift for a grieving family). Now I had somewhere fun to go with Arie, and eventually, my baby, Sophia. If I bought a family membership, I could invite an adult to join us for free. Family memberships usually include up to four kids. I have two kids, so I could also offer free entry to a fun attraction for up to two other children.

Don't Go It Alone. Bring a Friend. Arie, and eventually Sophia, still wanted to go to playgrounds. So, for a while, I took friends with me to the playground. Their conversation and fun spirits kept me in the present moment. Eventually, the real sting of playgrounds and other emotionally charged places wore off, and I could focus on the beauty of my children and the gratitude I have toward Jason for being their father.

Follow Your Instincts

I have discovered that grief reshuffles the deck of our friendships. Some friends who are on top will move to the bottom, and some seeming acquaintances will become very close. Some people are comfortable with grief, while others are repelled. We all say stuff that doesn't resonate with people going through loss, myself included.

When you are the one handling the loss, it can be tough to negotiate the potential landmines. You appreciate that people are there for you in a difficult time. It's all so fresh, and you are struggling to find your way. Probably, you are encountering emotions and stresses with which you have little experience. You simply have to learn to trust your gut, even in the face of extraordinarily helpful friends and family. You must grieve in a way that resonates with your spirit.

Case in point: A large contingent of my Latino family on my mother's side returned to visit just a month after Jason's death. Cousins, aunts, spouses, spouses-to-be—all in one fun-filled, good-natured group—all stayed at my house, sharing beds, couches, and bedrooms. They are a little crazy, and that's just plain fun. I needed fun, except I was still grieving. I learned a really important lesson during that time.

Even though *la familia* had come to see *me*, after a day, they became restless with just sitting around my house and chatting. They wanted to get up and do things, like go to our big mall. So we went to the mall, and that was good, if odd, since it was the same mall Jason and I had always gone to together. I went through moments of shopping mixed with waves of wanting to cry, but that was okay. It was nice to be around family who understood.

The next day, *mi familia* decided to see Zoo Atlanta. It felt surreal once again, planning to go to one of the fun places Jason and I had taken Arie only weeks before. It was a good exercise for me to engage with life, with my loving family joining me for a time on the journey.

As I was getting ready to go to the zoo, I felt that familiar sadness come over me. I knew I would need a solid five to ten minutes to cry before I could move forward with the day. I could get the feelings out and then resume normal activities. I had sensed that it was hard for my aunt to see me cry and learned to cry privately when she was around. Only this time, she found me in my master bedroom's walk-in closet.

Embracing me, she said, "Mimita, you have to let the past be in the past. He is with God."

"It's only been a month," I said through my tears. "I am so hurt, and I miss him so much."

"Yes, Mimita, but you cannot cry like this in front of Arie. It's not good for her. It will change her. You have to be strong," she gently replied.

My gut instinct rose up. I pulled slightly back from our embrace to look at her.

"I *have* to cry. Something horrible has happened, and I cannot hide it from my daughter. She will know when I'm happy and when I'm sad. We will work through it together. I cannot do this any other way."

We looked at each other for a moment and then hugged again. I knew my aunt was offering her best advice from love and not malice. It was simply the way she might process grief. I knew she loved me and was gracious for being there with me in my sadness. Yet, in that moment, I also realized that I had to remain living independently in Atlanta with my children. I had to find my own path in grieving, one that resonated with my own emotional needs and character.

You will find those who resonate with your grief, and those to whom you need to give grace and freedom because they have a different way that works better for them. Release your expectations, and search for solutions that encourage and uplift you. We all process grief differently. Don't take it personally if some move in a contrary direction.

I'll give you an example of my own stumbles: a few years ago, a dear friend of mine was diagnosed with cancer. My mom had died of breast cancer five months after Jason's death. I grieved for her while grieving Jason, but it was different with my mom because I'd had time to say goodbye during the years before she passed. I had been on my grief journey for long enough that I should have been able to walk with my friend through her tragedy, but I couldn't. It hit too close to home for me. I wasn't ready to do it, so I pulled away from her when she most needed a companion. I am not proud of my choice. We all need forgiveness sometimes.

It's possible that if people have a past loss that they have not processed or expressed healthfully, they are not going to be comfortable around your grief. Your grief resurrects a painful place in them that they are unwilling to visit, and they will pull away from you without knowing why themselves. It's not about you. It's not about your loss. Give them grace.

Journey to the Sunrise

Discover that some people, even close family members, may grieve differently than you.

Realize that it's not about you. It's not about your loss. They are not rejecting you, and they are not dismissing your tears. It's about their own grief journey.

Understand that part of establishing camp in the aftermath is deciding to stay still. Don't run, and don't make drastic changes to your setting or major decisions if you can avoid doing so.

Steps on the Path

- Don't make any major decisions while you are in Ground Zero. Grief is like being emotionally drunk with pain. You are not firing on all pistons at this time. Proceed with caution.
- Grieve in ways that are true to you. Guard your process as well as your routines, and respect your emotional needs. Find ways initially that resonate with you, and know that those ways will evolve.
- Find your center. Find your faith anchor, and hold on for dear life.

Chapter 3:

The Swim

L ong before I had even met Jason, I learned a hard-won lesson
that helped anchor my choices in every grief storm. I'm not
proud of this story, but there were two lessons from this time that later
became lifelines to me after I lost my husband, gave birth to my second
daughter, and lost my mom all in a five-month span. I hope that if you
are ever struggling with despair, you make the choice not to suffer in
silence, but rather to find a support group, cry out to God, and hold on.
Never forfeit your future because of today's pain.

One day, when I was in my early twenties, I was suffering through
a dry, desolate time when I felt anguish and depression bordering on
despair. I had been weeping on and off for several months, and my
grief was causing physical pain. I had even missed an important job
commitment that day because I couldn't bear to leave my house. Every
time I tried to move, I wept.

There was a storm brewing outside. The weatherman cautioned
that the ocean would be dangerous. The waves were high, and the rip
current strong. It was tropical storm season in Florida. Something in
me thought, *It's a perfect time for a swim*. Though there was still a
raging war inside of me, a calm resolve took over, and I stopped crying.
Almost as if I were running on autopilot, I drove to Hollywood Beach,
where I knew the sea was at its most unforgiving. I walked along the
ocean for a long time. The sky was stormy and the winds were strong,
but I was finally calm. There were signs posted prohibiting swimming
because of the storm swell.

I walked past them. When I saw that I was out of sight of any life-guards, I removed my clothes and stood motionless in the bathing suit I wore underneath. Then, I simply walked toward the ocean. For the first time in weeks, I didn't feel a thing, and the numbness was a relief.

As I entered the ocean up to my waist, the waves crashed into my chest and face, pushing me back. I dove under them and started to swim out. There was no one on shore. I swam, coming up for air and diving under the waves. I looked back as the beach became more and more distant.

Then I turned toward the horizon and silently prayed, "I won't do it myself, but take me if You want. I can't do this anymore. I see no purpose."

I knew I had put myself in this very, very grave situation. I received no answer. Increasingly larger waves washed over me, throwing me around. Fighting them, I started to gulp water.

It was the point of no return.
My reaction was, "No, no. I don't want to *die*.
I just want to end this pain.
I want to chat with Death. Perhaps a cup of tea
to discuss what it has to offer.
You know, kick the tires. Take it for a test drive,
but I'm not ready to actually buy! I'm sorry!"

As I tried to swim toward shore, I found that I couldn't. The meteo-rologist had been right. The rip currents were strong. I had never really paid attention to what a rip current was. All I knew was that no matter how hard I tried to swim toward shore, I kept getting pulled sideways, parallel to shore. The waves kept coming. No one was on shore for me to yell for. I was in deep and couldn't touch the sand.

I was very scared. I prayed again, "God, what do I do?"
A calm, clear thought replied, "Relax, Kitten. Don't fight.
Ride the waves to shore."

That's right. In my head, God called me "Kitten."

After I let the current take me parallel to the shore for a while, I sensed that I was not traveling parallel any longer. Then I rode the waves like I had done when I played with my brother and mom on sunny days at the beach. That turned out to be exactly what you're supposed to do in a rip current situation. I let the waves carry me in, and when I could touch ground, I scrambled ashore as quickly as possible. When I could finally sit down in the sand, I was exhausted. I knew I had been saved, and I knew that I had been very shortsighted.

As I drove home afterwards, a picture came to mind. It was of a net made from all the people in my life. They were each holding on to one another, actually making up the fabric of the net. I heard in my thoughts, "This is where you fall. Reach out to those who love you."

It was then I realized what kind of pain I could have caused my family. Pain that they didn't deserve, pain that wouldn't stop for their whole lives. I had not thought of it before because I had only thought of relieving my own unrelenting pain.

My thoughts shifted. In my mind's eye, I saw several buckets. Precious life-force water was being poured into my bucket by my mother and my father. Then I took that bucket and started to pour it down the drain.

The thoughts in my mind continued, "You waste the life and love that others have poured into you when you threaten your own life."

"Never again, Lord. Never again," I promised. "I'm so sorry. Thank You so much for saving me."

Years later, I can see even more clearly. My marriage, my children, friends to be made, wonderfully beautiful and terribly sad moments to experience, and my purpose would have all been forfeited. Life is unbelievably precious. I do not recommend tempting God like I did. When I look back on what I did, I see it as incredibly dangerous and deeply hurtful. The pain had seemed unrelenting, and I had just wanted to make it stop.

After Jason's death, I was enraged, depressed, and then driven again to the edge of despair. Only this time, I knew what to do when I felt overwhelmed with grief. The slithering lie is that choosing to die makes the pain stop. Now I know that when you try to end your pain through self-destruction, the resulting death doesn't erase the pain. It multiplies it. It takes your bucket of pain, turns it back on all the people who love you, pours that pain into them, and it changes them. Permanently.

The lesson in my early twenties taught me that no matter how intense the grieving got, I was going to purpose to create a legacy with my life. I cried out to God to help me and I simply held on.

The Coiled Secret

Immediately after Jason's death, I found myself battling similar suicidal thoughts, so I confided in my friends that I really needed someone to stay with me. According to an article entitled "Suicide after Bereavement: An Overlooked Problem," "The suicide risk of widowed persons is increased in the days, weeks and months after bereavement. Widowed persons are a clear-cut risk group."[7] Roxanne Dryden-Edwards, M.D., states, "The potential negative effects of a grief reaction can be significant. For example, research shows that about 40% of bereaved people will suffer from some form of anxiety disorder in the first year after the death of a loved one, and there can be up to a 70% increase in death risk of the surviving spouse within the first six months after the death of his or her partner."[8] How many widows or widowers are going to admit that they are having suicidal thoughts, especially when they have kids? What if the children are removed from the home and everything becomes exponentially worse? With no one to relate to them, with no community, those widows, widowers, and others who are grieving are left to suffer in silence.

The thoughts were particularly powerful on my first Mother's Day as a widow. Some of my married friends kindly invited me to their family's Mother's Day celebration on Saturday afternoon. It was a nice gathering with lots of children playing and polite conversation by the large backyard pool. Arie and I splashed around and enjoyed ourselves.

It was a lovely day. Husbands doted on the children and wives. I felt like I was observing a life I no longer belonged to, so I focused on my girlfriend's mom, Mimi, the widow who had encouraged me not to make decisions based in fear. It was good to know someone on this new path of mine.

During the party, my cousin, who had been generously staying with me for a month, called to give me two weeks' notice. She had previously offered to stay with me until after I gave birth, but she had to change her plans because of her husband's work. Though I told her I understood, I felt an intense wave of fear. How I was going to take care of a toddler and a newborn by myself after a C-section?

Driving home, I felt an overwhelming sense of isolation and abandonment as I contemplated my future life. I didn't know which way to turn. In our marriage, I had been the businesswoman, not the baby person. Jason had been the baby master—he had helped take care of his four younger siblings. He had taught me how to change diapers. He had been a wonderful, hands-on dad with Arie. Now I was alone. How was I going to get through this? I felt hollow in my stomach, coupled with an intense pressure on my chest, joined by a throbbing ache in my heart. Inescapable, unrelenting, exhausting pain hit me like I had never experienced before in my life.

I stopped off at a drugstore on the way home to pick up some Benadryl. My obstetrician had said I could take it at the suggested dosage in order to sleep, and it wouldn't harm my baby. As Arie ran up and down the aisles of the store, I stood in front of the wall of sleeping pills. Staring, I wondered if I could just sleep until the pain went away.

The lies began to quietly coil around me, and I could hear the whispers slinking into my mind, "Just do it. This is too hard. It will make the pain stop."

Then, Arie jolted me, running to embrace my leg. Looking up from under her chlorinated swaths of hair, she asked, "Mommy, can we go home now?"

I took a deep breath and walked away, but when I got home I couldn't shake that feeling of being overwhelmed. As a Mother's Day gift, Mimi had given me a CD by Dr. Charles Stanley entitled *Our Choices in the Midst of Tragedy*. It turned out to be an excellent gift. As I listened to it, one important insight came through: "We are not defined by tragedy, but we are defined by our choices within our tragedy." I played that CD in my minivan almost ceaselessly during that first year. Those words were another huge clue on my journey.

Like the Wind

The next day, Sunday morning, Arie and I went to church for Mother's Day. It had been about a month since Jason had died. As I entered the sanctuary, I felt a dismal, sinking feeling. Just several weeks before, Jason and I had sung worship songs together in that very place. As the music started to play, tears streamed down my face. I wanted my man back. The ache was so intense.

As I choked through singing the songs, Arie asked me to pick her up. It felt good to be with her. She of all people was in this with me. She sat as best she could on my hip, shifting around my prego belly. Looking into my face and seeing tears streaming down my cheeks, she then did something completely unexpected.

She put her little lips together and blew on my eyes and wet cheeks, and she said, "You can feel him, but you can't see him."

I was amazed. I had been telling her that when her daddy's spirit was no longer in his body, it was like the wind that you can feel but not see. She had remembered my analogy and reminded me of it at just the right moment. She wasn't even three years old yet. I hugged her tightly, and that's how I came back to church.

Returning home, after watching all the couples at church, thoughts of those sleeping pills at the drug store kept darting into my mind. As quickly as I tried to block them, another one would appear. The allure was palpable. I needed strength. I *knew* that this was not the legacy I wanted for my family. So, I did the only thing that I knew to do. I grabbed a lawn chair, brought some toys outside for Arie, and parked myself on the front lawn of my house, in a visible, public place. I brought a phone with me, and while Arie played, I called friends.

"I need backup. Can you come to my house?"

I kept calling until someone came. My friends didn't press me with questions. They just spent time with me. Widows and widowers will not readily admit to these feelings, but they are very, very real. The last thing you want to do is admit to overwhelming despair. There's already been enough change. So how do you handle extreme despair and sly thoughts of suicide in isolation? The answer is that you don't.

For the first nine months, I had friends, family, neighbors, or a nanny stay with me nearly around the clock. I was that broken, and I knew my limitations. I found the support I needed, at least, to take care of my children.

But there is so much more. You need support for your spirit, and oftentimes those around you may not be equipped to give you all the support you need because they are not experienced in this grief journey. They can be there for you, but they have not walked in your loss, so it will be hard for them to help you healthfully navigate through it.

When you go through loss, you need to recognize areas where you can no longer answer your own needs and adjust accordingly. Though it's frightening, you must embark on the journey to find a place that offers additional resources to help you heal. It's vital to find a support group that understands your journey. If you can't find one, create it. Start your own group using our leadership materials. You might not get all you need from one group. I believe you need the wisdom of grief counseling and the companionship of a grief support group. I lost years trying to tough it out on my own.

I'm not saying to leave your friends and house of worship. I am saying to find additional resources. When I found my support groups and a good counselor, I could finally exhale, because I had found people who understood my immense challenges. In some cases, they were further down my same road and could give relevant advice. I felt understood. How much better would it have been had I found these groups earlier in my loss? Dear Reader, seek out a group as soon as possible.

Dinner and a Movie

In that crucial time after Jason's death, two sets of friends from my church—Jyn and Steve, and Kat and Dave—did an amazing thing. They rotated one week on and one week off, drove an hour out of their way to work, and stayed with me for a week at a time. I can't tell you how much that meant to me. I could be myself with them. They made no stipulations about how much I could be sad. They were just there. Just present. Ready to surf the wave of grief with me.

On the first night that Jyn and Steve stayed with me, we were all sitting around on the couch in awkward silence.

Jyn looked at me and said, "Wow, it really hit the fan, huh?"

I laughed a little and replied with a hearty, "Yeah, it really did."

"Wanna order pizza and watch a movie?" Steve asked.

"Yes, I do!" I answered.

That was one of my all-time favorite moments. My friends recognized that there was no way to fix this mess. There was nothing to say right then that would make it all better. We were sitting in the middle of a hollowed-out marriage, but they were willing to camp out there with me and be along for the ride. That was all I really needed.

We did watch a movie that night and then later talked about Jason, laughing and crying through the stories we all told together. It was another important step in healing that night. My friends remembered that I was still myself and that I still liked to laugh, still wanted to have fun. They recognized that I just needed them nearby for a time. Sometimes, all you need when you are grieving is a friend to sit close by and not try to make everything okay.

Poodle Up

One of the first things to go when Jason died was our laughter. Jason had a rapier wit. We had laughed a lot through life. In the weeks after his death, my laughter had disappeared, and I wondered if I could ever feel happy again.

Then, one day, laughter came unexpectedly. Amidst all of the details and drama of grief, I looked down at Coco, my chocolate brown toy poodle, and noticed that he resembled some kind of Rastafarian dog. His hair had grown out until he was literally just a matted puffball, and it was the middle of the summer in Georgia.

When I took Coco in to be groomed, the man behind the counter asked me what I wanted done.

"Surprise me," I said, unwilling to make yet another decision at this time. "Poodle him up!"

"Oh, I'm on it," the groomer said, and told me he would be done in a couple hours.

When I came to pick up Coco, my groomer presented me with the complete package: full-blown grooming glory lavished upon my nine-pound, dainty poodle. Coco came prancing out of the back room like a diva, proud, preening, and fully conscious of his newfound fabulousness. He had blue nail polish on his claws, a blue bow on his head, and blue bows on each ear. He had a puffball just above each foot and bows on each puffball. He had a puffball on his tail and a blue bow on that, too. He was Poodle-Fabulous!

I laughed a great belly laugh like the ones I used to share with Jason, and the groomer laughed with me, as if he had known exactly what I needed. Coco swelled a little more just knowing he was the center of all this attention.

Wiping tears from my eyes, I told the groomer, "Thank you. That was amazing."

Walking with Coco in my arms back to my minivan, I thought to myself, "Maybe I'll be okay. If I can laugh again, that is half the battle."

Rediscover Laughter

Laughter is healing to the soul and a great stress reliever for the body. If nothing funny is happening around you, rent some comedy movies. Find your laughter again because laughter reminds us that life is still good.

Proverbs 17:22 says, "A cheerful heart is good medicine, but a crushed spirit dries up the bones." It turns out that this ancient wisdom is also medically accurate.

In her book, *The Bounce Back Book: How to Thrive in the Face of Adversity, Setbacks, and Losses*, Karen Salmansohn says, "When someone shares a good laugh with you, they are not only spreading joy but lowering blood pressure, boosting the immune system, improving brain functioning, lowering the risk of heart disease, as well as reducing depression, anger, anxiety, and stress. For me humor is a great 'enlightening' agent – helping to shed light on an event, so it no longer appears as earthshaking. I have often quipped that comedy is when bad things happen to people who aren't me. One day I realized this joke of mine was actually quite Buddhist. By removing my ego, I'm no longer personally connected to a situation's outcome or concerned about humiliation or self-pity. Thus it's a lot easier to see the humor in it. When you have a good sense of humor, you are better able to reframe the meaning you give an event so it no longer appears so devastating or shameful."[9]

The Mayo Clinic offers a number of healthy side effects of laughter:

> **Short-term Benefits:** A good laugh has great short-term effects. When you start to laugh, it doesn't just lighten your load mentally, it actually induces physical changes in your body...Laughter enhances your intake of oxygen-rich air, stimulates your heart, lungs and muscles, and increases the endorphins that are released by your brain...A rollicking laugh fires up and then cools down your stress response and increases your heart rate and blood pressure....

> **Long-term Effects:** Laughter isn't just a quick pick-me-up. It's also good for you over the long haul... Negative thoughts manifest into chemical reactions that can affect your body by bringing more stress into your system and decreasing your immunity. In contrast,

positive thoughts actually release neuropeptides that
help fight stress and potentially more-serious illnesses...
Laughter may ease pain by causing the body to produce
its own natural painkillers. Laughter may also break the
pain-spasm cycle common to some muscle disorders....
Laughter can help lessen your depression and anxiety
and make you feel happier.[10]

An article in the *Huffington Post* by Yagana Shah, "New Study
Proves That Laughter Really Is the Best Medicine," highlights the
research into the health benefits of a good laugh:

...researchers at California's Loma Linda University
set out to find out if humor can deliver more than just
comic relief. The study looked at 20 healthy older adults
in their 60s and 70s, measuring their stress levels and
short-term memory. One group was asked to sit silently,
not talking, reading, or using their cellphones, while the
other group watched funny videos.

After 20 minutes, the participants gave saliva sam-
ples and took a short memory test. While both groups
performed better after the break than before, the "humor
group" performed significantly better when it came to
memory recall. Participants who viewed the funny
videos had much higher improvement in recall abilities, 43.6 percent, compared with 20.3 percent in the
non-humor group.

Moreover, the humor group showed considerably
lower levels of cortisol, the 'stress hormone,' after
watching the videos. The non-humor group's stress
levels decreased just slightly.[11]

Melinda Smith, M.A., and Jeanne Segal, PhD., offer helpful suggestions on how to find laughter if you happen not to run across a
poshly primped poodle:

Checklist for "Lightening Up":

- **Laugh at yourself.** Share your embarrassing moments. The best way to take yourself less seriously is to talk about times when you took yourself too seriously.
- **Attempt to laugh at situations rather than bemoan them.** Look for the humor in a bad situation, and uncover the irony and absurdity of life. This will help improve your mood and the mood of those around you.
- **Surround yourself with reminders to lighten up.** Keep a toy on your desk or in your car. Put up a funny poster in your office. Choose a computer screensaver that makes you laugh. Frame photos of you and your family or friends having fun.
- **Deal with your stress.** Stress is a major impediment to humor and laughter.
- **Pay attention to children and emulate them.** They are the experts on playing, taking life lightly, and laughing.

Creating Opportunities to Laugh

- Watch a funny movie or TV show.
- Go to a comedy club.
- Read the funny pages.
- Seek out funny people.
- Share a good joke or a funny story.[12]

Journey to the Sunrise

Do not believe the *slithering lie* that choosing to die makes the pain stop. **Realize** that it takes your bucket of pain and turns back on all the people who love you, and pours that pain into them, changing them permanently.

Understand that though the pain is excruciating, it is only temporary.

Steps on the Path

Grief can be caused by many of life's experiences, but you are not alone.

There is a way to handle the rage, depression, and despair connected to grief.

Start your journey toward transforming tragedy into triumph by:

- Crying out to God for help. Even if you two aren't on great terms at the moment.
- Calling your friends until they come and sit with you.
- If friends can't come, go to them. Do not isolate yourself.
- Find help through connecting with others.
- Honestly tell them how you are feeling.

Try to take a five-minute vacation from grief and look around you. I promise there will be something to smile about.

Chapter 4:

Green Grief

I n the meantime, I was only getting more pregnant. After the initial shock wore off, I found I wanted to eat everything, and I moved very little. My developing baby considerately camouflaged any weight gain brought on by the ample funeral foods and my own poor cooking skills. However, the "comfort food" I kept inhaling was doing damage to my system, even though at first I didn't notice it.

At the time, I had bigger fish to fry—dipped in a beer batter with a side of thick-cut fries and an extra dollop of tartar sauce. In fact, I continued to flounder (my deepest apologies for the pun) in the early stages of grief for far too long.

Although I had found grief groups, gone to counseling, and eventually made it through the diaper years as a widowed parent, I could not manage to overcome the sadness, the mood swings, and the grief fog. I was surviving, but I wasn't thriving. The grief did not magically lift with the passage of time.

Finally, I discovered another seldom-addressed key to overcoming grief: *proper nutrition*. Learning how to nourish our bodies while we are grieving can create a more efficient journey through grief.

The Importance of Eating Right

The first thing I had to recognize was that grief is physical, mental, and spiritual. However, I was struggling to sustain myself only mentally and spiritually during my Ground Zero. I discovered that grief physically depletes our bodies in a host of unique ways. In an article entitled "Understanding How Grief Weakens the Body," Cari Romm shares, "Previous research has found that following the death of a spouse, people were likely to report more self-medication and worse overall health. Grief has also been found to aggravate physical pain, increase blood pressure and blood clots, and exacerbate appetite loss—possibly because it also caused people to find less pleasure in food."[13]

When we feel bad, we eat comfort foods, which are mainly comprised of refined sugars and simple carbs, which stimulate the same pleasure centers in our brains as love and cocaine do. Refined sugars do not nourish us properly and actually leach nutrients from our bodies, causing us to further bankrupt ourselves physically. It's just not realistic to expect to make wise decisions in such a depleted state.

The "comfort foods" that we habitually turn to during grief only serve to aggravate our already-challenged mental balance. Think about the casseroles and desserts that appear as kind-hearted gestures from friends and family: they are usually starchy or sugary, carb-laden affairs that our bodies will treat as sugar. In fact, most of the foods we are tempted to reach for during times of stress—even the ones we know we shouldn't—fall into the category of "simple sugar." These include breads, pastas, desserts of all kinds, alcohol, even nicotine. I asked Atlanta-based nutritionist and licensed dietitian, Ilana Katz, MS, RD, CSSD, about the effects of bad sugar, or simple carbs, in the diet, and she explained that they offer "comfort" because of the way our bodies process them:

> Sugar is a stimulant that causes a rollercoaster of high to low energy due to its insulin response. Insulin is a hormone that is surged into the bloodstream to clear the sugar into cells, with the resultant of fat storage, as well as a quick drop in blood sugar. And then the cycle starts all over again. In other words, sugar causes the need for more sugar. Why? Because the physiological response to sugar is like an addiction. Sugar temporarily elevates the levels of various neurotransmitters and endorphins. The "feel good" chemicals, serotonin and dopamine, are released when sugar is metabolized, giving a sense of pleasure. Sugar cravings, therefore, are best explained as an addiction to endorphins, which is a reaction similar to the high of a drug addict. More sugar causes more fat to be stored and lower energy; low energy stimulates the release of the counter-regulatory hormone called glucagon, which then sends messages to the brain to eat more sugar. It is an addictive and difficult cycle to move out of. These peaks and valleys are symptomatic of fatigue, further cravings, fat storage, and low energy, but the low energy is not one that parallels sleep.

So is this addiction a serious or dangerous one? The answer is both yes and no. Our bodies do need sugar. The required fuel for the brain is, in fact, glucose. The metabolism can thus effectively metabolize what we eat and provide the energy source required thereof. The key phrase here is "amount required." The danger takes effect when the amount of sugar that is consumed is way more than required for the optimal source of energy. Furthermore, sugar that is refined has no nutritional value, resulting in empty calories. Calorie-dense nutrient-free foods, if making up most of one's diet, will lead to an array of health problems, from overweight and obesity to diabetes and cardiovascular disease, just to name a few.

Ilana Katz has some suggestions for how to stave off sugar cravings, a battle that for me involved an unending replay of Good Cop/Bad Cop inside my head, with my psyche the exhausted prisoner who had never even been read her rights. When I asked Ilana if there are supplements that can help curb sugar cravings, she replied:

The best way to curb sugar cravings is to eat smaller meals throughout the day and make sure each of the mini-meals contains a source of fat and a protein—for example, an apple and almonds, or whole grain crackers and avocado, or a protein shake made with fruit, protein powder, spinach, flax, or chia seeds and almond milk. The protein and fat help to suppress hunger; eating smaller meals at shorter intervals helps to maintain an even balance of insulin, which suppresses cravings.

It is always better to rely on real food rather than supplements, but of course a supplement is just that, a "supplement," when the real thing is difficult to accomplish or satisfy. Supplements known to suppress cravings include:

Vitamin B. Vitamin B complex has been hypothesized to help with carbohydrate metabolism so better use of carbs can result.

CoEnzymeQ10. Also known as ubiquinone, this is a key component of every cell's energy mitochondria – the energy source. It is an element found in all carbohydrate utilization processes. Many multi-vitamins and supplements already include CoEnzymeQ10, so it may not be necessary to get more if a multi is already being utilized.

Resveratrol. A component of red wine and grapes that has been hypothesized to improve insulin sensitivity. This means a better response for glucose to enter muscle tissue for energy storage.

Fish oil. Similar to resveratrol, it is hypothesized to reduce carbohydrate cravings because it enhances insulin sensitivity. The triglyceride form of fish oil is more expensive, but is the recommended form for the intended result. It has better absorption capacity than the simple "ethyl ester" form of fish oil.

Chromium. Since it is part of the glucose metabolic pathway, chromium has been hypothesized to ensure the glucose is used as fuel and thus increase insulin sensitivity.

Lipase. Lipase is hypothesized to reduce sugar cravings based on the logic that it is deficient in people who have blood sugar fluctuations. It also aids in fat metabolism and is hypothesized to ensure fat is used as a fuel source rather than stored. It is usually part of many digestive enzyme supplements, so those alone may be just as good to try, versus lipase alone (suggested recommendations are based on brand, so read the labels).

Note that the research on these products is equivocal, meaning that some studies support their positive effect while some studies do not. There are no studies that can claim that any of these supplements definitely work. So be aware and appropriate whenever you choose to "supplement" your food – always go with real food first. If all else fails, these may be safe and worth a try, but there are no guarantees. If it is your choice to use supplementation, follow the labels on the bottles for recommended dosage. Remember, more is not necessarily better.

Since I was not an enthusiastic cook, I gladly indulged in the cascade of casseroles that appeared after my husband's funeral. Those dishes eventually gave way to ordered pizzas and warmed-over frozen dinners, and I considered myself successful to be putting food on the table at all some days. Eventually, my food choices and grief avalanched, and I developed walking pneumonia. To recover my health, I went on a quest to learn how the body, mind, and spirit are deeply intertwined. I needed to understand human chemistry and how our foods affect our moods.

Learning to nourish our bodies for our optimum life is a key ingredient in crafting a life we love. There are logical reasons why we should stay away from certain tempting foods and why we should incorporate others. When we are educated about what a food is doing in our bodies, we can make rational rather than emotional decisions about our nourishment choices, especially while we are physically depleted by loss.

One of the first places I turned for help was Dr. Joan Mathews-Larson's book, *Depression Free, Naturally*. I knew I needed to deal with my grief on a physical level, and I knew also that I had been surviving on auto-pilot and not making healthy food choices. I was inspired when I read that "chemistry, not personality" might be "the culprit that causes your emotional woes."[14] Of course, I was grieving specific losses—my husband and mother, my daydreams of a fairy-tale marriage and family— but long-term grief can actually change the chemistry of our brains, making them less able to adapt, and making our bodies less able to fight disease.[15] According to *Depression Free, Naturally*, "Ongoing losses and heavy stresses are also a setup for depression. Such life events, if prolonged, profoundly affect the brain's chemical balance."[16] Dr. Mathews-Larson writes that "'emotional' symptoms develop as a direct result of the unavailability of brain and body chemicals. These important chemicals create our stable emotions, behaviors, thoughts, and sanity"—and I was ready for a dose of stable emotions and relative sanity.[17]

Depression Free, Naturally explains how the chemicals in our bodies affect our behaviors and mental states, and then pinpoints specific nutrients and their effects. Dr. Mathews-Larson systematically identifies what our bodies need and how we can get them through the foods we eat and through supplements, and also what we need to eliminate from our environment if we want to function at our best. Although I had been grieving for years before I found her book, I first had to do nutritional triage to begin to reset my body's balance. Essentially, for the purposes of Ground Zero grief, I think we simply want to coddle our chemistry: to keep from doing damage while our system is responding to the shock of great grief, and to nudge it along the path to recovery with the right foods and activities.

What I learned from researching the links between nutrition and depression convinced me that various nutritional deficiencies are found in those suffering from depression. Eating healthy by reducing carbs, particularly from grains, along with detoxing, which helps clear up an inflamed digestive system caused by stress and poor nutrition, will aid in helping a grieving person heal emotionally and physically.

The stress of grief causes the brain to produce an adrenocorticotrophin (ACTH) hormone, which ultimately results in the production of cortisone by the adrenal gland. Cortisone activates the sympathetic nervous system, preparing our bodies for a "fight or fight" reaction. When the sympathetic nervous system (which speeds up the body's processes) is working, the parasympathetic nervous system (which slows down the body's processes) must be suppressed.

It's the parasympathetic nervous system that runs our digestion, and under stress, it shuts down; that's why, when I first became a widow, everything tasted like sand in my mouth. After a while, something switched, and I got really hungry. At first I didn't want to eat and I lost weight, but not in a healthy way. Then I craved the simple sugars in comfort foods, and I gained weight.

When the stress lasts a long time—as when we're processing grief—our overstimulated and out-of-balance nervous systems suffer. As Dina Aronson, MS, RD, explains, "Imagine what goes on in a cortisol-flooded, stressed-out body when food is consumed: Digestion and absorption are compromised, indigestion develops, and the mucosal lining becomes irritated and inflamed.... And, of course, the resulting mucosal inflammation leads to the increased production of cortisol, and the cycle continues as the body becomes increasingly taxed."[18]

Our compromised, inflamed digestive system then has more trouble processing the necessary nutrients, so we reach for a quick fix of "comfort" foods, which provide a burst of energy but insufficient nutrients. But this is exactly the time when it's more important than ever to eat nutritious, anti-inflammatory foods. She recommends avoiding foods that contribute to inflammation, such as those with a "high glycemic load" (simple carbs), saturated and trans fatty acids, caffeine, and alcohol (Aronson 38). Dr. Mathews-Larson connects the negative effects of these to our moods, explaining that "Sugar, caffeine, and alcohol all increase the lactate to pyruvate ratio in the body, resulting in anxiety."[19]

Beyond the important types of food that could work to stall our progress through grief or add to the fog that we are already muddling through, there are a few foods we can add to our diets that will not require much thought, preparation or actual gagging—and that will offer the nourishment our over-stressed systems actually crave.

We can turn to healthy foods to minimize inflammation of our system, such as organic vegetables (eat raw as much as possible, since cooking reduces nutrient effectiveness). Some of the best vegetables are tomatoes, lettuce, celery, Brussel sprouts, spinach, squash, and onions. Avoid potatoes, sweet potatoes, and gluten (wheat). Keep dairy products at a minimum except for goat cheese, cottage cheese, organic butter, and raw cheese. Whey is a great source of protein in your protein shakes.

Eat grass-fed beef, organic chicken, duck, and wild-caught fish (try to avoid farmed-raised fish unless it is responsibly farmed). These are excellent sources of protein. Raw fruit and apple cider vinegar contain essential nutrients for your emotional healing—as do organic apples, grapefruit, raspberries, and blueberries. Avoiding alcohol altogether is ideal, but if you decide not to go cold turkey, consider shifting to drinking a glass of Organic Red Wine once a week. Eating fruit with protein helps you keep your carb intake to under twenty-five grams a day. Remember that stress causes your body to store excess carbs around your belly, rear end, and vital organs, including your heart, pancreas, and liver. Weight gain from poor nutrition in itself is depressing.

Avoid all processed sugars. Read labels and stay away, as much as you can, from all processed foods. Processed sugars and grain products can produce inflammation in your gut and diminish brain function, which leads to depression. "Nutritional Therapies for Mental Disorders" is an article that will provide you with more specific research on this topic and will give you a list of nutritional deficiencies that can be alleviated through good nutrition and supplements. Most important to helping your brain are "healthy fats" and the B vitamins, in particular B12.[20]

Foods with "healthy fats" (omega 3 and 6) help reduce inflammation and promote healthy brain function.

Vital Nutritional Information on Essential Fatty Acids

Here's the bottom line to what nutritionists, chiropractors, medical researchers, and health-conscious physicians recommend for good nutrition that promotes brain health and supports the healing of your emotions and thoughts.

Remember that your brain needs healthy fats, which you can get from almond butter, walnut and cashew butter, organic butter, coconut oil, avocados, and pure virgin olive oil, as well as raw nuts. As a rule, avoid peanuts.

The good fats containing essential fatty acids provide us with our most efficient source of energy. The body absorbs them more efficiently. Wild-caught fish and fish oil supplements are excellent sources of essential fatty acids, and our body uses these fats as well as vitamin-rich foods to produce the hormones we need for healthy metabolism and pH balance.

Speaking of that, proper hydration is essential for your body processing and metabolizing all your healthy foods. I will talk more about that later.

According to Dr. Michael Gershon, chairman of the Department of Anatomy and Cell Biology at New York–Presbyterian Hospital/ Columbia University Medical Center and author of the 1998 book *The Second Brain*, our enteric nervous system, which controls our digestion, constitutes a "second brain" because of its complexity and ability to control our moods. "It is this brain that could be responsible for your craving under stress for crisps, chocolate and cookies," claims Emma Young, author of *Gut Instincts: The Secrets of your Second Brain*, "the enteric nervous system (ENS) has long been known to control digestion. Now it seems it also plays an important role in our physical and mental well-being."[21] So the foods and nutrients we eat directly fuel the brain and the "second brain" with what we need in order to control our moods and our energy. In other words, sometimes the key to minding my moods is through minding my diet.

That said, Ground Zero is probably not the best time to start a diet. Early on, I would have felt triumphant just getting out of my pajama pants. I think it's important to recognize a few easy steps to begin with: a few key foods to avoid, a few foods to make sure you have on hand. In addition, there are some supplements that are particularly helpful for a body that has been overwhelmed by grief toxins.

Help Your Body While You Are Grieving

Joan Mathews-Larson, PhD, recommends a formula for overcoming depression caused by a chemical imbalance. The formula consists of specific amounts and types of elements necessary for the body, including Free-form amino complex, Tryptophan, Vitamin C (Ester C), Multivitamin/mineral, Antioxidant complex, Omega-3 Fatty Acids, Omega-6 Fatty Acids, Pancreatic enzymes, and Betaine Hydrochloride. *Depression Free, Naturally* explains how each of these ingredients contributes to the brain's ability to process stress. Dr. Mathews-Larson then offers more symptom-specific formulas for individual needs, and explains the roles of each of these ingredients in maintaining mental balance. Many of these nutrients and minerals can be found in foods, and Dr. Mathews-Larson offers recommendations for foods to increase or avoid as we attempt to lift ourselves out of the "grief fog." I encourage you to read her book and visit her website for the full nutritional details on healing your emotions nutritionally.

As you move through the grieving process, you need to help your body heal nutritionally. That can begin with detoxing as you move yourself to a fat-burning machine instead of relying solely on carbs for calories and energy. To transition to this nutritional lifestyle, you may begin with detoxing.

Using a three-day green juice detox can kickstart your progress toward a healthy nutritional lifestyle. Detoxing before moving toward a healthy diet will cleanse your digestive system and allow it to more readily absorb your healthy foods loaded with essential fatty acids, minerals (use Sea Salt), needed vitamins, and antioxidant rich foods. Bookstores and the Internet provide an abundance of detox plans and recipes, and list the benefits derived from detoxing. You will feel better after detoxing and see feelings of depression, sadness, and grief begin to moderate. Of course, consult your physician before making changes to your diet.

Proper hydration helps to balance your body's chemistry and metabolism. All of my reading and experience in this area from medical experts make two essential points about hydration—

1) Drink ½ of your body weight in ounces daily. If you weigh 150 lbs., then drink 75 ounces of alkaline water daily. Don't drink soda or diet soda—too much sugar and it dehydrates you.
2) Drink alkaline water (drops for that are available at stores like Whole Foods).

Ground Zero can be an effective time to re-balance our body's chemistry and take control of what we are eating, and here's why:

1) You probably don't want to eat anyhow, so you might as well eat healthy foods.
2) People want to help, and they often think of making food. You can give them healthy recipes to create for you, found in this book, which makes it easier for friends and neighbors to feel truly helpful. Look for the "Taste of Triumph" recipes in Appendix 2.

When the rest of my life seemed completely out of control, I could exert my own order within the firestorm simply by eating healthy foods.

Never in your life is it more important to be on your A-game than when you're going through loss and change. You need to have your body in as balanced a position as possible so that your brain can make the calm, rational decisions that need to be made for your family in the aftermath of loss.

To Sleep, Perchance to Dream

During Ground Zero, natural sleep aids seemed like a drop of water on a raging fire for me. It got to the point where I couldn't sleep without Benadryl. Even then, my sleep was still not entirely restful. During my recovery from pneumonia several years later, I learned to take out certain foods (sugar, alcohol, caffeine) and add others (green juices, super foods, green smoothies, and veggies), and I also found some alternative therapy items. This got me off of sleep meds and helped me tap into vibrant health.

My #1 choice is a natural sleep aid that contains powered magnesium. The magnesium in that supplement helps me relax and have a good night's rest. In my opinion, even natural sleep aids are like a Band-Aid on a major wound. They can work for a while, but they are not the long-term solution. Eventually, I had to address the bigger health issues in my body that were brought on by the grieving process.

The next big question was what and when was I eating my last meal before bed. It's going to sound crazy, but dropping sugar, caffeine, and artificial sweeteners (for a start) and adding fresh green juices and smoothies, combined with not eating after 7:00 p.m., have made a world of difference in my life. You don't have to do it all at once. Make one change, and then when you feel comfortable, try another.

Exercising on a consistent basis is a *huge* part of good sleep, but what you are eating and when you eat it is just as important. We have to give our bodies the opportunity to create the right hormones, which is affected by the foods we eat.

In addition to learning how to streamline our digestion, we also need to plan for effective sleep.

I again turned to health researcher and nutritionist Ilana Katz for recommendations for getting the best night's sleep, and she offered some helpful suggestions:

How Can You Get a Good Night's Sleep?

The most important hours to sleep for the full recovery and washing of cells is between 10:00 p.m. and 4:00 a.m. You should adjust your individual sleep cycle to ensure these hours are taken the most advantage of, and should be a part of the healthy 7–8 hours per night.

Get ready for sleep–turn off all electronics (unless they have a dull backlight and are used more for relaxation than mind stimulation, for those who like to read themselves to sleep). Watching TV (especially the news), playing games on cell phones, laptops, and computers— these are all mind-stimulating activities, and should be avoided as you prepare for sleep.

Try to get workouts in earlier on in the day rather than in the evening. Although it may seem like a workout may tire you and ready you for sleep, it is actually stimulating and keeps the body more awake than preferable when you are attempting to wind down.

Darken the room, draw the curtains, and dim the lights close to bedtime. It is even recommended to get into night clothes (pajamas or sleepwear) when you are winding down for the evening.

As far as nutrition goes, do not eat within two hours of bedtime, and preferably reduce simpler carbs even earlier than that (simpler carbs, such as fruit, bread, and potatoes, stimulate insulin and keep the cells more awake while the body metabolizes them). Higher protein with a gut-soothing effect are preferable for the last meal of the day, such as almond/hemp/rice milk. Proteins also aid in muscle recovery through the night.

Avoid caffeine (or any other stimulants) and alcohol before bed.

Finally, be sure to stay constantly hydrated throughout the day, every day, but also make sure you stop your water intake within two hours before bed, to reduce the risk of disruptive sleep (needing to go to the bathroom in the middle of a deep sleep).

Healthy Power Tools (Good Grief Gift Ideas Instead of Flowers)

Sleep is at a premium for those who are grieving. Here is a list of gift ideas that have helped me get healthy and stimulate good rest. For more ideas, visit 180YourLife.com.

- **High-powered blender**: truly liquefies my green smoothies. There's nothing like chunks of partially pureed celery to turn me away from drinking a healthy smoothie.
- **High quality juicer**: helps me quickly make great green juices.
- **Infrared sauna sweatbox**: I've used it at least once a week for over three years now. An inexpensive, collapsible, personal

sauna (mine was about $250.00) purges my body of impurities, which helps me rest. You may want to start slowly with 5-10 minutes of sweating to start. The sauna process renews my skin and detoxes my body. Use as directed and consult your physician.

- **Dead Sea Epsom Salt** soak in the tub: Helps me sleep like a rock. Of course, consult your own physician before starting a new health regimen and use these products as directed.
- **Ionic footbath**: It is said to pull the heavy metals from your system. It can be pricey, but it helps me rest, and feeling energetic is priceless to me.[22]

Power Tools for Your Spirit

I also recommend journaling. Writing a letter to the loved one you have lost when you cannot sleep is really helpful. It can mirror, if only in the dimmest way, the times when you had that person as a sounding board or a comforter. It cannot take your pain away, but part of the transformative process is sitting with grief. There's no way around it. It's part of the love you have for the person you lost. So, write when you need to, talk with God, and try one idea listed here, then try another. That's how you begin to wade through the wreckage of broken dreams to a renewed life. One step and one good decision at a time.

Speak Life into Your Darkness. I suggest reading from a book of timeless wisdom. For me, I started with the book of Proverbs in the Bible. There are thirty-one short chapters, which coincidentally line up with the thirty-one days in the month. I always find some nugget of wisdom, some new insight that helps me make wise decisions. Proverbs 3:18 says, "Wisdom is a tree of life to those who embrace her."

Want to go a bit deeper? Try the Psalms, which is right next door to Proverbs in the Bible. When I was too steamed with God to say anything, I could read a Psalm out loud, and fortunately, King David, the author of most of the Psalms, had his struggles with God, too. This was a great place to start pouring my heart out to God.

I would have despaired unless I had believed that I would see the goodness of the Lord in the land of the living. Wait for the Lord; Be strong and let your heart take courage; Yes, wait for the Lord.
(Psalm 27:13-14 NASB)

While grief is incredibly painful and uncomfortable, it's also the fire that is going to remake your heart, mind, and soul in potentially spectacular ways. That transformation takes time, and if you are running away, you will miss the opportunity to craft a life you will eventually love. Hold steady, even when it feels like your feet, or your whole person, are in the fire.

Ship of Gold

One evening when I was nursing Sophia, I saw a documentary on the History Channel that offered another clue on this journey. The show was called *History's Mysteries,* and the feature was named "Ship of Gold."

This true story was about a ship, the SS *Central America*, a side-wheel steamer that left Panama in 1857 and went down in the Atlantic while carrying gold from California (then valued at over $2 million, now valued at over $100 million). This was during the years of the California Gold Rush, and the SS *Central America* was transporting about 600 passengers and a heavy cargo of gold coins and bars. Onboard was a newly married couple named Ansel and Addie Easton, and during their journey there arose a terrible storm at sea.

After three days of battling a fierce tropical storm, on September 12, 1857, a storm-damaged rescue ship, the brig *Marine*, responded to Captain William Lewis Herndon of the SS *Central America,* who had been sending Morse code cries for help. The crew and men on board transported women and children across the choppy seas in lifeboats from the ailing ship to the rescue ship. In that transference, the new bride was separated from her husband. They said goodbye, and Ansel assured Addie that he would be on a following lifeboat, but that never happened.

The tropical storm whipped into a fierce hurricane, driving the rescue ship farther and farther away from the SS *Central America*. Many of the men didn't have a chance to get to the rescue ship. In the throes of hurricane-force winds, the SS *Central America* finally gave way and sank to the bottom of the ocean. She came to rest in the darkness 8,000 feet below the surface, about 160 miles offshore from Charleston, South Carolina. Loss of the ship led to the "Panic of 1857," the first worldwide financial crisis.

Ansel Easton found himself in the storm-tossed ocean, holding desperately to the remaining wreckage of the perished ship. The surviving men gathered together as best they could in the unforgiving waves. All looked completely hopeless. In that devastation, a man of faith encouraged some of the shipwrecked men to band together to pray and sing songs to God.

As the the men huddled together in the ocean, they could hear the cries of others being picked off by sharks. Night was upon them. Some men, looking at the bleak situation, simply let go of the wreckage and sank into the sea, but others sang songs of hope into the cold darkness, staying together, while clinging to the wreckage.

On another ship, the Norwegian ship *Ellen*, something bizarre happened. Her sea captain, Captain Anders Johnsen, having no idea the SS *Central America* had sunk, was guiding his ship when a seagull dove down and hit the captain's head. The sea captain perceived this as a sign from God and *changed the course of his ship*.

On this new course, the *Ellen* drove directly into the path of the remaining survivors who were clinging to the SS *Central America*'s floating wreckage. The *Ellen*'s crew found the survivors by the sound of their singing. It was nighttime, and there would have been no other way for Captain Johnsen to know where the survivors were. Ansel Easton, along with other determined men, was saved and eventually reunited with his new bride, Addie.

All of this is documented in newspaper stories of that time, which report the tale of this harrowing journey. In an expedition in 1988, a remote-controlled underwater vehicle recovered gold and artifacts from the SS *Central America*. Among the recovered treasure was also the trunk that held the marriage trousseau of Addie Easton. By the end of the SS *Central America* disaster, about 426 lives were lost. Only 153 were saved.[23]

I was stunned as I watched this documentary, and this is what I took away from it:

Don't...Ever...Give...Up!

Even when hurricane-force winds break apart your ship and it's dark, the ocean is cold, the sharks are circling, there's no hope of rescue, and others are releasing their hold on the wreckage and letting the ocean swallow them, don't give up! Stay together, pray, hold on, sing when you can, cry out to God, have hope, make good choices, and wait. You never know when a seagull will dive-bomb a captain's head, he will think it's a divine sign, change course, and steer his ship into your wreckage. The world is filled with more miracles than we realize. Your story of despair might become one of determination that will inspire others for years, maybe decades, or like the SS *Central America,* for centuries to come.

This is the stuff of a lasting legacy.
It begins with determination and faith,
and some crazy signs of hope.

When I felt most overwhelmed, I would say, "'I shall not die, but live and declare the works of the Lord' (Psalm 118:17 NKJV). I shall not die in body, mind, or spirit. I will live. I will not be a victim, but a Victor. I will stand firm in the hope that God will show up in my circumstances, and then I will tell of His faithfulness."

While I am waiting, I will purpose to make good choices.
Sometimes those good choices are simple prayer,
staying in community, holding on, and doing the next best thing.

I held onto that story of the SS *Central America* when I didn't know how to navigate the wreckage of my life. Now, looking back from the standpoint of eight years, I can see that God did rescue me in thousands of small and big ways. I wasn't lifted out of the cold, dangerous ocean of grief in one fell swoop, but there were people on my path and decisions that I made that did eventually help guide me to a place of peace and hope.

The SS *Central America* was a ship of gold, not because of the gold coins it carried, but because of the endurance, faith, and determination that Ansel and Addie Easton and many others displayed in the face of fear and destructive circumstances. The story reminds me that God is God, and sometimes hope comes in crazy forms.

Journey to the Sunrise

Discover that grief does not magically lift with the passage of time.
Realize that nourishing your body while you are grieving can create a more efficient journey through grief.
Understand that grief is physical, mental, and spiritual.

Steps on the Path

- Do something soothing for your soul—pray, walk, get in the sunshine, reach out, and meet someone new.
- Be gentle with yourself, be patient, trust the process, forgive yourself and those around you for being messy.
- Don't worry too much about taking away bad foods right now. Focus on adding a few good things to your diet. When you get comfortable with those, add a few more.

Speak Life: Ground Zero
(Please Say Out Loud)

I will not lie down in the Desert of Grief. That is not my destiny. I am on a quest. Though the grasses have browned, the ground has cracked, and the night is full of the unknown, I sense a presence. I ask God to show me the way to the flood lands of the soul. I rise, taking one step and then another, moving forward into the night, pressing on toward the waters of renewal and the light of day.

Forge Your Team

Step 2:

Forge Your Team

"Behold, I Myself have created the smith who blows the fire of coals
And brings out a weapon for its work…"
Isaiah 54:16a NIV

The Blacksmith

I stood before the darkened shed, cool air behind me, hot air wafting on my face. The fire pulsed as the blacksmith worked the bellows and he gathered his heavy, hard tools around him. As he began his project, he first took an old iron railroad spike in his tongs and placed it in the fire until the black iron became red with heat. He pulled it from the fire and placed it on the anvil, where he struck it over and over with his hammer. Then the blacksmith hit the metal hard, but carefully, as he methodically turned it and began to shape it. When the metal cooled off, back into the fire it went. The blacksmith repeated this process until the form of the spike slowly faded away. The head of the spike began to change into the shape of a leaf, and the long part of the spike now curved into a hook.

There is a historic village at Stone Mountain Park in Georgia, where I watched the blacksmith work. I visited this village while Jason and I were married, several years before his death. On the day that I visited, the blacksmith was taking old railroad spikes and re-making them into decorative hooks. The spikes had seen better days. They were rusted and worn out, and common as dirt. But in the hands of the blacksmith, something transformative was taking place. I had to wonder if the

89

hardened, artisan hands of the blacksmith could be likened to God's hands when He gets to working on us.

As the blacksmith's work began to take shape, his tools and process changed. After the major reshaping of the spike was done, he pulled out chisels, which he used to detail the veins of the leaf. He then used a vice to hold the metal completely still so that he could bend it into a hook. He used a poker to punch a hole at the leaf's base so that the hook could be hung on a wall.

At the end, he dunked his new creation in the water, sending a sizzling steam into the air. A quick coat of black paint, and he was done. I bought two of his hooks and nailed one near my front door as a reminder that God's renewing work in us is often achieved through the heat and blows of fiery trials.

Several weeks later, I returned to the blacksmith to ask a couple of questions. I brought with me one of the hooks he had made. I was hoping to get him to add a small decorative curl on the end. It was an October weekday, and the blacksmith didn't have a crowd around him. We struck up a conversation. I showed him my hook and asked for the minor change. What happened next was unexpected.

As he worked, he gave me insights into the blacksmithing process. For one, if he tried to work on cold metal, it would break apart at the first blow. The fire makes the metal soft and malleable. The blacksmith knows exactly how much heat the metal can take before it would be destroyed under the pressure. A good blacksmith will cool the metal from time to time before continuing to work, so as not to over-stress it. Sometimes a blacksmith will change one of his creations and fashion it into a specific tool that he needs for a specific job. Then, when he is done using that unique tool, he may change that metal again into something else for another purpose.

**Nothing is garbage in the blacksmith's hands.
With his fire, anvil, and hammer, he can create
and re-create as he sees fit.**

While he told me these principles, his hands were at work on the hook. He had heated it in the fire and now was hammering out the leaf again. He broke the leaf from its base, and the hook section fell to the floor. He explained that he could work on it better that way. By hammering it out, he changed the rather small leaf into a larger, rippling, more intricate one. It was beautiful.

Then he took the hook and placed it in the fire until it glowed red-hot. With his tongs he placed the hook in a vice and began to twist. He twisted until the hook became even more ornate, with the four straight angles of the spike now curved into a lovely spiral running up and down the hook. Then he added my requested curl at the end.

He re-attached the two pieces, soldering them together by adding part of a melted steel rod.

"Stronger than before," he told me.

I held the hook in my hand. It was more beautiful than the other I had at home. An extra request for the fire had done that. The blacksmith had added my curl, and much more, with his creative hands, rough-hewn from years of working with simple tools and the heat of the fire.

I was not on good terms with God after Jason died. My bitterness and anger came with a host of other emotions, such as numbness, terror, guilt, loneliness, and depression. At first, I tried to resist these feelings, but they still found a way into my soul—like boorish, unwelcome guests that put their shoes on the furniture, make a mess of the place, and eat all your food.

Later, exhausted from trying to outrun my pain, I stopped fighting and would let these unwelcome guests have their way. Somehow, when I relaxed into accepting that such feelings would come, they eventually lost their power and stopped coming by so often. Now, when they do visit, their shadows don't loom so large, and they don't stay so long.

Looking back, I wonder if the emotions that invaded me might have been the tools used to reshape me.

I still have many questions for God, but the image of Him as a blacksmith working to bring purpose out of pain was one I clung to in the aftermath of Jason's death.

Chapter 5:

Ground Zero Posse

"...believing that someone is by your side—someone who makes you smile,
but also someone you know you can count on when you need support—
is one of the great secrets of supersurvival."
- David B. Feldman, Ph.D. and Lee Daniel Kravetz[24]

Though I found comfort in object lessons about my relationship with God, I still suffered deeply after Jason's death. I would have many angry, frustrated conversations with Him. I had been told in my first week of widowhood that I was not actually without a husband. Several women tried to console me at Jason's funeral with, "Well, now God is your husband." It was obviously meant to offer me some comfort, but at the time, I wasn't ready to accept it. I was imagining, among other things, the hundreds—nay, thousands—of dirty diapers that would be mine alone to change.

One afternoon, Arie was screaming while I was wrangling her into the car seat. I was eight months pregnant, I was frazzled, and I was running late. I had to run back into the house to get something I had forgotten.

Once I got back inside the house, I stamped my foot, thrust my finger at the ceiling, and yelled to God, "Fine! If you want to be my Heavenly Husband, I'm giving You the Stink Eye! I've had it!"

Then I stormed out of the house, slammed the door, and retreated back to my minivan.

I knew, of course, that I needed help, but at the time, my need was a vague, all-encompassing feeling of frustration. The crux of my struggle, and of my salvation, was that I had to have support: a team of specialists who would teach, guide, prod, encourage, or just plain yank me out of bed to get me going. Some days, I could not even manage to do simple, everyday tasks, such as tackling the laundry or planning the meals. There were times I couldn't breathe or think outside my pain.

During the first few days after a tragedy, friends and neighbors will want to help because they want an outlet for their grief. Before long, however, life returns to normal. Schedules are busy, and grief can be isolating for the surviving family. The silence from the huge hole in your home caused by the absence of a loved one can be crushing. The parade of casseroles will be replaced by the sound of crickets. Where's the group that once swarmed your house? In time, you will discover that more than just a loss of a loved one has occurred.

A life-shift has taken place for you and your family. Therefore, you must strategically harness the goodwill that is so plentiful. Here's a secret: your friends and neighbors want to help. Your friends care about you, and they need to work out their own feelings of grief and sympathy. You can give their grief a direction by asking them for specific, concrete help.

In **Appendix 1**, "Casserole Killer: A Practical Guide to Empowering the First Few Weeks and Months of Your Grief Journey or the Grief Journey of Someone You Know," I offer specific, practical advice for moving efficiently through the weeks and months following a great loss. It includes detailed and time-sensitive plans for managing the logistics of the grief journey and enlisting help from neighbors, friends, and community resources.

Your need can be a gift to your friends and neighbors; you are offering them a chance to feed their spirits. You also open the door for your new Team—those among your acquaintances who are uniquely equipped to usher you through your transition.

As I tell the following stories, I ask grace from those who know me. Please forgive me if I leave something out. There is so much to tell, and each story I share here has a specific point I want to convey. The truth is, I have had lots of help in my grief journey, and it didn't necessarily come from sources I expected.

Your first priority is to find an emotional posse that will come to encourage you. These people are like the firemen who will run into a burning house while everybody else is running out. When you are feeling overwhelmed, they are the ones running toward you. They are not afraid of the arrows of grief, anger, or sadness that are flying. They understand. These people know how to be effective in an extreme grief situation and how to get you away from the destructive fires of negativity.

When I told my friends that I didn't want to be alone at home, they didn't ask questions. They didn't talk around me in hushed tones. They didn't have any particular words of wisdom; they just offered their presence. They simply rolled up their sleeves and plunged into the muck with me. They took care of me in the ways I most needed.

For example, I was never the cook in my family. After Jason died, I used to burn myself just defrosting pizza. Friends who knew me well would call to ask, "How are you holding up, Mishael, and what are you eating?" They did not send flowers; they ordered me a catering service for a few weeks. This was a brilliant grief gift!

In the first few weeks, a dear couple from church hired a nanny to stay with me during the day, and then they stayed with me on the nights that the nanny wasn't there. That was one of the best, most practical grief gifts I could have received. I was too much in the "fog of grief" to consider hiring a nanny, but what a relief it was to have someone make meals, clean the house, and play with my daughter while I took time to rest.

Kiki and her husband Don, a fellow news colleague, were also creative in their generosity. About a month after Jason died, they flew my daughter, my cousin, myself, and even my toy poodle to their horse farm in Dallas, Texas. The change of scenery, being with friends who were comfortable with grief, and spending time outside with the horses were all very healing. Mind you, I cried for hours at a time, sometimes with their horses—which I personally found quite soothing. (Nothing like being nuzzled back to peace). I was really messy and really pregnant then. They couldn't fix my grief, but they could be there with me. They conveyed the hope that even though I was hurt, in time I would be healed.

My cousin came to stay with me about four weeks after Jason died. There was something peaceful about having family around who knew who I had been before becoming a wife. She called out my former self in the way only family can. Her laughter was infectious, and while she helped me with Arie and found fun things for us to do, she also introduced another important element. *She educated herself about grief.*

I hadn't thought to read books on grief, but she had. My cousin would read them from time to time to better understand what I was going through. She introduced to me ways of understanding grief that made it feel less like a random, swirling morass and more like a chartable journey. I will always be grateful for the love, fun, and time she gave me.

Diamond in the Darkness

When it came time for me to give birth to Sophia, Kiki flew from Dallas to Atlanta to be in the delivery room with me. I had asked for her specifically, because I knew that her spunky spirit and sense of humor would be just what I needed to set the tone for my new child's entry into this world. I didn't want sadness or melancholy. I crafted that moment by consciously placing people around me who would set the right mood and create the right memories.

I remember wearing a hospital gown, walking down the hospital hall with Kiki, prepped for my scheduled C-section. The doors to the delivery room opened, and the doctors and nurses all looked up from their preparations around an operating table, all masked and ready for action. There was no turning back. I lay down on the table. Kiki sat on a chair near my head. My arms were strapped down so I couldn't move them during the operation.

"Do you want to see us deliver your baby, or do you want the blue screen?" my OB asked.

"I don't really like to encounter my innards," I replied. "Let's put that blue screen up, and let me know when you get to the good stuff."

They set up a little blue curtain of sorts starting at my chest, so that I couldn't see what was going to happen in my baby-making zone.

Jason and I always liked the surprise of not knowing the sex of our children until birth. I kept that surprise going even after he passed. Kiki, a very spiritual soul, was convinced I was having a boy. I agreed, because my basketball-looking belly was so different from the super-fluff belly I had sported when I had my older child. Although I wondered how I would raise a boy without my husband, I mainly just wanted a healthy baby to love.

My doctor asked, "Kiki, would you like to tell Mishael the sex of her baby when the time comes?"

"Yes," she replied.

"Okay, then let's get this party started," replied my OB.

Kiki and I waited quietly while doctors were working behind the little blue curtain.

Kiki leaned over near my ear to quietly comment, "I just want to say right now that I am *really* outside my comfort zone."

"Really?" I turned my head to look at her, because that was the only body part I actually had control of. "That's something to know, because I'm *really* outside my comfort zone too!"

We laughed, taking my mind off the procedure. My plan was already working. Kiki asked for some good Christian tunes to be pumped in, and we waited while the doctor and nurses worked. The time soon arrived: I heard the cry of my baby.

My doctor said, "Okay, Kiki, tell her."

As she lifted my child up, Kiki stood up and, in utter shock, said, "It's a *girl*!"

"*What!*" I replied. "Are you *sure*?"

"Do you need me to show you again?" asked the doctor, smiling.

"Yes, I'm sure. It's a girl!" chimed Kiki.

"A girl!" I said. I felt my heart swell and burst with happiness. "I know how to raise girls!"

I felt like a child running to my presents on Christmas morning, with the joy of a thousand Christmas mornings.

A *girl*. I would name her Sophia Tigerlily Mikaela, all names Jason and I loved. Each name a gift and a spoken destiny: Sophia for wisdom, Tigerlily an exotic princess, and Mikaela, after the archangel Michael, a warrior. She is my "Wise Warrior Princess."

Once I was wheeled back into my hospital room with Sophia, swaddled like a soft, pink present, my girlfriends, Amy and Jyn, brought up Arie to meet her new sister.

Arie walked in wonder toward my bed and I said, "Big Sister, welcome your Baby Sister," leaning a swaddled Sophia toward Arie.

Her hands splayed out in joyous surprise, "A sister! I always wanted a sister!"

She climbed onto my bed, and we three snuggled together.

I had my posse of *chicas* around me. Like my sweet friend, Melinda, who drove from Florida to watch Arie while I stayed at the hospital. Jyn slept overnight in the post-delivery room and bears the distinction of changing Sophia's first diaper. Kiki alternated nights with Jyn until

I went home from the hospital. Neighbors helped me by mowing my lawn, taking care of my family, and later inviting us to social gatherings, even though I was still struggling.

I was thrilled to be a new mother, but there were times I struggled almost daily with grief. During those times, I would take Arie and my new baby Sophia and walk, sometimes in my pajama pants, to visit my neighbor, Lenore, who was an older widow. She would make food for us and let me sit with her. I'd laugh and cry and eat dishes she had made from the *Betty Crocker Cookbook*.

> **If you are the friend of someone facing loss,**
> **your primary gift is just showing up.**

You don't have to have the answers, and you will probably say the wrong thing. Just be open, and I guarantee that your grieving friend will be glad simply to have someone in the room. Later on, *being there* can evolve into helping with estate issues, exercising with your friend, and cooking a healthy meal for her.

Practical Support: Designate an Organizer

When I began my grief journey, I simply flew on autopilot and tried everything that came to mind in order to cope with my new condition. Afterwards, I had to clear away the rubble of those efforts in order to create the life I could love once again. With the benefit of hindsight, I can offer some suggestions for someone who is facing loss.

Grief is physically exhausting. The fear and the stress can actually create a brain fog, and it's harder to make decisions, harder to function through your normal day. You need a support system around you while you are in shock, and then while you are readjusting to your new life. Even simple tasks can feel overwhelming when you are grieving. The extra energy brought by having friends alongside you is important.

You may have to be proactive and organize friends for yourself. Start by making a list of your friends and the talents that they have. Then ask them to help you with their specific talents. If some people are good at cooking, don't ask them to mow your lawn. Ask them to cook some meals for you, and then in the future, ask them to guide you in bulk cooking healthy meals.

If you have a family member or a friend who is willing to act as your secretary and bodyguard during the first week, then pin that person with an official title. This person need not be a best friend, but rather someone who is tactful, firm, organized, and most importantly, willing. Titles are free, so make up a good one for your organizer. "King" or "Queen" has a nice ring to it. If such a volunteer doesn't materialize, then these lists can help through the first few weeks.

The "King" or "Queen" Posse Organizer's job duties are:

- First, take down the names, contact information, and skillsets of those wanting to help.
- Second, have these volunteers commit to a schedule of help.
- Third, run interference for you when you are in the midst of meltdowns.

Through websites like signupgenius.com, you can email a link to all the friends and neighbors who want to help. Volunteers can view the schedule and sign up for specific tasks on specific days. Other useful volunteering websites are volunteergenius.com and caringbridge.org.[25]

The Organizer should also make a list of all the items given to the grieving family and write the thank you notes. I don't think this task should be done by the grieving person, unless he or she wants it. Have someone make the list, get the addresses, and write the notes, leaving the signature area blank for the grieving person to sign.

Ideally, your Posse will consist of several key Go-To Captains, in charge of:

1. Finances: This trusted person is in charge of gathering all the bills, contacting a financial planner, and gathering the information that you will need for the Social Security office so that you can possibly start collecting Social Security.

2. Food: This person coordinates healthy meals so that you don't have casserole after casserole, cake after cake. He or she could send out a list of recipes that takes into account your family's tastes and allergies, and provides healthy, easy-to-store meals. (Refer to "Taste of Triumph" recipes in Appendix 2). Your Food Captain can also offer a place where families can order meals for the grieving person. A meal-prep service such as dinnerafare.com or insteadofflowers.com can be a great help. The website at 180YourLife.com will have healthier recipes, as well as ongoing links and helpful ideas. Most people will want to do whatever is most helpful and will be grateful for very specific guidelines.

3. Home Care: Helping to organize the house is a great way to bring a sense of order and calm to a situation that feels out of control. You need somebody to help with laundry, lawn care, home repair, and general cleaning of the house for the first couple of months. Friends and family might lend a teenager or pay a teen to be a helper to a grieving parent. Even doing laundry, which can pile up and feel overwhelming to a surviving spouse, is a helpful gift. I suggest sending teens in groups of two or three. Use wisdom and gauge your own comfort level. If you can afford it, you could look into gonannies.com or post a job notice for an assistant to help with the kids and house. (You must interview the applicants and perform background checks, of course). Early on, I depended a great deal on babysitters to help with my laundry and clean the house with me.

4. Write it Down: Lists are a big help, too. The trauma of grief affects your memory, so grieving people forget stuff all the time. I took to writing lists for groceries, getting the kids' supplies ready for school each day, daily financial details, and errands.

5. Mobilize the Family: Your Home Care expert can help organize a chore chart for the kids and help get it started—instructions coming from other adults are generally easier for kids to take. Ultimately, you can't sustain an outsourced system of home care—although it would be a wonderful relief if you can do so for a couple of months.

6. Exercise: This person will be in charge of making sure you exercise about three times a week. It doesn't have to be the same person who exercises with you each time: somebody can volunteer to walk with you on Mondays, and another can come by on Wednesdays. That way, you will be getting outside for a ten-to-twenty-minute walk from the beginning. You need to get out into the sunshine. It will to elevate your mood. The vitamin D from the sun has a calming effect on your nerves. You need to have friends who will prod you with a simple, "Let's go for a walk," and if you respond with, "I don't feel like it," who won't take "no" for an answer too easily.

7. Activities: This person will put together a list of all the contacts for the family, the teachers, etc., so that volunteers can step in to help with specific events. For example, if someone at school needs to meet with a parent, maybe a friend can go with you to do that. If there's a "Donuts for Dads" or "Muffins for Moms" event at school, your Activity Captain can designate a volunteer stand-in.

You have to remember that the surviving children of loss are still kids. They need to get outside to play and run around. Families and friends can also schedule activities and outings—for example, going to the playground or the zoo. Volunteers can do all the organizing and planning for the activity, freeing the grieving parent from that stress. It will be much easier for the parent to leave the house and enjoy the afternoon if all the prep-work and packing has already been done. If the parent doesn't feel up for an activity, a friend could offer to take the kids for an afternoon or even overnight if possible. Mostly, kids need to have the freedom to be kids, even in a grieving environment. Use your wisdom and discretion when sending children to play with volunteers. Sometimes it's great to have someone else join you at an event with you and your kids.

8. Organizations: Church groups, small faith groups, and volunteer groups such as Floodstudentmissions.org are great for quarterly or biannual help for single-parent families who need repairs and yard work done around the house. Flood Student Missions helps mobilize middle school and high school students in local service projects. They have been a Godsend in my home. The Organizations Captain can identify these resource groups, schedule time for them to help a grieving family, and identify household projects that will need attention in the next few months.

In time, connecting the grieving family with a support group and grief counselor will also be a great help. I have seen a grief counselor off and on during my grief journey. It may seem best to throw yourself back into work, but if you don't deal with the issues, vibrant healing might never materialize for you and your family. These are concerns that a newly grieving parent may not know to think of, but will be a great source of help and healthy healing in the long run. Resources that were helpful to me were Katesclub.org, TheLink.org, and Loveloud.us.[26]

9. Spider & Insect Removal: If you are like me, wherever you are on your grief journey, spiders or various insects will always be unnerving. I'm afraid you may have to gird your loins, take off your shoe, and take charge of this role yourself. Be brave! You can do it!

10. Ask for Help: My best advice is to ask for help as often as you need it—don't save up requests or postpone your needs. Also, respond with grace and gratitude whenever someone cannot help at the moment.

One benefit of organizing your Ground Zero Posse is its emotional economy. It's important to spread your grief support thinly among your friends and neighbors. Frankly speaking, anyone who is not in the throes of tragedy cannot live long amid the power of grief emotions, but many people can visit you there and offer you strength. If good friends appear to pull away, offer them the same quiet grace that you are depending on receiving. Different friends will likely phase in and out on this journey. Some friends only seem to have left, and you may run into them again farther down the path.

Life marches on. It's inescapably true. You want it all to stop, but it just doesn't. Kids still have to eat, lawns will grow, laundry will get dirty, and you will have to establish kind and firm boundaries to honor your life and home environment. Don't be afraid to speak up and take the reins when necessary. It will feel tough sometimes. Some folks may not take kindly to it at first. That's okay. Don't be afraid to stand as the leader in your life and home, but draw around you a protective mantle of supporters.

Journey to the Sunrise

Do not be surprised when life marches on in spite of your grief.
Realize that you may have to speak up and stand up as the leader of your life.
Understand that you should ask for help as often as you need it.

Steps on the Path

- You need a support system around you while you are in shock, and then while you are readjusting to your new life.
- You need people around you, because even simple tasks can feel overwhelming when you are in grief. The extra energy brought by having friends alongside you is important.
- The three primary steps in getting the help you need:
  * Identify ways others can help you.
  * Realize that people want to help.
  * Ask for it.

Chapter 6:

A Posse for your Journey

E stablishing a posse for a widow's journey will look different for each person. For a long time, I basically stayed in survival mode. I hired a live-in nanny, Caroline, from GoNannies.com. She helped me until Sophia was seven months old. In many ways, she rescued me. Besides providing help in the difficult chore of caring for a toddler and a new baby, she weathered some of my fiercest storms. She was cheerful every day and inspired me to find my own fun again. Caroline called herself a Plain Person, which is like a pioneer from the 1800s who uses technology. She wore a head covering and dressed like Laura Ingalls Wilder. She played a cappella worship music from the same CD all day, every day, until it got so far into my brain that I would hear it in my thoughts when I woke up in the night. I'm not making this stuff up; God has a sense of humor. She was adventurous, loving, funny, compassionate, and strong. She had the *flair of fun* and a passion and love of life. Just being around her relit my creative fire.

Only a few days into her stay, she gently but firmly set me back on my feet.

"You realize that the three-year-old (meaning my daughter Arie) runs the house," she declared. "And she is not doing it well."

That was one of many calls for me to step up and establish order in my home as a single parent. I didn't want to believe that this was actually my life and that I had to steer this ship myself. What if I didn't do it? Would that make Jason come back?

**Eventually, I had to accept that I needed to own my life —
even though it was in tatters at the moment —
and claim my family space, organize it, and work with my
daughters to move forward.**

God as Posse: The Night Shift

I remember a night, just before Caroline came to us, when a new-born's cry jarred me out of slumber. I lay face up in my bed. Bleary eyed, I could dimly see the time on the digital clock blink a furtive 2:13 a.m. Sophia, about four days old, was in a co-sleeper bassinet next to my bed. I reached my hand over the edge of the bassinet and tried to soothe her.

"Shhh. It's all right. Go back to sleep, Bunny," I whispered as I rubbed her back.

My other daughter, who was in the midst of her ninety-day blitz of not leaving my side after Jason's death, was sleeping in a toddler bed on the other side of my bed. I had to act with the speed and precision of a one-woman bomb squad. If Sophia's crying lasted long, Arie would be joining her early morning chorus, and then it would be a full-tilt-boogie for hours.

A girlfriend was staying overnight, but she was sleeping in the bedroom across the house from mine. We hadn't had the forethought to set up a baby monitor connecting her room to mine. Or maybe that *was* by design, but not *my* design. Well played, Girlfriend, well played.

Sophia was still crying, and as I tried to sit up, my lower abdomen, sporting a new C-section incision, felt like it was being tasered *and* burned with a branding iron. I had backed off my pain pills a few days after my C-section because I was breastfeeding. In that moment, I realized that this might not have been the best plan.

I took a deep breath and propped up on my elbows. *Holy heavens!* The pain was psychedelic. Between the searing sensation of my lower gut and Sophia's cries, I was definitely awake. It was clear that the simple act of pulling myself up into a sitting position, turning my torso, and then lifting Sophia out of her bassinet to breast-feed her, would not be possible.

I lay back staring at the ceiling. In a hoarse whisper, I called my friend's name, but couldn't yell too loudly because it hurt my lower abdominals, and I didn't want to wake Arie.

No answer.

God and I weren't really on great terms, but hot, tired, and feeling helpless, I prayed in desperation, "Lord, Jason used to take the night shift when Arie was a baby. I really need you to help Sophia get back to sleep. Please."

About ten seconds later, Sophia's cries quieted and then there was blessed silence. Sophia was asleep. From the time she woke up to the time she went back to sleep was only a minute or two.

I lay there in the darkness of my room, and the thought occurred to me that maybe I wasn't in this alone. Maybe there was something to the Heavenly Husband promise. Could God actually be that practical?

As I drifted back to sleep, I felt a new measure of peace while my baby slept beside me.

So I repeat my advice: *don't go it alone*. It doesn't matter where your relationship with God is, or even if you don't have one: reach out in honest prayer. Even when we don't understand God's ways, my experience is that God shows up in one way or another when we are real with Him. Sometimes it's timely, and sometimes God's timetable is entirely different than ours.

Even though I was steamed with God, I couldn't help but remember a verse during that time. Hopefully, it will help you too.

> *Do not fear, for I am with you; do not anxiously*
> *look about you, for I am your God.*
> *I will strengthen you, surely I will help you,*
> *surely I will uphold you with My righteous*
> *right hand.* (Isaiah 41:10 NASB)

Fun Posse

Laughter brings healing both mentally and physically. Look for ways to have fun.

When Jason died, we had been living in a rental home in Cumming, Georgia, for only three months. I had already made fast friends with my next-door neighbor, Rachel. Rachel was also pregnant, and she was due only a month after I was. She and her husband were a fun, relaxed couple—the type that strummed guitars to play background music while you sipped tea.

By the winter of that year, however, I was stalled in functional mode. Even though I wasn't the most fun person to be around, Rachel would come over to spend time with me. One especially cold winter's day, when it had snowed in Georgia, we both had our babies in their snowsuits. After playing outside with our kiddos, I invited her to come over to my place.

I had just cleaned the house, so it was prime hosting time. She noticed that the slick, faux-wood floors of my home were perfect for "baby hockey." If we put the hoods on our kids, their little bodies glided nicely on the smooth floors. We lined our babies up, set a shoe as the goal, placed our babies on their backs, and one at a time, gave our cooing children a gentle shove.

To our delight, it worked! Our babies giggled with glee as they slid on the floor, and we laughed hysterically. I'll never forget that day. Rachel wasn't afraid to walk into my emotional mess and help me find a place of laughter. I was reminded again that life is indeed beautiful. I could not change what had happened to me, but I could take a momentary break from grief and enjoy what I had been given.

Push-Me Posse

I also needed people who knew me well before my life had been changed by loss. I needed someone who would not see me as just a weeping, pregnant widow. I needed to be reminded of who I was and who I would be again. I didn't want pity. I wanted someone to help me find real hope, empowerment, and purpose.

About six weeks after Jason died, I was on the internet (couldn't sleep at all) and saw that one of my dear friends, a news colleague, was also online. Living in another state, he didn't yet know about Jason's death. So, I sent him an instant message. He called me within moments.

We had known each other for almost fifteen years at that point. Our first assignment together had been on a Coast Guard cutter, shooting for ABC News as the crew was rescuing Cuban rafters in the Florida Straits. We became fast friends. He has always challenged me to dig deep and work hard on my craft in television journalism. A seasoned network news producer, Bert listened as I tearfully shared the details of my devastation.

I could just imagine him sitting quietly in his New York home, thoughtfully sipping a scotch as he took it all in. I unburdened my heart to him that night. In a litany of stories, my grand finale was from that very day. Eight months pregnant and with a toddler clinging to my side, I had inadvertently run the vacuum over my belly-obscured right foot and torn off part of my big toenail.

When I finished with the story, Bert paused and then laughed a hearty laugh. He had that smooth, deep, basso profundo broadcaster voice that should announce the evening news. Now that I thought of it, it was pretty funny—the not seeing my feet part. So, I joined him in a much-needed laugh.

Then he said, "I'm so very, very sorry for your loss. It's tragic and unfair. There also seems to be a book in you. You should start writing these stories down and eventually put together a book."

He didn't see me as a victim. He knew who I had been before. He reminded me that I was a strong, capable woman, an overcomer, and that I could do something productive with my pain. That night, Bert reframed my journey. He spoke hope and strength into what I was going through. Amazingly, that moment was the seed of my purpose, which has grown to this very day and to this very moment with you, Dear Reader—right now, in this book.

Composite Spouse

Part of your posse could include what I call the Composite Spouse. For me, a composite husband is comprised of the expertise of several male friends and neighbors—which means "he" will probably be more competent than any one person. For example, I have a neighbor who is an excellent handyman, and I call him if I have a non-urgent plumbing issue or help jumpstarting my car. Another neighbor is an expert gardener and offers gardening advice for my yard. I have a friend who helps me with legal issues, and another who volunteers to go to Father-Daughter events with my girls.

I appreciated a man's perspective as well as the advice of my female friends. Having trusted male and female voices in your life after loss can provide a wise counterbalance. Mostly, I restrict my requests for help or advice to single men. Occasionally, I may need the expertise of a man who happens to be married. I want to emphasize the very delicate position I am in if I call for the help of advice from a married man. First and foremost, I must respect his relationship with his own wife. I would only approach a married male friend for advice when his wife was present or we were in the company of other people. I would not call him just to have a chat. I am careful to avoid any one-on-one situations. When a married man offers me help, I do not accept that help in an isolated environment. I respect the fact that I'm receiving both his and his wife's generosity. She will only be comfortable with his charity if we are all completely above reproach.

Posse for your Healing

When Arie was six years old, she met me at the bottom of the stairs one morning with a troubled expression on her face. She looked up at me with her piercing eyes and asked, "Did Daddy know that the coals would kill him?"

She was asking *the* question. Was his death an accident, or did I think he had chosen it? I had my own decision to make in that moment. I want my daughter always to trust me, so I decided to tell her the truth. As much truth as "her little backpack can carry," as a counselor once phrased it. When she asked questions, I answered them. So, she knew that daddy had died in his car. She knew he had died at a campground. After she asked how he had died, she knew that the coals he brought into the car emitted fumes that caused his body to stop working, but now she was asking the Big One.

I hadn't expected it to come so soon. Arie was only six. However, I was also not surprised. She has always been a truth-seeker. She cracked the code on Santa at four years of age. Not long afterwards, she woke me up one morning by slapping her dollar from the Tooth Fairy on my bed and demanding her tooth back. She wanted to make an aboriginal-inspired necklace with her baby teeth. It seemed only natural that her quick mind would eventually want to sort out her dad's death.

I had attended individual grief counseling after Jason died. After a while, I wanted to move on with my life and not focus on this pain. I thought that providing fun experiences for my kids would help us re-engage with life and move forward. That did work, to some degree, but it didn't erase the questions.

Now, my daughter was asking whether her dad's death had been an accident or his intentional decision. It was a fundamental question. After the dust settled, about six months after Jason had died, I remembered a conversation he had once had with me. He had graduated from Life University with his doctorate in chiropractic medicine. One day, after class, he came home and warned me never to bring a Hibachi grill into the house for warmth, because the coals emit carbon monoxide, and some families have died this way. It must have been something he learned in class and wanted to share with me. For that reason and others, I felt strongly that he had known the result of his actions.

The Bible verse kept running through my head, "The truth will set you free" (John 8:32). I had to believe that speaking the painful truth now, even to a six-year-old, would give us the opportunity to manage the pain of this type of loss together over the course of her childhood. I didn't want her to be blindsided later when she put two and two together and then become furious with me for lying. I believe that telling the truth now protects the trust later—even when that necessary truth-telling is going to result in a painful present moment.

So, I took a deep breath, sat on the bottom step, brought her onto my lap and said, "Yes, Baby, I think he did know."

With that, her innocent and seeking eyes started to well with tears.

"Why would he leave me? Didn't he love me? Was I a bad child? Why wouldn't he stay to be my dad?" I prayed for wisdom and said, "Have you ever had a bad tummy ache?" Arie nodded. I continued, "And maybe that tummy ache makes you throw up, but you are not doing that on purpose, right?" She sniffled and nodded again. "Sometimes that tummy ache makes you feel so bad that it just happens. Well, that same ache can happen with the brain, and sometimes someone makes a sad decision that he wouldn't normally make. We know now, that it's so important to tell other people when we are really sad so they can help us. Do I ever make mistakes as your mommy?"

"All the time," Arie smiled.

"Very funny. Do you still love me even when I make a mistake?"

"Yes, I do," Arie replied.

"Well, then we can still love Daddy, even when he made a mistake that he can never take back. He was such a good daddy and he loved us so much. I bet he even loves us from heaven right now."

I tried to answer these questions as best I could, to help her to have compassion for his pain, but these questions kept coming up for about a week. Arie, who was normally a cheerful child, was now expressing anger and crying off and on. My six-year-old child was grieving. Again.

I knew I couldn't do this alone. I needed backup. Professional backup. So, I called Kate Atwood, who started the group Kate's Club, an Atlanta-based non-profit that empowers children who have lost a parent or sibling

(KatesClub.org). We knew one another through media connections, but I had resisted such grief groups. I wouldn't elect to join a group that might make me feel sad, because I was working so hard to be happy.

Now, in trying to manage the pain of my grieving child, I knew I needed help. So, we joined Kate's Club, and it has made all the difference in our lives. Arie found her Posse of Kiddos who understood what it was like to lose a parent. Kate's Club engages the children with art therapists and counselors who use creative ways to help children express their grief. Counselors eventually worked with both of my kids, and I became connected with other parents who were widows and widowers. Somehow, I had thought that joining a group like this would make everything too real, so I had avoided doing so for a long time. The reality was that it was already too real, and I needed tools to empower my life and the lives of my children with truth.

I wish I had made this decision earlier in my grief journey. I have met widows in support groups who are healthier at one year after loss than I was at four years out. From Kate's Club, I learned about TheLink.org, another counseling center in Atlanta, which specifically helps adult and child survivors of suicide. I also didn't want to join a Survivors of Suicide Support Group. I didn't want to admit to myself or to those around me that suicide was the way my husband had likely died. I felt like it would be a public admission of failure, like I should have seen the signs or known what he was thinking. Was I a bad wife? What could I have done differently? How could I have saved him? This way of thinking can get you lost in a horrible house of mirrors. It's a mirage of lies.

Don't stay there. Get help. Find support.

Studies show that the grief associated with processing a suicide is extremely complicated, and it can take a person five to ten years to find a healthy recovery. I suffered alone needlessly for years. Once I finally joined a grief group for survivors of suicide, I felt a relief that comes only from connecting with people who understood my specific pain and experience.

An added benefit is that you eventually come to a place where you can use your experience to help others in their pain. When that happens, the feeling of healing and purpose is surprisingly joyful. It's hard to explain. I was completely shocked to discover that when I could help others in my area of grief, a joy bubbled up in me. That was new, and it made me want to do it again and again.

**The joy your heart feels when you help others
in your grief zone leads you and changes your life.**

I couldn't change what had happened in the past, but I could change my response to it. Each time I went to a grief group, each time I connected with those who understood my loss, I felt freer, more myself, and I saw my children start to thrive. We no longer had secrets to hide. Loss became part of the landscape of our lives. We found compassion and understanding. We found community, and that has been a vital part of the healing of our family.

The Reset Button

One key lesson I remember from my talks with other widows was what I call The Reset Button. Just being in community with other widows helped me to put my circumstances into perspective and eventually find gratitude.

The Widows' Group at First Baptist of Woodstock met at the early morning hour of 8:00 a.m., and I needed the community it offered more than I needed the extra sleep. Under the best of conditions, it wasn't easy wrangling my then three-year-old and six-year-old children through breakfast, getting dressed, and commuting to church by 7:45 on Sunday mornings. On one particular Sunday, the struggle was downright epic. Sophia was in no mood to be wrangled, and the girls were fighting in the back of the minivan, while contemporary Christian music lilted in the background. I was tired and hungry. I felt crabby. I don't remember what set me off, but I had one of those meltdown moments. I was yelling at my kids even as our car pulled into the church parking lot. We all felt emotionally off. I was embarrassed that I had lost it with my girls, and my children felt shocked and sad. Not the way I wanted to start our Sunday.

Once I got my kids settled into Sunday school, I flopped into one of the chairs in the Widows' Group. As I was complaining about my morning to the other ladies, a young, slight woman named Brooke asked how old Sophia was.

"She's three," I answered, sighing through my exasperation.

"Oh, yes, I remember that age," she said softly.

111

"You have children?" I asked eagerly.

I craved meeting other widows with young children.

"I did," she answered as she looked at me with compassion and longing.

I just stared at her. My mind was moving quickly. She was in this class, so she was a widow. Surely, not more than that?

After a pause, Brooke shared with me that she had lost both her husband and her toddler son in a car accident. I realized that Brooke would love to have my problems. She would love to be mad at her kid, love to hug her son and hear his laughter. She would love to feel her child in her arms again.

I had nothing to say. Brooke had positively and permanently pushed my "Reset Button." Our eyes met for a moment, and I hugged her. Her loss was greater, so much greater. I was so thankful that Brooke had said something to me. She gave me a deep gift, a costly gift, in that moment of her honesty. I walked out of the group that Sunday morning forever changed. I was so grateful for what I had.

**If I focused on what I had lost, I was going
to miss what I had been given today.
The time is precious. I had been given wonderful
children to parent.**

Other widows or people in your grief zone can offer perspective, the wisdom of their experience, and training in the coping mechanisms that they have learned. You need support for your spirit, and oftentimes, your current friends may not be equipped to help on certain topics because they don't know this specific journey. They can be there for you, but if they haven't walked in your loss, it will be hard for them to tell you how to find the way through. People who keenly understand your loss from experience can warn you about specific landmines and what's coming up around the bend. I'm not saying to leave your current friends, only to add some new ones. Remember, some of the old friends cannot go with you through certain parts of your grief, but God, in His grace, can bring into your life new friends who will help you with wise advice based in experience.

This specific kind of support group is also better able to understand the intimate family relationships after loss. The death of a family member usually means new stresses to manage, and all kinds of new family dynamics to navigate. If your husband was the buffer between you and your in-laws, that buffer is now gone, and you will have to find positive ways to deal with them. If there was tension in a family relationship before a death, that tension may escalate afterwards. You need a support group around you that will give you positive feedback and encourage you when you feel stressed.

Identifying and collecting this specialized support might be difficult. People don't usually walk around with labels on their foreheads. You have to approach this challenge as if you had just relocated to another country and started a new job. You will have to learn new skills and make new friends. Find new friends who can speak your language—people who understand your specific trials and who can match your energy and personality. People who have worked through their losses positively and know how to move forward.

As I met with other widows in those first few months, I started to notice a difference. While I appreciated their presence and encouragement, I could see that some widows were still struggling, still somewhat wilted by their grief, even years after their loss. Other widows became empowered, leading healthy, vibrant, wonderful lives. I realized I had a choice before me. Was I going to allow my spirit to become wilted, perpetually overshadowed by grief, or was I going to fight through the pain and toward a wonderful life?

Behind the Upholstery

Church groups sometimes look different from the inside than they do from the outside. From the outside, they might be well-organized, cheerful, energetic dynamos. From the inside, they are just people. My church friends certainly rallied around my daughters and me, and provided practical and spiritual support. Friends slept at my house. Others ordered catering. They helped me plan the funeral service, activated people to care for my yard, cook meals, and donate lots of diapers and baby supplies for Sophia's upcoming birth. I am forever grateful for their love and help.

One pivotal moment early in my widowhood eventually motivated me to create my first Team Lady 180 group. This is one of the messy stories. I don't want to dishonor the gift of sincere friendship that friends from church gave me at that time, but I also want to offer insight into what a widow feels and how awkward it is to re-enter your life after a massive loss. Maybe if more people understood, they would push past the awkward feelings and reach out to those who are grieving.

Religion that God our Father accepts as pure and faultless is this: to look after orphans and widows in their distress and to keep oneself from being polluted by the world. James 1:27 NIV

By telling this story, I hope to encourage more churches to create long-term support group environments specifically geared for the unique needs of widows, widowers, their children and those who are grieving. No person or church is static but grows and changes over this passage of time, so this story is a snapshot of what happened to me in 2007.

At this church on Sundays, the children separated into a performance group that harnessed their creative energies while their parents were in the main service. I had been a part of the production team for that children's performance. Several months after Jason's death, I decided it was time for me to step out of the shadows of anonymity and rejoin my production group. I was finally able to put my older daughter in the nursery, and I wanted to show off my new baby to my friends and re-establish myself in this smaller community. There were always snacks, great conversation, and a creative production vibe that was fun to be around on Sundays.

However, today was different. People knew my story. I was greeted by welcoming hugs from the mostly twenty-something crowd. One or two brave souls said they were sorry for my loss. The production team leader, an older man with life experience, kindly chatted with me before he had to start the children's church program.

But the remainder of the group, mainly younger adults, quickly looked away and busied themselves with random tasks. They didn't know what to do with me. They didn't know what to say. Maybe they were afraid to say the wrong thing or they were just uncomfortable. I was trying to re-enter my old life, but I wasn't the same. My whole family wasn't the same, and everyone around me knew it. I wasn't part of a fun power-couple anymore. I felt isolated in a room full of people.

Then Sophia stared to stir. She was waking up and was hungry. I felt a lump in my throat. I missed my husband. I missed our lives together. I missed my friends. By now I knew this feeling. I could feel the tears coming. So, I picked up Sophia and scanned the room for a hiding place where I could feed her and cry privately. The kids' service was now in full swing, and I could hear kids and families laughing together. The green room only had a few people in it, so I found an overstuffed armchair in the corner of the room and sat down on the floor behind it. I still remember the feeling of sitting on the carpet behind this pretty armchair, trying to make myself as small as possible while I breastfed Sophia.

In this little corner, I couldn't hold my tears back. Sophia looked up at me and smiled while she nursed, wrapping her little hand around my finger, and I smiled back at her though tears were streaming down my cheeks. I could hear a few young people chatting on the other side of the room. I wondered if they even knew I was there.

Younger people often don't know how to deal with grief, because many haven't had to yet. Young married people don't want to think that life is so fragile that their amazing Christian marriage could disintegrate so publicly. Parents with small children don't want to think that their lives could change so drastically. It's easier to give a casserole and look away than to walk with someone through her grief journey.

I knew then that I couldn't go back. Not that I couldn't go back to church, but that I couldn't go back to my old life. That feeling of isolation, of wanting to make myself as small as possible, became a seed in my heart. I never wanted to feel that way again. I never wanted another widow to feel that way, either. That was the moment that changed me. I vowed then never to be that small again. I vowed to find a better way, to find purpose in this pain.

It was this moment that started me on my quest. I craved appropriate environments that met the needs of families grieving the loss of a loved one. I started to seek out other widows. I discovered a widowed Sunday school in one church, a widowed ministry at another, and a widowed home group at another. Each one had a clue for me about the importance of a supportive community that understood my grief journey. I was in search of my Team. There had to be a better way.

Journey to the Sunrise

Look for that moment when the seed of purpose is planted in you.
Realize that focusing on what you've lost causes you to miss what you've been given today.
Understand that your choices can make your life wilted or wonderful.

Steps on the Path

- You need your own community. You need the encouragement of others who have been on this journey longer than you have.
- Other widows or people who are in your specific zone of grief can offer perspective, the wisdom of their experience, and training in the coping mechanisms that they have learned.
- Those mentors can warn you to watch out for specific land-mines: what's coming up around the bend.
- Find support. Updated resources and links are available at 180YourLife.com

Chapter 7:

Forge Your Team

Your posse rides in like the cavalry to rescue and re-establish order in your life after the chaos of loss. Posses help establish healthy boundaries; they help us gain control of chaotic territory; they defend us and help us feel safe. Your *Team,* on the other hand, develops after a certain measure of peace has been established.

Your Team works together with you to successfully achieve a common goal and empower your vision for the next chapter of your life.

Once you have a vision for the next chapters of your life, you can create your Team. There may be some overlap, naturally, with your posse. Some of your posse may migrate to your Team, and that's a good thing. You share a common goal with your Team.

Grief can make a person feel isolated and disconnected, which can lead to addictive behaviors in an effort to relieve extreme stress. Addictions can be a way that we avoid reality or dull our pain, and those behaviors can range in intensity from an addiction to social media, texting, or constantly checking emails on your cell phone, to consuming simple sugars, excessive shopping, porn, prescription drugs, alcohol, or even illegal drugs. I believe that none of those addictive choices lead to a vibrant life. Author Johann Hari stopped me in my tracks with this quote from his book, *Chasing the Scream: The First and Last Days of the War on Drugs*: "The opposite of addiction isn't sobriety. It's connection."[27]

I have totally felt addicted to sugar, Facebook, and television as ways of escaping the pain in my heart. But you miss out on the life you have been given when those light interests become addictive behaviors. That's why I believe it's so important to find a support group and connect with a mentor (someone who has navigated your kind of loss in a healthy way).

Creating positive relational connections is a vital step in your healing and in the healing of your family. I cannot emphasize this point enough. You may not find everything you need in one group. I am a part of at least four groups that help support my grief and the grief of my children, even now, almost nine years after losing my husband. I love being connected to my fun, active widows and single moms through Team Lady 180. Kate's Club, which is the Atlanta-based nonprofit for children who have lost a parent or sibling, is a great way for my kids to feel connected with other children who understand their loss and for me to find widowed friends who are also parents. I also occasionally attend a support group for survivors of suicide. Finally, I enjoy occasional meetings at Modern Widows Club, a sister organization that also helps widows. Each support group offers wisdom and connection with others who understand my journey from their unique perspective. That connection keeps me on a wise, accountable path of wellness after loss.

Finding those who will mentor you is vitally important, and (add comma) those mentors can come from many sources. If you also want a grief group that is active, then visit 180YourLife.com to learn more about starting a Team in your area using this curriculum. Our leadership guide and our online videos will help lead your bi-monthly meetings.

For the purpose of this book, the Teams we create will have the common goal of getting healthy and creating peace in our hearts and home environments as we train for an athletic event together. My Team trains with me to participate in races—5K, 10K, and sprint triathlons. The aim is to work together to achieve a defined goal so that we succeed both individually and together.

Over time, I was able to hone in on what inspired me about other widows and widowers. I was able to clarify what I wanted in my family and what worked for us. I did this by cutting magazine clippings of things that inspired me, such as eating healthy and having a strong body, going on adventures both with my kids and on my own, laughing with my family, creating a big garden, being spontaneous, and having a peaceful home. So, I made friends with the people who were already living this lifestyle.

I can be a pretty independent woman. Before connecting with support groups, I didn't think having a Team was important. What do I need with some Chick-flick, Ya-Ya group? *The answer: My Team is my backbone. It supports me and helps me carry my burdens.* The more I focused on befriending people who understood my loss, inspired me, and made empowered choices, the lighter my burdens became and the more delightful our lives became together.

Another benefit was that once I had my community in place, once I knew I had friends who understood my grief journey and could advise me, then I was able to better appreciate my other friendships. I wasn't expecting my best friend who was married to understand the mindset of a widow. I had other friends for that. When I felt happier, more understood, it was easier to have fun with friends I'd had for many years.

Identifying Your Mentor: A Queen Widow

Around my third year after loss, anger was my internal default emotion. I was angry that I was in this position of widowhood. Angry because I missed my husband and my daughters missed their father, angry that I was so exhausted, and angry that there was this huge hole in my family.

That was when I heard of a Bible study at First Baptist of Woodstock led by an extraordinary widow named Lori Apon. She amazed me. She homeschooled all eight of her children, and, at the time of this writing, all but one of them (who is still a high schooler) have left the nest to attend good universities. She is a woman of great faith and great discipline. She is strong and fit, has bright, piercing eyes, and inspires me with the way she structures her family. The family has Bible study every day at 6:30 a.m. No television in the house. One movie a week allowed for family time. She eats no sugar. *Wow*, I thought. *Hard core.* Then I met some of her children and found them well-spoken, intelligent, kind, and compassionate people. I do not emulate Lori in all her choices, but I am continually impressed and inspired with the empowered way she has approached her widowhood.

I've taken to calling her "Queen Widowed Mom." It was my way of acknowledging that, for me, she was a mentor figure. There were aspects of her journey that I wanted to incorporate into my own grief journey. I wanted to be healthy, I wanted to have a strong faith-base at home, and I wanted to homeschool. This lady was doing it. Her presence alone gave me hope. Your Team may look different, resonating with what you need, and that's good.

That's the power of your Team—inspiring hope and action.

I sought out Lori because I was tired of being angry. It was exhausting and alienating to some people I knew. I felt hardened, and I knew it was not where I wanted to be. Stylistically, I had entered a black, biker phase (not a terribly flattering fashion choice for me, especially since I owned a minivan). So, in black jeans, black turtleneck, and black vest, I walked through the halls of First Baptist of Woodstock. I started attending Lori's Sunday school class for widows, and I met many inspiring widows there, including Brooke, whom I mentioned earlier in this book. It was my first real exposure to a support group for widows. I spoke to Lori for the first time after her class, and she asked me how I was doing.

"I'm really angry right now," I replied.

"What year are you in?" Lori asked.

"Year three," I answered.

"Yup, I was angry too in year three," she observed, which shocked me.

"You mean there is a path to this? It's not just random? This will pass?" I asked.

"Yes, with God, it will," she assured me.

It was then that I realized that there was a pattern in the chaos of grief. There was a way out, but it wasn't a solo journey. I attended her class for the next six months. During that time, I realized that grief could make us flounder like the Israelites as Moses led them to their promised land. Because of their grumbling and lack of faith, the journey to Canaan, which should have taken them less than forty days, caused them to wander for forty years in the wilderness. Processing grief can be an efficient journey, or it can include aimless wandering and loss of precious time. By seeking out my Team, I was learning how to travel on my grief journey more efficiently, wasting less time in getting to the place of promise. These principles are the tools you can use to empower your journey, in your style.

Six-Pack Abs

I will never forget one widow who helped inspire my Team, even though I only met her for a short time. She had an unassuming personality. She was the sister of a church friend I was visiting. Somewhere near my last month of pregnancy, I was lying on their family room couch watching TV when this woman came in from her daily run.

I looked up from my comfortable position on their sofa as she entered. Lifting the bottom of her tank top to dab her sweaty brow, she revealed part of her stomach—her six-pack ab stomach. She was a widow with *five* children. This woman was *strong,* and the first physically active widow I had ever met. She ran marathons in honor of her late husband, who tragically collapsed from a coronary complication one day, instantly catapulting her, a young mother, into widowhood.

That simple moment was a game-changer for me. I never forgot meeting her. She didn't say anything earth-shattering when we spoke. Her peaceful demeanor was in stark contrast to my "jazz-hands" outgoing personality. She simply offered her listening ear and compassionate understanding as I tried to wrap my head around the still scorched and smoldering landscape of my life immediately after Jason's death. Nevertheless, her quiet but powerful example gave me hope and inspiration that lasts to this day. I thank her for taking the time to be with me in my grief, because her gift was the seed that grew into my gift to you today.

This woman illustrated with her positive daily decisions that she could be a strong and vibrant leader for her children and herself, even in the aftermath of massive loss and life change. If she could successfully lead her family and train for races while single-handedly raising five children, then maybe one day I could do the same with my two kiddos.

You never know when your positive life decisions are actually a *lifeline* to others around you.
Don't ever underestimate the power of your presence.
That simple hour-long meeting with this quietly powerful widow changed my life,
and I hope this resulting 180 Your Life Program helps change your life for the better, too.

Tiny Team Members and the Importance of Play

In those first days and weeks after my husband had died, I wanted someone to swoop in and save me from all the chaos. I craved the continual presence of people because I felt hollow inside. At seven months pregnant, I wanted to curl up in my bed, getting lost for hours in romantic comedy after romantic comedy to deaden my pain. My strong-willed toddler, Arie, had different plans.

One morning, she stood at my bedside and said, "It's time to get dressed, Mommy."

"We are going to stay in our pajamas today, Arie. It'll be fun!" I responded, faking excitement to distract her.

"I don't want to be in my pajamas, Mommy. I want to get dressed," she answered, crossing her arms in deadpan seriousness.

Then we proceeded with the almost-three-year-old-daughter and the thirty-nine-year-old-pregnant-mommy stare off.

"Fine. I'll get you dressed," I caved and forced myself out of bed, put on a robe and helped her pick out clothes from her closet.

That was just the first step in her mini-master plan.

Freshly dressed, she then said with sincere toddler excitement, "Let's go on an adventure, Mommy!"

"Wait, what do you mean?" I was planning to attend my own film festival taking place in my bedroom.

How could I redirect this child into sitting down to start watching another movie?

"Let's walk outside and pretend to be Dora the Explorer on an adventure!" she replied.

How could she have guessed that this was the absolute *last* thing I wanted to do?

"No, Baby. I don't want to do that. Let's watch a movie," was my counteroffer.

"No, Mommy. Let's go on a walk outside. Just for a little while. It'll be fun," she said, smiling up at me with what was clearly the same distraction tactic I had just tried on her.

"Fine, but I'm not getting dressed," I threatened.

"That's okay." she smiled and ran to get her shoes on.

I had no plans to get out of my pajamas for, like, months. I wanted to hibernate. Sleep away this pain, both literally and figuratively.

I put on a robe and took my daughter's hand, and she gently pulled me into the sunshine. I took a deep breath. The air was cool, and it felt good. We lived on the edge of the country, in what felt to me like the outskirts of civilization. There were pastures near our subdivision, and I could actually hear cows lowing in the light morning mist. The sky was a soft blue, and I realized this was still my favorite time of day — early morning, when the air is crisp.

Our neighbors knew our situation and were very kind and understanding. In any other scenario, I would have looked like a crazy woman shuffling in slow circles around the cul-de-sac in my bathrobe with a toddler. Well, maybe I did look a little crazy, but sometimes the first steps toward your new life are messy, and that's okay.

I was planning to satisfy Arie with the least effort possible and then go back to the house.

Arie quickly redirected, "Let's go on a Dora adventure!"

By now I realized that this really wasn't a suggestion.

"What? I'm not sure I'm up for that, Baby."

"It'll be fun! Let's walk in the woods back to the house," she pleaded.

We lived in a neighborhood with large half-acre to two-acre lots, and we had a common creek and a pond near our home. I knew Arie wanted to go through the little wooded area and pretend to be like Dora on an adventure. We had played that game together often while Jason was alive.

"Okay. Let's go," I smiled.

It was a way to get back home, and I knew it would make her happy. Two birds with one stone. Having majored in Theater in college, I loved to pretend and tell stories with Arie. But that was before everything changed. After Jason died, a part of my heart — the fun, playful part — was devastated. It was hard to want to play again, because playing meant innocence and hope. I felt I had lost both.

"Where are we, Mama?" Arie asked as we entered the little thicket of trees that surrounded the pond.

This was her cue that she wanted to start imagining with me.

I took a deep breath, "We are in a magical forest. Be careful! I think I see a crocodile in that lake!"

For a while, Arie and I got lost in our adventure where we dodged talking crocodiles, discovered fairy doors, and figuratively returned some monkeys (which looked a lot like squirrels) back to their mother, all before we returned to my backyard.

I remember wishing for a close friend who truly understood my circumstances and who would intimately walk this path with me. I realized then that Arie was one of those people. She was just really, really short, and her spirit had only been on this planet for a brief time. She had so much to share if only I had ears to hear her.

Now, I say this carefully. I did not expect my young daughter to support me like an adult would have, or for her to be the person that I unburdened my heart to. But that didn't discount the fact that she was going through this massive loss as well. She terribly missed the same person I did. We were in this thing together. In her almost three short years, she had gained wisdom and insight to share in her own special way.

She had the hope and imagination of a child,
and the desire for adventure
that is a powerful force for healing if it is
recognized and honored.

Arie was part of my most intimate Team, and I was a part of hers. In time, my new baby, Sophia, would belong to our Team as well. Together, they brought laughter, wonder, and love in their purest forms into my heart and life. Spending time exploring life together was healing for all of us.

Often, it's the people directly around us that we sometimes overlook. We take for granted the wonderful treasures they have to share, even if it's just the profoundly simple treasure of their presence and love for us.

Here are a few things I learned from that time:
1. My daughter, Arie, instinctively knew as a child that it was good to get outside, take a walk, and play. She was inviting me to re-engage in life even if I was in my pajama pants. *Getting the endorphins moving is key to healthy grief recovery.*
2. Get out in nature and let the healing beauty of your surroundings remind you that life is still good.

124

3. Learn to imagine again. Let yourself open up and play with your children or the kids in your extended family. Practice the hope and innocence of imaginative play.

4. The last lesson is to keep your childhood innocence. I have probably watched the movie *Under the Tuscan Sun* at least twenty times, (it has some adult themes, so take appropriate measures). The main character creates a whole new life for herself by refurbishing an old villa in Italy after her husband divorces her. While on her adventure, she befriends a beautiful former actress who has a wonderful ability to love life and live in the moment. This character shares her secret in a brilliant one-line quote from the Italian director, Federico Fellini:

"No matter what happens, always keep your childhood innocence. It's the most important thing."

Team Lady 180

While I believe purposeful grief processing is very important to the healing journey, I also discovered a missing component. In many grief groups, both secular and faith-based, I found a pattern. We got together, we ate donuts and shortbread cookies while we talked about our loss, we listened to the newest loss, we processed problems, and then we did it again the next month, and the next, and the month after that, until the months became a year, and then the year became several years.

Verbal processing is a necessary step in the grief journey, but I believe it's not the only step. I also wanted an empowered way to heal that was age-appropriate. Something that was active and fun. I was always that theater geek, the one picked last for athletic games in school. So, doing something crazy—like the Iron Girl Triathlon— seemed like a big challenge that would take me out of my head and forward to a finish line.

I joined a "couch-to-tri" team, meaning that they took rookies and trained them to do a sprint triathlon. They trained for the Calloway Triathlon at Calloway Gardens, which included a quarter-mile swim, a nine-mile bike ride, and a two-mile run (or, for me, a power walk). I successfully completed that triathlon as my test case, and the next week did the Iron Girl Triathlon at Lake Lanier. That event was a third-of-a-mile swim, 24-mile bike ride, and 5K run.

I hired a trainer, Robert Haddocks, for that initial race, and he helped me commit to a race finish line. He pushed me to achieve my goals even when I felt grief. Exercise tends to lower our emotional walls, so sometimes I would cry or get angry when I worked out. That didn't faze Robert one bit. He was determined to get me across my first finish line, and we did. In both triathlons, crossing that finish line gave me such a sense of hope and accomplishment.

**My first thought after crossing my finish line was,
"If I can to this, I can do anything!
What's the next big thing I want to tackle?"**

When I felt stronger and healthier, I slept better and felt happier when parenting my children. I felt younger. I wanted to run around on the playground with my girls. I didn't feel slowed down by my weight. We had more fun together as a family.

So, a few years later, I had a crazy idea. What if I put the two together? What if I put the supportive community I found in my grief groups together with the health and self-confidence I found in training, and we all trained for a triathlon as a Team of widows?

That is how our Team was born. My personal Team, my group of widows in Team Lady 180, includes women of differing strengths. Some women really like to exercise; they are my exercise buddies. Some women are calm, thoughtful organizers. Since I'm one of those exuberant, big-idea people, I find it useful to get the advice of practical planners on upcoming projects, helping me scale them down to a manageable workload. Other women are great at being cheerleaders. One widow is a very level-headed, positive person who has been a widow longer than I have. She is a really strong Army widow; I am always amazed by Natalie. When I start to stress out as a parent, I call her, and she always has a sage word to share. She is a ray of sunshine in our group as a wise encourager.

Our group started out as Team HOT Widow: Healthy, Optimistic, Thriving! We trained together for five months, meeting once a week. I thought Team HOT Widow was a great name, but I learned that some people thought we were a specialized dating service. To end any confusion, we migrated to the name Team Lady 180. We also wanted to open up the option of starting other support groups that had the same principles, but addressed other types of loss, not just widowhood. What we discovered was that Team, Train, and Triumph was a way of transforming our loss into a life we loved, and my hope is to empower many existing grief/support groups to get healthy, empower one another, and cross finish lines together as a form of grief recovery.

While we trained and learned more about healthy eating, the members of our Team were getting to know one another. Our children would play together while we exercised at boot camps on the weekends. We buddied up and kept one another accountable during the week. If one Team member didn't have tri equipment, we worked together to help her get what she needed. We started doing *life* together.

By the time the race came, we were a tight-knit group, like an extended family. At the hotel where we had all booked rooms, our children played together while a few of us watched over them at the pool. We were like a pride of lionesses: strong, spirited, and watchful over our cubs.

I discovered that accomplishing a goal of training for a 5K, 10K, and Sprint Triathlon with a Team of ladies who understood my grief was an enormous turning point for all of us. We were in the sunshine. Our children began training with us—they were inspired to get strong like their mommy. Our process made our kids proud of us. We loved going to races, and family members and friends would cheer us on. We felt beautiful, and we felt understood by our Team.

At the end of the race, one of our widows proclaimed as she crossed the finish line, "I got my life back! How awesome is that?"

This gave me such a deep feeling of accomplishment, of community, and of belonging. My children were inspired, and they were in community with other kids who wanted to exercise, too. We had a whole Team of "aunties" who watched over our brood. That was the path of 180-degree change in my life. That's why we chose Team Lady 180 as our new name.

The Power of the Team is the power of understanding,
support, and the shared journey.
It's not about finishing a certain race length,
but about joining together
with the goal of getting healthy and inspiring
one another to be the best that we can be.

**It's about creating an understanding community
that strengthens one another.**

Speak to the Bones

I've talked about several of the seeds for this book, and moments when ideas sprouted that would lead me to create a healthy, active Team. These were all part of the process of reshaping my life and working through my grief, but the journey was a long, arduous, and sometimes wandering process. Before so many years had passed and I formed my Team, God and I were still in a heated discussion. Actually, it was pretty one-sided. I felt cheated. I mean, I had gone to missionary training school as a young adult; I was a loyal wife and active in my faith community. I unconsciously believed that I deserved protection and blessings, not trauma. I felt that I had the right to be happy. My family had the right to have a safe life. I had the right to be happily married. I had the right to be a wife. *Right?*

However, horrible things happen every day to people who are much better than I am. So, clearly those rules aren't God's rules. Relatively good behavior does not always shield us from tragedy. In my quest for grief recovery, I have concluded that there must be a deeper truth to this life than my comfort and safety. Clearly, comfort doesn't appear to be one of God's main objectives for me.

I had to decide to make peace with that tension between my perceived rights and my reality. I ultimately chose, and still daily choose, to relinquish my perceived rights and accept what has been given to me. This became my valley of bones—the bones of the dreams I believed were mine, but that now lay bare and baking in the sun after many years of battles.

When Sophia was seven months old, Caroline, the nanny who had been with me for the last six months, decided to move back to her farming roots in Vermont. By then, I felt I could handle my girls—but still, the prospect of managing bedtime for a baby and a toddler on my own was slightly terrifying. So, I concocted a plan. Often, I would drive my girls about thirty minutes to a nearby mall where there was an indoor playground. We brought packed dinners or sometimes bought a meal there. Afterwards, I would take the kids to the playground and let them run around until the mall closed. I then packed them, half dozing, into the car and—*voila!*—they would be deep in REM sleep by the time I arrived home.

On one of those days, as I was working the intricate contraptions that were my children's car seats, I said a short prayer. It went something like this: "God, I really need to hear from You. I am so hurt. Are You still there? I have no idea how to trust You again. Why are we going through this? Are You hearing me? Where are You in all this?"

No answer. Then I drove with my children to the mall. I fed Sophia a bottle as I watched Arie climb around on the foam sculptures of the indoor playground. A man sitting nearby struck up a conversation with me. He was a good ole' Georgia guy, thick as a bull, with close-shaved red hair and a deep Southern accent. He had some kids playing in the playground, too. We'll call him "Bud."

As Sophia fussed, Bud said, "Looks like she's teethin'. A really great trick for teethin' is givin' a baby frozen waffles to chew on. They break down as they defrost, so they're not a chokin' hazard, and they make babies' gums feel better, too."

I smiled a tired smile and said, "Thanks, that's a great idea."

As we continued to talk, Bud asked what my husband did for work. I was still wearing my wedding ring back then, so it was a natural question.

It was one of those moments that you connect with a stranger and tell him things you may not normally say. I told Bud the whole story—not just the sanitized version, which was that my husband had died in his car, implying that he had died in an auto accident. No, this time I went into all the details, and Bud quietly listened. When I was done, his blue eyes seemed to look right through me.

"I'm a mechanic, and I own my shop," he said. "Today, when I was working, I felt God's Spirit nudging me to close up early and come to the mall. He had someone for me to meet here. I think that person is you."

My eyes widened. I was stunned.

Bud went on, "He has somethin' to tell you. He wants you to know you are not alone and that He sees you. He is with you on this journey."

I refused to be impressed with the coincidence of this message, and instead issued a challenge.

"Why would I have a baby in the middle of such terrible grief?" I asked. "How can He be in this?"

"Sometimes God gives us the task of focusin' on being a parent for a while until we can handle the harder stuff. He has given you a gift to enjoy, the gift of your children, while you are grievin'," Bud answered. "I see that several years from now, you will be talking to lots of other people about this. You will be teaching others."

"How can that be?" I asked. "I'm so damaged and hurt. I'm just holding on minute by minute, day by day. What could I ever have that other people would want?"

"It's like this," Bud answered. "There is a story in the book of Ezekiel about a valley of bones. Ezekiel is askin' God for an army, and God tells Ezekiel instead to speak to the bones. First he speaks muscle, then flesh, then breath. You have to speak to your life in the same way. Speak hope, speak purpose, and speak life."

I sat in silence. Arie came to hug me and run off again to play. Sophie was gnawing on a rattle.

Bud gave a slight smile, "Yup, that's all I was supposed to say. Spirit's done now. Look up the story in the book of Ezekiel. It was really nice meetin' you."

With that, Bud rose and left. I never saw Bud again, and I never forgot our meeting. For me, that was one of many significant signs that God had not left me. My path had changed, to be sure, but God had not left.

My chance meeting with Bud spoke to my bones, as I hope it speaks life into you and your circumstances. Bud's meeting with me wasn't just about me and my family. It reflects the words of Ezekiel, which are a message to all of us. Speak hope to the bones that are left from our broken dreams. In time, if we allow God to work in our lives, we will be renewed with strength, life, and even an army of hope-filled warriors.

Vision of the Valley of Dry Bones (Ezekiel 37:1-10)

The hand of the Lord was upon me, and He brought me out by the Spirit of the Lord and set me down in the middle of the valley; and it was full of bones. He caused me to pass among them round about, and behold, there were very many on the surface of the valley; and lo, they were very dry. 3 He said to me, "Son of man, can these bones live?" And I answered, "O Lord God, You know."

Again He said to me, "Prophesy over these bones and say to them, 'O dry bones, hear the word of the Lord.' Thus says the Lord God to these bones, 'Behold, I will cause breath to enter you that you may come to life. I will put sinews on you, make flesh grow back on you, cover you with skin and put breath in you that you may come alive; and you will know that I am the Lord.'"

So I prophesied as I was commanded; and as I prophesied, there was a noise, and behold, a rattling; and the bones came together, bone to its bone. And I looked, and behold, sinews were on them, and flesh grew and skin covered them; but there was no breath in them. Then He said to me, "Prophesy to the breath, prophesy, son of man, and say to the breath, 'thus says the Lord God, "Come from the four winds, O breath, and breathe on these slain, that they come to life." So I prophesied as He commanded me, and the breath came into them, and they came to life and stood on their feet, an exceedingly great army.

The Vision Explained (Ezekiel 37:11-14)

Then He said to me, "Son of man, these bones are the whole house of Israel; behold, they say, 'Our bones are dried up and our hope has perished. We are completely cut off.' Therefore prophesy and say to them, 'thus says the Lord God, "Behold, I will open your graves and cause you to come up out of your graves, My people; and I will bring you into the land of Israel. Then you will know that I am the Lord, when I have opened your graves and caused you to come up out of your graves, My people. I will put My Spirit within you and you will come to life, and I will place you on your own land. Then you will know that I, the Lord, have spoken and done it," declares the Lord.'" (NASB)

The power of this image reverberated within me, as its significance radiated out towards the conversations and concerns I was having with God and my life. God had spoken to me in an audible voice, and He had directed me to speak as well. To speak in faith what I needed, to design the answer to my needs, to trust Him, to step out and create my Team and allow it to help me improve my strength. It didn't matter how dry the bones were, how long it had been since they had seen life and moisture. Each one of us has the opportunity to speak to the bleached bones of our broken dreams, to speak our vision and back it up with action, to build an "exceedingly great army of hope," and God would give it breath.

Moving forward from "Wilted" to "Wonderful" isn't based on our feelings or circumstances. It's based on our faith, goals, planning, and decisions. Plain and simple. This process works. I know because this is how my life changed from surviving to thriving.

Are there times when I feel overwhelmed and accidentally eat an undisclosed amount of chocolate? Yes, I still struggle with emotional eating when I am stressed, but now I know what to do. I take time to pray and speak my goals, call forth my Team, draw upon their support, and then make plans to exercise. It's my go-to pattern for moving forward in my life. It doesn't matter how I feel when I start. I simply start and get others to join me, even just one person.

Give time for your Team to grow. Eventually, positive feelings will follow your wise decisions, and that's how you keep moving to the light of dawn.

Journey to the Sunrise

Create your Team and establish a common goal to work toward.
Invest in the power of your Team to inspire hope and action.
Realize that there is a pattern in the chaos of grief.
Understand, "If I can do this, so can you!" So ask, "What's the next big thing I want to tackle?"
Remember to play, even when you don't feel like it.

Steps on the Path

- Moving forward from Wilted to Wonderful isn't based on our feelings or circumstances. It's based on our goals, planning, and decisions.
- Once I could stop asking, *Why did this happen to me?* and started asking, *How will I choose to live my life?* I gained some hope, a light at the end of the tunnel.
- Which question are you asking?
- What have you done to begin to establish your specific community?
- Your Team works with you to successfully achieve a common goal and your vision for the next chapter of your life. How have you seen this manifest in your own life?

Speak Life: Forge Your Team
(Please Say Out Loud)

As I press into this journey, I will join others who understand my loss around the campfire, so we may strengthen one another for this quest. We will come together in trust and confidence, for protection, friendship, and renewal. We will speak hope, speak purpose, and speak life to one another. Though the plains are arid, we take refreshment at a watering hole, encouraging one another, content to know we are not alone.

Train Your Mind

Step 3:

Train Your Mind

In the Grips of Kathy the Reticulated Python

Years ago, when I was in college, I took a summer job at a children's science museum in Ft. Lauderdale, Florida. At the time, it was a small operation housed in a quaint historic building along the Intracoastal Waterway. I was to give insect and reptile shows to groups of school-age children. Since I have always been geared toward adventure, this job was right up my alley—although I have to admit, it took some time before I was able to hold a hissing cockroach in my bare hands. Under their exotic exterior, they look just like regular roaches. When I flipped one over to show its head, abdomen, and thorax to the audience, I couldn't keep from squealing and dropping the roach in its cage. I always had to overcome the urge to spray it with Raid. (Which, of course, I didn't, since it was an *exhibit* and all).

When I wasn't giving an insect or reptile show, I would occasionally walk through the halls of the museum with a creature for the kids to pet. There was Buckwheat, the three-foot iguana, who could pee like a racehorse—which I discovered firsthand. There were box turtles, various frogs, and several other small reptiles.

By far the greatest crowd pleaser was Kathy, the sixteen-foot reticulated python. Her skin was sleek and exotic. Her head was as big as my hand. Ever the show-woman, I would wear Kathy like a boa all wrapped around my body. She would start wrapping herself around my ankle, continue up one of my legs, curve around my stomach and chest, and then rest her head on top my head. I walked down the halls, and kids would flock to pet Kathy's midsection.

Occasionally, she would shift her head downward to my shoulder. That was always an odd sensation. She would slowly slither through my hair, and then hiss as she brushed pass my ear, which would make every hair on my body stand on end. Nevertheless, I liked walking around with Kathy. It felt a little edgy.

Eventually, Kathy's instincts would kick in. She was a constrictor by nature, so after a while, she would start squeezing me. It was nothing major, just a slight squeeze across my ribcage after I exhaled. Barely perceptible. When I inhaled again, I couldn't take in as full a breath. As I exhaled, she'd squeeze a little more. This was the slow train toward dinner for Kathy. It's how she suffocated her food, which ordinarily was comprised of rats and the occasional stunned chicken.

After a couple of these slight squeezes, I would take control of the situation and say, "Okay, Kathy, that's enough."

Then I would gently but firmly take hold of her just behind her head and unwrap her from my body.

Like that sixteen-foot reticulated python, despondent grief can wrap itself around you and slowly constrict your movements, your life, and your sense of adventure.

At first, you are too steeped in sorrow to realize that the loss that has changed your family dynamics has also changed your social dynamics. For me, it took some time before I recognized that not only was I a widow, I was also now an unmarried woman. Jason and I had been part of the young married set in our neighborhood and at church. We participated in a regular round of barbecues and dinner parties. After his death, even if my friends wanted to be there for me, their activities were centered around a couples' dynamic, and my Jason-and-Mishael identity no longer existed.

Grief can constrict everyday life as well. You may find yourself avoiding places that hold memories of your loved one. You abandon activities that once took up part of your day because you had been doing them for another's sake, like cooking a full meal, or exercising, or dressing up. The incentive is gone. Now, as you view this enormous crater that seems to be expanding before your eyes, you try to fill it up.

Jason used to quote Aristotle, saying, "Nature abhors a vacuum," meaning nature responds by filling a vacuum with whatever material lies nearby. I found a dozen ways to fill the new holes in my life and my day: food, activities, shopping, and projects. For every new gap in my social life, I could find an alternative activity. The wounds from missing my mate were temporarily plugged with a stick of furniture or a pair of shoes. For every frustration with my new role as a single parent, I could soothe that vacuum with an elaborate project, or at least with some chocolate cake.

One day it hit me. I was being constricted out of my own life.

I wasn't moving freely, and, what was worse, it was slowly killing my soul. My fear was slowly affecting my children and their lives, too. While the grief constrictor was slowly squeezing away the possibilities for joy, movement, and wise choices in my life, I was busy drowning myself in the debris of distractions.

I could not take a deep, soul-cleansing breath until I figured out a way to uncoil the serpent from my psyche, clear away the clutter, and survey the scorched landscape to assess the actual state and shape of my new life. So, I remembered what I had done with Kathy.

I calmly and firmly took hold of the situation.
I purposely unwrapped the constrictor from around myself.

Chapter 8:
Bargaining with Grief

The first step in training for a new life, after we have gathered around us a supportive Team and stabilized the home front, is recognizing our distractions and clearing them away. That process includes neutralizing the poisonous habits and influences that have inserted themselves into the holes in our lives, and then replacing them with positive, intentional steps that will improve our health, create peace in our home, and build confidence for this new adventure.

Be aware that the constrictor comes in different forms. It can take the shape of any emotion that inhibits life, such as depression, fear, unforgiveness, resentment, or anger. The constrictor can also come as a craving for something that isn't good for you—in my case, too much sugar. You want so badly to dull the pain, and the constriction is so subtle, that you hardly notice it happening.

You have to take charge, because constrictors play for keeps. So, calmly take a firm hold and make choices to unwrap the fear and destructive habits from your life.

It takes time, but such is the journey to the holy grail of grief— the much-lauded "New Normal." The secret is that your new life is not a destination, a conclusion, or even an understanding. It is a continual discovery, including an occasional wrestling match, which leads to eventual acceptance of—maybe even gratitude for—your life as it is today.

Someone told me recently, "It hurts to heal."

Yes, it does, but the alternative is much worse: emotional suffocation.

Surveying the Suffocation

At first, I thought I had found a handy way to avoid the insidious snake. Lots of projects, travel, home renovation, bargain hunting, romantic relationships, and running my girls around to activities. Constant motion.

It started about a month after Jason died. Even though I was grieving heavily, I began nesting, as pregnant mothers do. I was getting ready for Sophia's upcoming birth. Shopping to create a fun space for my new baby was a nice distraction. It took my mind off the pain temporarily, and it felt good.

Later, I found that closing up Jason's estate was an effective way to distract myself. I treated it like a project. I accomplished in six months what takes most people twelve months to complete. I had to supplement Sophia's breastfeeding because I was in so much motion that it affected my milk production. The consequences were already starting to show.

Whenever I would finish a project, I would soon hop onto another. Fifteen months after Jason had died, I moved to a different house. Over time, I fully renovated the new house, and installed a huge garden that took up my entire half-acre plot. I planted fourteen fruit trees, two herb gardens, ten blackberries bushes, fourteen blueberry bushes, two strawberry patches, and over a thousand flowers in my yard.

That's not all. I hit a furry, feathery phase, too. I collected two dogs, two rabbits, and two cats that almost immediately gave birth and produced ten kittens all together. Plus, until the Cobb County Code Enforcement officer paid me a cordial visit, I also had twenty-eight chicks.

I made plans to sell my house and become a missionary. Instead, I had a kiln installed, bought a pottery wheel, and began to pour and paint ceramics in my home. I also started a home daycare and then closed it a few months later when I discovered I wasn't cut out for the continual care of other people's children. I learned to edit for NBC News. I enrolled my girls in competitive gymnastics. Then, I began going to yard sales to find stuff to sell on eBay to make up for the extra expenses of the gymnastics classes. I trained and competed in the Aflac Iron Girl triathlon twice.

At one point, I wrote out a schedule for my week, and I was amazed to find that the girls and I were booked solid from morning until night.

Arie was starting to ask if she could skip a gymnastics class just to be with me. She missed me, and I missed her.

Dating was also a distraction. I got in and out of relationships. I even hired a professional matchmaker. I became intrigued by the euphoria of liking a man, but usually felt compelled to end the relationship if it started to get serious. I didn't ever want to experience a broken heart like I had with Jason.

I also travelled with my girls. We took a road trip from Atlanta to Vermont when Sophia was fourteen months old, staying with friends and family along the way. I took the girls to Costa Rica for three weeks, where we visited more friends and rode horses on the beach. After reading all the *Little House on the Prairie* books to them, I vacationed with my girls in De Smet, South Dakota for the Fortieth Annual Laura Ingalls Little House on the Prairie Festival. We camped in pioneer prairie attire on the original Ingalls land claim among predominantly Mennonite families.

It was chaos—although, I must admit, a beautiful chaos.

The Bargaining Phase

Eventually, however, I ran out money to fund my big projects. Even more, I had run out of energy to do them. Then, all I wanted to do was watch TV and eat. I had crashed. My energy had bottomed out, and I also felt like I wanted to jump out of my skin. I gained fifteen pounds in a month.

The stuff I had collected started to swallow my kids. Well, one of them. One evening while I was finishing something on the computer, I was startled by the cries of my older daughter, Arie.

"Mom! I can't find Sophie!"

It was nine o'clock on a summer's night, and my then-six-year-old daughter, Sophia, was M.I.A. Where could she be? I hadn't heard any of the home alarm beeps that indicate an outside door had been opened. As I frantically searched for her, I was already trying to suppress a number of horror scenarios that were speeding through my head.

My eldest and I raced around the house calling for Sophia. No answer. I opened the back door and called into the night for Sophia. No answer.

I opened the front door and called for Sophia. No answer.

I ran around the house outside and scanned my front and back yards in the dark.

"Where is she, God?" I prayed in a growing panic.

Afterwards, a sense of calm came over me. I decided to give the house a more thorough look-through before I called the police.

I went upstairs to my bedroom. I'm sure this has never happened in your home, but it has happened more than once in mine. There was a huge pile of laundry on my bed, waiting to be folded. When I say huge, I mean cover-the-whole-queen-bed, up-to-my-ribcage huge.

I almost walked by it in my rush to find Sophia. But wait…is that some blond hair and an ear? Upon closer inspection, I realized that my six-year-old had burrowed into my mountain of laundry and fallen asleep. I swear, I am not making this up.

My laundry was so massive that it had apparently swallowed one of my own children.

Perhaps I had been accumulating more clothes than strictly necessary. My daughters and I have an eclectic sense of style, and we enjoyed indulging in such non-chocolate treats.

I used to cruise yard sales on Friday mornings as a reward for getting through the week. One day, I found a darling solid wood pedestal dining room table with ball-in-claw feet and carved roaring lion heads in its base. It came with six matching solid wood chairs. All for $175.

So I bought them. It took three trips in my minivan, but I moved it all. I squeezed the six dining room chairs into my already-stuffed garage by snaking among the paths already carved through the clutter. There was nowhere to put the dining room table. So, in my minivan it stayed. For two weeks, I had the table placed upside down on the floor of my minivan. Whenever I looked in the rearview mirror, I could see its legs sticking up like those of an enormous dead beetle. I jammed things around it. Grocery store attendants tried to stuff my food in the nooks and spaces remaining. It was getting embarrassing. Was I becoming a hoarder?

I took a look around my house. There was stuff everywhere— although not in cascading piles or roach-infested nests. I looked out of my kitchen window and noticed all the stuff I had accumulated outside: the empty chicken coop, a 275-gallon water tank to collect rainwater, an A-frame support holding a swinging bench, a plastic playhouse the girls had outgrown. Now there was a dining room table in my van, and I had no place to put it. It was time to rethink this.

By this point, I knew of the five stages of grief: Denial, Depression, Anger, Bargaining, and Acceptance. It was that bargaining phase that I never fully understood. Did it involve trying to bargain with God that Jason hadn't died? When I got his wedding ring from the funeral home, I knew it was really over. When his ashes were in my house, there was no mistake. He wasn't coming back, so no need to bargain there.

Was it bargain *hunting* then? Was there a whole phase of grieving when you just shop? Was it like a happy kind of commercial break in the program of grieving? For me, the answer was, "Yes."

I come from an artistic, slightly eccentric family. I remember once visiting my grandparent's house with my soon-to-be husband, Jason. Some people may have had grandparents who put plastic coverings on everything to preserve their items in store-bought condition. Not mine. My grandparents were antique dealers and had priced everything in their house. We family members didn't even notice it anymore.

Jason couldn't help but notice the adhesive neon price tags affixed to everything, and wondered aloud if my grandfather was moving.

"No," I replied. "He just likes to sell stuff. It's all available for sale."

"Really?" Jason paused for a moment, taking it in.

Then he said, "I'm kind of digging those antique candle sconces on the wall."

It was another moment I knew Jason was a keeper.

While my Grandpa Theo was always ready to wheel and deal, I think it's safe to say that his wife, my Grandma Nelly, was the Queen of All Yard Sales. She was like a foreign bargain-hunting spy. Part covert ops wrapped up in a sweet, adorable grandma skin. No one could hold his ground in her presence.

She was Peruvian and an exotic beauty even in her seventies. She was petite and power-packed, like a pearl-handled pistol. She wore red lipstick and had nearly black eyes. Couple that with her sweet, sexy Spanish accent, and she could have talked Adam out of his fig leaf.

She was a force of nature to watch at yard sales and antique shows. She didn't seem threatening at all, until it was time to talk money. She could low-ball and hard-ball all at the same time. She had a way of asking for the most impossible discount and then wearing down people's resistance until they were happy to give their stuff to her, wondering what hit them as she scurried away to her Volkswagen Fox with her new deal. We were sure to see it in her antique shop, marked up by 100 percent or more. She was a bargaining goddess, and I was in awe of her.

So, when I thought of the bargaining phase of grief, it didn't look like such a bad phase to go through. I had learned from the best. If I had to go through a shopping, bargain hunting phase in my grief journey, I was well-trained and ready for action.

However, as I gazed at the upturned table in my rearview mirror and the fabric landfill in my bedroom, I realized the Bargaining Phase of grief was not about trying to bring Jason back.

Bargaining with grief was about creating distractions for myself because I did not want the life that Jason's death had left me. I didn't want to be a widow.

I felt that if I kept in constant motion, I could stay ahead of the pain. I was chasing the sunset, unwilling to see the day's end. I couldn't slow down. I couldn't stop running, or the grief would come in like a tsunami. I was scared to find out what would happen if I just sat still without the TV or a project to do. How much would it hurt?

Overwhelmed and anchored by all this stuff, exhausted by the endless activities and projects, depressed from the excess carbohydrates and the resulting fat, and fed up with the senseless drama, I knew something had to give.

Looking back, I realize that my crash was a gift. When I stopped running from the grief, I began to clear out the clutter and that huge mound of debris I had collected to fill the vacuum that pain and loss had left in my life.

To establish order in your environment, simplify your home, relationships, and lifestyle.

This is not a quick fix, but in the long run it makes for a peaceful home life. I began to cleanse my home room by room. It was hard to let go of some things, but each time I released stuff, I felt a lightening of the load in my heart. It freed me to stop managing the stuff and instead do things that made me happy, like exercise with my daughters or help them with art projects.

There is power in simplicity.
It is the power to find peace and successfully manage
your life and the life of your family.
That simplicity gives you space to discover
what sparks your soul.

Oftentimes, in the desire to give my girls everything they wanted, I was also taking away what they really needed: my time. The time for us to enjoy one another, play together, relax together, read a book, laugh, and think quietly. Clearing the clutter makes space to create new memories that will last a lifetime.

When I simplified my home and lifestyle, I began to sense a peace and calm coming over my girls and me. I yelled less and listened more. I was not on the edge of myself all the time, overwhelmed with activity. I stopped running.

Journey to the Sunrise

Realize that there is power in simplicity.
Understand that it hurts to heal.
Remember to establish order in your environment. You need to simplify your home, relationships, and lifestyle.

Steps on the Path

- **Be aware that the constrictor comes in different forms.** It can take the shape of any emotion that inhibits life, such as depression, fear, unforgiveness, resentment, or anger. The constrictor can also come as a craving for something that isn't good for you. You want so badly to dull the pain, and the constriction is so subtle, that you hardly notice it happening.
- **You have to take charge, because constrictors play for keeps.** So, calmly take a firm hold and make choices to unwrap the fear and destructive habits from your life.

Chapter 9:

Uncoiling the Snake

Minimize Clutter

One day, I watched as my daughter slid from her Ikea top bunk bed to the floor on laundry alone, like a Jamaican bobsledder. Something had to be done. Calls to action from me had been met, at the time, with looks of bewilderment because my children didn't know where to start. Too many clothes and too many toys were threatening to crowd them out of their living space.

I'm not some kind of neat freak. I'm really not. But I have found that when I craft my home, I am also taking the time to intentionally decide what I want my life to look like and what my future goals are. I read a little book by Marie Kondō entitled *The Life-Changing Magic of Tidying Up: The Japanese Art of Decluttering and Organizing*. In those pages, I discovered a principle that was helpful in creating a peaceful, inspiring home. She says, "Keep only those things that speak to your heart. Then take the plunge and discard all the rest. By doing this, you can reset your life and embark on a new lifestyle."[28] As Kondō suggests, "The question of what you want to own is actually the question of how you want to live your life."[29]

I find that sometimes, after loss, I can become a curator of the past. Keeping things because I should. I want to give you the freedom to make your home fabulous (within your budget), and it can be as easy as simply purging what no longer gives you joy. Sometimes that is hard to do because we can get emotionally attached to our things. Kondō advises, "When we really delve into the reasons for why we can't let something go, there are only two: an attachment to the past or a fear for the future...The process of assessing how you feel about the things you own, identifying those that have fulfilled their purpose, expressing your gratitude, and bidding them farewell, is really about examining your inner self, a rite of passage to a new life."[30]

So, armed with my determination and what I imagined a Zen-like peace might be, I began to purge my home of clutter. Starting with the exterior of our house, I grabbed my camera and took some pictures of the items I wanted to get rid of: the chicken coop, the water barrel, and the outgrown plastic castle. I put them up for sale on Craigslist, and a few days later I had cleared my backyard of clutter and made about $500 in the process. Now, instead of looking like the opening credits of *Sanford and Son*, my backyard was inviting and fresh.

Then onto my sunroom, which included a dual-station home gym I had purchased from a yard sale for $100. I had thought I would use it, but in six months I hadn't touched it, so I flipped it on Craigslist for $245.[31] With that space now cleared in my sunroom, I finally had somewhere to put my pedestal dining room table and chairs. Sweet relief! No more dead wooden beetle legs in my minivan.

Then I moved to my guest bedroom, which had become a catch-all for all the bargains I was finding and would theoretically flip on eBay. In one day, I had boxed things up and put them in my garage. I made a deal with myself. If I didn't put the items on eBay within sixty days, I would unload them at Goodwill. Now I had a free guest room and could invite friends and family for visits.

Next was the girls' shared room. Drastic measures had to be taken, so I pulled out the big guns. I invited them to a mini-film festival. I popped popcorn, snuggled up with them under our favorite leopard-print blanket, and queued up Season Two of the reality show *Hoarders*. For those who have not watched this show, the title says it all. Full-blown hoarding, featuring rooms packed to the gills with years of stuff, paths eked out for daily navigation between towering masses of junk, combined with decaying garbage and insects.

At one point, my older daughter turned to me with a look of grave concern. We were watching some child try to climb over a noxious concoction of toys, clothes, garbage, and dirt, all mixed with rodent fecal matter. The child on TV asked some grown-up why there were so many spiders in her room, which sealed the deal for Arie.

She said to me, "Our house never gets like that! My room doesn't look like that!"

"Yes, my love," I calmly replied. "But some of these people say that they didn't learn to be neat when they were kids, and so it spread to their whole house as grownups."

Quiet child-processing followed.

Sophia, in her four-year-old wisdom, declared, "They need a yard sale!"

Don't get ahead of me, Sweetie.

After a few episodes of *Hoarders*, I decided to top off our mini-film fest with an episode of TLC's *Clean House*. It's like *Hoarders* only kitschier, with a yard sale and design tips that end in a happy reveal. Now the pump was primed. Timing is everything.

I turned to my girls and said, "Ready to clean your room?"

They replied with a resounding, "Yes!" and ran up to their room, ready to do anything to avoid cohabitation with spiders.

We started with the toys. We pared down their toys by half. While we pared down, I immediately bagged the toys that the girls purged. I've read that when simplifying, you tend to keep what you let linger in your hands. So, we got the items out of sight and out of reach on the spot. Then we went through the toys again and got rid of more. My goal was to get the content down to a size they could both easily put away in a few minutes. The surplus went to Goodwill.

If you saw my girl's rooms today, you would notice a minimal amount of toys. I kept whittling things down until my girls could manage their room themselves. We kept enough favorite toys in their rooms to fill a small toy box. I gave some other favorite toys a "vacation" in a bin in the attic or garage. When the rooms had been kept clean for a few weeks, my girls could trade out toys with the bin of extras. I asked that their rooms be cleaned at the end of each day and beds made in the morning for the privilege of trading out toys.

Then we hit the clothes. I can thankfully say that my girls are set for clothes. I have such amazing friends who have supplied us with high-end hand-me-downs of their daughters' clothes. The downside is that when my daughters were rifling through all their clothes to put together a fabulous outfit, all the folding I had spent hours doing was undone in less than five minutes. Add to that their daily, multiple costume changes, and the laundry alone became its own black hole of work, sucking my time and energy on a consistent basis.

So, we began simplifying their stock of clothes as well. I went through all their clothes and asked them to point out their favorite pieces, which cut the amount in half. Whatever my younger daughter didn't need, I bagged for donation. I stored what my older daughter didn't want in a bin marked with the clothing size for Sophia to go through later when she had grown. Clothes for nice occasions went in the guest bedroom closet or another bin, except for a few dresses and favorite clothes, which were hung back up in my children's closet.

Then we cut their favorite clothing selection in half again. I took the newly purged clothes and put those in bins marked by size for the girls to trade out with later. I had to make my daughters' closets bite-size, or they would get overwhelmed by the sheer amount of clothes to manage. We kept six t-shirts, four skirts, three pairs of pants, three sweaters, one or two nice occasion dresses, and four pairs of shoes. It may sound sparse, but it was what I believed to be a manageable amount for the girls at that time. The idea is to empower your children to take on the responsibility of their clothes themselves.

As my girls showed me they could take clothes to the hamper, take them out of the drier, fold them, and put them away in an organized manner, I was willing to add more clothes to the mix. Having available fashion choices was a great motivator for my girls. When their roster of clothing options got stale, my daughters were very motivated to do their laundry. Of course, I would give a helping hand, but I wanted to set a precedent: *Mama ain't the maid.*

I am not the mother of boys, but generally speaking, some boys may be less likely to notice a lack of fashion options. For kids who don't care about a smaller wardrobe, I would try to find something that motivates them and offer that as a reward. Sophia may not be motivated like Arie to hang up all her clothes, but she loves to swim. If I "sweeten the pot" with time at the gym pool at the end of the week, Sophia will be happy to earn points by doing chores.

Finally, the girls' room was clean. There was space and peace. I was not dogging their steps, getting angry with the mess, or resenting mountains of laundry. The girls felt successful, which was a big "Win-Win" all around. After I had vacuumed and dusted, we had the chance to cheer over the newfound open spaces and cleanliness.

I am not saying this will be an easy process initially, but the free time you are creating for you and your family is worth the effort.

**Teaching my children to be content with less, to successfully manage what they have,
and to help out in the house starts to craft a peaceful family environment.**

When my children help in the house, I am happier as a mother, and when I am happier, I have more time to play with my girls, and they are happier as well. With this discipline, we have learned to function as a family Team, tackling problems together, and creating time and space to create fun memories with each other.

**Enjoyable down time with your family promotes peace.
Peace is a great space to fall in love with your life as it is today.
Then you have the space and grace to muse about what you want to create in your next life-chapters.**

Minimize Audio Clutter

Another step on my road to a peaceful house involved minimizing the audio chaos. Once I cleared the clutter of my schedule so that I wasn't seeing my life only as blurs in my rush from one activity to another, I realized that I was still bombarded by constant noise from the TV, computer, phones, and animals surrounding me. I found I could only half-listen to my children because so much else was clamoring for my ear.

I cut down television time by making our normal TV room into a family game room, adding kids' books and craft bins. Then I reduced the number of animals under my care. My two dogs were constantly fighting and racing around the house. The cats were shedding on my furniture and occasionally bringing in bloody "gifts" of vermin they had killed. The rabbits didn't like to be held. It was a mess. Backtracking in the pet department is no fun with little kids, but you have to do what is best in the long run. So, I re-homed a dog, created an outdoor home for the cats, and re-homed the rabbits. Now we have two outdoor "barn cats" that keep vermin off of my garden's produce and one indoor dog, which is more than enough. My house is more peaceful, and that makes for a happier mommy.

Finances and Schedule

As a new widow, the last thing I wanted to do was create a budget and stick to it, so I didn't. I had some life insurance money and let that savings account float our family for a time. Eventually, my savings account could no longer support our extra expenses, and I absolutely had to create a budget.

When I finally buckled down and set a budget, I discovered that I had freedom to spend more time with my family because I knew what our budget was. I didn't have to do extra work outside the home or dip into savings because of overspending. It became engaging for me to see where I could trim from our expenses and meet my goal to save money every month.

I'm here to report to other creatives and procrastinators like me: Creating a budget was not the personal Armageddon I thought it might be. Actually, it was freedom.

Eventually, I engaged a financial planner to help me sort through my debt and assets, and plan for the future. I encourage you to do the same. If you are married and reading this book, I strongly encourage you to see a financial planner *with* your spouse so that together you can create an emergency financial plan in case life throws a curve ball. I can tell you from personal experience that creating a financial plan while you are grieving is not the optimal time. Peacetime, exactly the time when you don't want to do this, is the perfect time to wisely build a financial fortress for your family.

Though I am not a financial planner or an investment guru, I can tell you that creating peace in my life has included the task of organizing my finances. My booklet, "Love Prepares," details some important ideas for preparing your finances for unexpected events, like losing a spouse.[32] For now, you just need to get the basics down so you have an accurate picture of where your funds are going every month. It is imperative that you have control in this area of your life, or someone else will, like a debt collector, and it will most certainly become a source of stress.

If a financial planner isn't in your budget right now, I have found that an efficient way to simplify my financial life is to list my monthly and annual bills and use a simple budget plan. In addition, there are charitable organizations, such as the Salvation Army and Consumer Credit Counseling, which may help you create a workable budget and deal with debt management.

To help inspire some ideas, I'm including a sample budget that I recently created. There are certainly wiser financial minds than mine, so I recommend using this as a springboard to get started and then engaging with a professional financial planner as soon as possible.

Create A Budget:

Income:
   Monthly:
      Annual Assets/Investment income:
      (Divide annual assets / investments income by 12 for a monthly income total):
      Monthly Assets/Investment income:
   Annual Expenses
      Services:
   Exterminators: $ per year
   Alarm company: $ per year
      Insurance:
      Life: $ per year
      Flood: $ per year
      Car: $ per year
      Home owner's: $ per year
      Taxes:
      Property taxes: $ per year
      Car tax and tag: $ per year
      Car emissions test: $ per year
      Pets:
      Animal medications: $ per year
      Vet visits $ per year
      Memberships:
      Annual internet memberships $ per year
      Area attraction memberships $ per year

Annual Expenses Subtotal: $ per Year

**Divide Annual Subtotal by 12 for Monthly Total:
$ per Month**

Monthly Expenses:
    Savings:
        Monthly savings:
        Savings for vacation:

Giving:
        Charitable giving:
    Mortgage(s):
        Home:
        Rental:
    Utilities:
        Garbage:
        Gas:
        Electricity:
        Water:
    Insurance:
        Health insurance:
        Dental insurance:
        Vision insurance:
        Pet insurance:
    Monthly Needs:
        Gas for car:
        Internet:
        Cell phone:
        Food:
        TV:
    Charges:
        Monthly bank account charges:
    Memberships:
        Gym:

Animal Costs:
    Animal food:
Education:
    College investment plan:
    Monthly educational costs:
Retirement Plan:
Family:
    Allowances:
    Entertainment:
    Clothing:
    Sports Clubs:
    Childcare:
    Hair appointments:
Business Expenses:
    Dry cleaning:
    Childcare:
    Cell phone:
    Internet:
    Client meetings:
    Website and online costs:
    Continuing education:

It may take a few days to think of all the expenses you have per year and per month. Keep a running list and then add the expenses as you think of them. Once you have written every expense down, you will have an accurate map of where your money is going.

Take your Annual Expenses and divide them by 12 for a monthly expense subtotal:

' Next, add the above number to your Monthly Expenses for a Total Monthly Expense:

Now, take your Annual Income and divide by 12 for a monthly income subtotal:

Add this number to your Monthly Income for a Total Monthly Income:

Now subtract your Total Monthly Expenses from your Total Monthly Income:

Analyze your result. Can you save some money? Can you cut corners?

Stop the Bleeders:

Now it's time to play with numbers.

Take some time and see if you need to cancel some annual or monthly expenses. Ask these important questions:

- *Are you saving at least 10 percent of your income every month?*
- *Do you have financial margin enough to make charitable donations?*
- *Do you have the ability to save for a family emergency, family vacation, and monthly family entertainment?*
- *Do you have six months of savings in place to cover an emergency?*
- *If not, what "fat" can you trim?*
- *Can you cook more and eat out less?*
- *Are there some memberships you can downgrade or cancel?*

**By being fully present in your finances,
you will intentionally create the financial peace
you need for your home.**

This might be time to engage a financial planner to help you sort through everything and create a live-able budget for you and your family. You may have to make some tough financial decisions, but if you choose to do the hard work, you will create the space and grace to heal for yourself and your family.

There's nothing like feeling freedom from financial stress.

Simplify the Family Schedule

To simplify both my finances and my schedule, I took my girls out of most of their activities. When I began to clear my schedule for my girls, I was able to spend more relaxed, unstructured time with them. Those broad expanses of free time scared me at first, especially in the summer. Just the thought of almost three months with no childcare, endless cleaning, and sweltering temperatures seemed a recipe for the perfect storm.

So, I structured our time by instituting a schedule and chore charts for the kids, with special activities as rewards.

I used lots of colors and pictures, and made the chore charts as fun as possible. Most importantly, they clearly outlined what needed to be done, and my children could take as long as they wanted to finish them—they just couldn't play until the chores were done.

The idea of involving my family in everyday chores rather than in extracurricular activities appealed to me. It taught my children that we were a Team, working together. We had been reading *Little House on the Prairie*, and the routine on the frontier always included morning and evening chores in addition to the day's work. I wanted my girls to contribute to our family and housework, and to build this work ethic into a habit.

On the first day of the Chore Chart Project, Arie took until 4:00 p.m. to complete what should have taken her forty-five minutes (sorting laundry and mopping the kitchen floor). The girls got themselves put together for bed all on their own. They straightened their bedroom and bathroom, picked up all their toys, and put them away. In my enthusiasm and relief, I wanted to lick the floor, it was so clean, but I restrained myself.

Behold, the Power of Shoes

A confluence of circumstances brought about a delightful discovery. One Sunday after church, we went to the nearby outdoor plaza for a bite to eat and strolled while window-shopping.

All was well until the girls ran ahead of me and entered a high-end kids' clothing store. I knew I had made a mistake about two seconds after we set foot in the store, in the time between Arie's squealing over flamenco-inspired shoes and Sophia's grabbing a multi-layered mini-skirt and exclaiming, "I've been waiting to wear leopard print all my life!" Which was curious, since she was actually wearing leopard print at that moment. Clearly, I had made a tactical error.

Or had I?

Myself a savvy Goodwill shopper, I rarely take the girls into a retail children's clothing store. But this was a sale, and the bikinis were salsa-themed. Before I knew what hit me, the girls were emerging from the dressing room looking adorable. I was caught in the clutches of seriously cute kid-wear.

Quickly formulating my strategy, I said, "You realize that you will have to earn these clothes, girls?"

"Yes! Yes!" they eagerly replied while clutching their shoes, which perfectly coordinated with their tops.

A method to the madness was beginning to crystallize. About this time of year, my yard took on a life of its own. It was lush and full of flowers. However, if it was not weeded often, it could quickly turn into a horticultural monster that threatened to engulf my house.

There is a fine line between a lush garden and a jungle. In the past, I have hired out the weeding work or done it myself for hours while the girls pulled a weed or two and then went inside the house for a costume change.

"There will be weeding to do, and household chores," I said as I coolly swiped my credit card.

In other words, *indentured servitude*, though I did not express it in quite those terms.

"No problem, Mom," they chorused.

Back at the house, the girls naturally wanted to try on their shopping conquests. They paused, slack-jawed, when I said that they *must wait and earn every piece of clothing*.

"We can do that in a day, right?" Arie asked.

"Unfortunately not," I calmly answered.

I dusted off the dry erase chore chart that Sophia had been using as a coloring board. I explained that there were common living chores, such as making their beds and keeping a clean room, as well as extra chores that earned clothing, such as weeding the garden and laundry.

The girls fell silent at the full realization of the cost of those cute clothes and shoes. They could earn one item per week if all chores were fulfilled on a daily basis. With this plan in place, I was set to cruise right into mid-July without touching a weed or laundry basket.

After a moment of looking deflated, Arie and Sophia rallied. They were determined, as only females of any age can be, to work for beautiful shoes. They started the chore chart that night. My dad had to stop them from sweeping the kitchen so they would go to bed. It was like stumbling onto pure gold.

I wondered if the concept would continue into the next day. It did. Without my having to ask, the girls referred to the chart and executed chore after chore. The table was set, the floors swept, the garden weeded for an hour, baths taken, and homework done. I actually danced a little jig when I saw Arie unloading the dishwasher without being asked.

At least for the day, I felt like I'd cracked some kind of parenting code. I reveled in this brief victorious moment when parenting, fashion, and home life were in glorious harmony. I was able to sit at the dinner table and relax while Arie and Sophia cleared the dishes, and I thought, "Thank God for little girls and the power of shoes!"

Journey to the Sunrise

Realize that creating a budget is not the personal Armageddon you think it might be.
Understand that enjoyable down time with your family promotes peace, and peace is a great space to fall in love with your life as it is today.
Remember, there's nothing like feeling freedom from financial stress.

Steps on the Path

- When motivating children to help around the house, include positive reinforcement for their completed chores, offering items or activities they like as rewards.
- Shoes and salsa-inspired clothing may not spark your kids like they do my girls. So, find out what does inspire your children. I'm sure they will be happy to tell you!

Speak Life: Train Your Mind
(Please Say Out Loud)

I have met the constrictor, which stealthily coiled around me while I grieved, almost imperceptible, threatening to constrict my movements and even my very breath. With courage, asking for God's help, I will take conscious steps to firmly unwrap its coils from my life, minimizing chaos and creating healthy boundaries, as I purpose to create calm and peace in my home and my mind.

Chapter 10:
Triggers

Once you get your exterior environment and family processes into a state of peace, it's time to go a little deeper. I never thought of the concept of "triggers" until I met Scott Rigsby. Scott is the first double amputee in the world to complete the IRONMAN Triathlon in Kona, Hawaii on two prosthetic legs. The IRONMAN Triathlon is a race consisting of a 2.4-mile (3.86 km) swim, a 112-mile (180.25 km) bicycle ride, and a marathon 26.2-mile (42.2 km) run, raced in that order and without a break. When we first met through a mutual friend, Scott and I spoke about the similarities between widows and amputees. I suggested to Scott that, in my opinion, losing a limb or limbs is possibly more difficult than an emotional loss.

With the clear vision of an eagle, Scott said, "I wouldn't say that, necessarily. Both are great losses. I have three sisters who have become widows. At least when you lose a limb, you know your limitations. In widowhood, there are triggers everywhere. A widow looks normal on the outside, so people can't see her loss."

I was stunned at his insight: he had summed it up perfectly. I was walking around with this phantom amputation influencing my thoughts and habits, but nobody could see the extent of my loss. I was to discover that my amputation was still as sensitive as an open wound, and if anyone touched it in the wrong way, it might send an electric current shooting through me and cause unpredictable responses.

Little and big things can trigger grief, and the triggers can be anywhere.

It takes conscious work to reclaim your territory and desensitize emotional triggers. Here are a few ideas:

1. Consult with a professional counselor as you move forward to reclaim emotional trigger zones.
2. The first time, or even the first several times, of returning to a trigger area location may really hurt. You may cry a lot and that's okay.
3. Talk to a counselor and consider taking an understanding friend with you to shift the mood in "trigger" spaces. Don't suffer alone.
4. Purpose to layer a good memory in the present moment over an emotionally charged space.

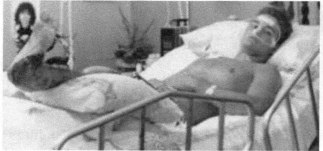

Scott Rigsby: Scott after his accident, resulting in one amputated leg. His other leg was badly damaged and, after multiple surgeries, Scott later elected to have his remaining leg amputated so he could move more freely with dual prosthetics. Years later, Scott is the world's first dual amputee to complete the famous Hawaiian IRONMAN triathlon race. Scott is also the author of *Unthinkable*, which chronicles his journey from his tragedy to triumph. Learn more about him at **ScottRigsby.com**.

Top four photos provided by Scott Rigsby. Bottom two photos provided by photographer Joe Kelley.

Loss Is Like an Amputation

Yes, there will be emotional triggers, some expected and some unexpected, and you may have to learn to manage them for years to come. Some of this is hard work, but Scott taught me something else. Whether an amputation is physical or emotional, if you learn to accept it, the circumstance can become the door of purpose that leads you to a life of helping others, which will fulfill your soul and spirit in ways that you never thought possible.

Scott Rigsby says it best:

Twenty-nine years ago today, (July 23, 1986), I had a catastrophic accident that would eventually lay claim to both of my lower legs while leaving me to survive and struggle with the very devastating effects of a Traumatic Brain Injury.

One of the most commonly asked questions I get as I travel around the country speaking is, "Would you, if given the choice, ever want your 'real' legs back? If there was a magic wand to wave and instantly return your birth legs, would you want them back, or would you make the choice to keep living with prosthetics?"

My answer to that question is easy, but the journey to that answer was not. I would want to keep my prosthetics and live the rest of my life with them, because I know that I can make a bigger difference and a more profound impact in the world and change more lives than if I had my birth legs miraculously given back to me. I know that decision may confuse those who struggle to find comfort in their own skin, and my heart goes out to them with great compassion, but my body doesn't define the kind of person I am, and neither do my legs, whether they are made of shiny metal or smooth, blemish-free, tanned skin.

The truth is, I have my real legs now. These shiny metal sticks which I balance upon every day have taken me farther and allowed me to reach higher than my birth legs ever could. These legs are a blessing. They are a gift to share and not a burden to bear.

I believe that I am playing a role in a much bigger story. That role is in living out God's beautiful masterpiece that He has been writing for me since the beginning of time. It's a role that He has allowed me to play so that I might inform, inspire, enable, and love the broken, in mind, body, and spirit. I am to reach out and render aid to the outcast, the underdog, and the defeated. For me, it is to live a sometimes wild, wacky, crazy, frustrating, stressful, chaotic, rewarding, fulfilling, amazing life, an unthinkable journey, and encourage others to join me along the way.

Thank you to all who have loved, supported, comforted, nurtured, and cared for me when I was lost and unlovable. It was/is your gracious and merciful love that allowed me to get to this day once again! There's no way I could have ever made it this far without you. I love and appreciate each of you, and out of respect for your investment in me, I will continue to pay your gracious gift forward by laying down my life in the service of others!"

We have often heard the saying, "Less is more." Maybe that applies to loss, too. Our loss makes us more. Loss can make room in our hearts and lives that causes us to live to the fullest. That's the paradox of grief.

Covert Triggers

Psychologists tell us that eighty to ninety percent of our actions and responses come out of our subconscious mind and triggers that have been planted there by our past. Feelings, thoughts, and behaviors that we have learned since childhood have been scripted or written into our subconscious mind. So, when passing a stranger on the sidewalk, we may automatically look away, or nod, or smile. We don't consciously think about that response; we default to scripts that have embedded into our subconscious from years ago—even as far back as something we learned from our parents, like, "Never talk to strangers."

When you find that some of your automatic responses—thoughts, feelings, and actions—are not working for you, then stop. With an accountability partner, counselor, or friend, talk through what you are doing and why it's hurtful or painful to you or others. This will help you bring what's subconscious to the surface. It may take some time and multiple conversations to pull out the root to your "dysfunctional" response. When you feel that you have reached the root, then choose to glean wisdom from a counselor, reference timeless texts, like the biblical book of Proverbs, and develop new attitudes that will help you respond to triggers in healthier ways.

What do triggers commonly set off? Bombs, explosions, guns, bullets, flying objects, serious wounding, and even death. So, it would be wise to take stock of what sets you off. What are the situations that, as my oldest daughter puts it, set off a "Mommy-Meltdown"?

I discovered my nuclear trigger after a few disastrous dating attempts. Even the slightest whiff of possible abandonment could set off a strong reaction in me. Over time after losing Jason, I started dating again, but I generally kept the relationships light. I was not willing to open myself up. I would guard my heart like a well-trained ninja. These earlier dating attempts would metaphorically end up like a movie scene with me standing in front of a flaming building, with randomly clawed overturned cars in the background, smoke rising from my frizzled hair, and the sound of a distant scream as male figures ran away towards the horizon.

We are not going to unpack my whole dating life right here, but I will share a little background and a recent highlight.

RTS: Reverse Trigger Situation

Recently, while writing this book, I met a man with whom everything seemed to click. It was delightful to feel like I had a high school crush. Our get-togethers were electric, full of fun flirting and good conversation. As we continued in the relationship, the attraction deepened.

I thought, "I'm so proud of myself. I'm getting past this major dating/abandonment trigger. Maybe this is a new chapter in my life. Maybe I am over the part where a guy gets too close, and he makes some random mistake that looks remotely like abandonment, and that triggers a series of relational bombs that would rival any blockbuster movie. He then walks out of our relationship dazed and shell-shocked, wondering what just happened."

"Look at me," I thought as I got ready to meet the man we'll call "Leo" for a joint get-together with his child and my girls. "I'm all *Triumph*. I am *living* this book, Baby. This could be the last chapter!"

I was thinking this as my daughters and I pulled into the Atlanta Botanical Gardens for our play-date. Little did I know, something had changed. His child was amazing, and our kids were playing together well. It was a gorgeous spring day. The temperature was in the low seventies. There should have been an upbeat musical score swelling in the background, a cool theme song about loving your life, and a slow-motion camera shot with sunshine highlighting my good hair day and his winning smile. The set-up was that good.

Except it wasn't. After a cursory hug, "Leo" could hardly look at me. He wouldn't sit next to me. He was polite, but not engaged.

He looked at his phone a great deal. I tried to talk to him. It fell flat. Something had shifted. I was confused. Why was he here if he didn't want to connect with me?

I didn't let my displeasure show, although I was internally protecting myself because of his sudden distance. We both managed to go through the motions of a nice afternoon get-together, and then said polite goodbyes.

We were able to communicate about it later, and that's when I discovered the existence of the **Reverse Trigger Situation**. "Leo" said he was "triggering" because our good chemistry had somehow set off fears for him of becoming too close and getting hurt. That scenario had the lovely effect of setting off his triggers *and* mine. Think Hiroshima and D-day with lots of tulips blooming in the background.

I hadn't even known that scenario existed. The trigger table had turned on me. Can you do that to a widow? I'm not denying the narcissism of the moment, but that is exactly what I thought.

A friend told me of a Buddhist maxim years ago,
and it's always stuck with me.
"The first person you meet on the road to
enlightenment is yourself."

This means that the stuff that other people do that makes you crazy is likely a reflection of a part of yourself. I was being confronted, in living, breathing color, with a version of myself who was fearful of falling in love again and being abandoned in the process. This was my own trigger behavior.

This otherwise good, kind, intelligent, and wonderful man had taught me another valuable lesson. In the past, I have often, without realizing it, made good men who tried to date me pay for my grief over my late husband's death. If I were really honest, I'd have to admit that I am battling a belief that I could be abandoned at some point, so I have been known to push a man away before he can leave. It's my effort to preempt the pain.

Looking back, I know I'm believing a lie. My father, numerous amazing male friends, and wonderful male family members have not abandoned me. Jason, my late husband, was caught in so much pain that it undoubtedly skewed his judgment, so I cannot term his passing as abandonment, no more than I can term one of my kids' getting ill as an intentional event. I choose to frame his passing with compassionate understanding.

Operation Preempt Pain

I realized that I'd been boxing a mirage. My "Operation Preempt Pain" was only trapping me and fulfilling my own prophecy. The painful experience of Jason's death has passed. I have to choose to keep letting it go. We all have our triggers. Certainly widows haven't cornered the market on triggers or grief, though for a while I was convinced maybe we did. I learned a hard lesson that day in the botanical garden.

**I cannot make others pay for my past pain.
It's neither fair nor kind, and it limits my own life adventure.**

So what do you do when you find yourself in a trigger situation? This is the list that has worked for me.

Reframe. Realize it's not about you. In the book, *The Four Agreements: A Practical Guide to Personal Freedom (A Toltec Wisdom Book),* Don Miguel Ruiz states that one of the primary life agreements is, "It's not about you." What people do, the reactions they have to you are, for the most part, *not about you.* Their reactions to you are about the internal, psychological, and experiential grid that they themselves see life through. Their reactions are how their life experiences have shaped their thoughts. So, take a step back, give grace, and don't take it personally.

Take a Break. When I feel my emotions ticking like a bomb about to go off, I need to defuse the situation for myself. When having a fight-or-flight response to a trigger situation, the best thing to do is take a break, walk away, give yourself time to calm down, and gain wise perspective. Sometimes, this can take a few hours or a few days. Triggers can skew our thinking. That's okay, but be honest and communicate that you need time to yourself to process in a productive, positive way.

Communicate with grace. Give favor and kindness. Generally speaking, peace is more energy-efficient for your soul than an anger attack. I'm not saying that you should be someone's doormat. You can set healthy boundaries in a firm, gracious manner. We are all fighting invisible battles. Maybe you're not the *only* person with triggers in the room. Try to understand the other person's point of view and respect his or her life journey.

Practice Gratitude. Finding gratitude gives you freedom. When you can be thankful for what a person has given you, it shifts the focus from what you are not getting to what you have been given. People are finite, limited, and fallible. They can't give you everything you need. Only God can do that for you. You craft your best life with wise decisions. Let people be who they are meant to be on their adventure. Give them freedom, and you'll be surprised at how much they may want to be around you. Even if they don't, giving grace and freedom from expectations is a more peaceful way to live.

Love More. I have a refrigerator magnet that has offered a continual life lesson for me. It reads, "The only solution to love is to love more." When I have been tempted to remain in anger against someone, I remember that magnet. The only workable solution to loving Jason after he died was to love him more. To love him into understanding, into acceptance, and into freedom to be who he needed to be. I could stay angry, hurt, or depressed, wondering what happened to the good old days. Instead, choosing to love more gives us the freedom to accept life as it is today.

Release in Peace. Make a decision to release someone in peace. Will it hurt? Yes! Do you have to give up your expectations of them? You bet! Will you make mistakes as you try this? If you are like me, most certainly! Choosing to release people to be who they *are* is a healthy way to approach grief. It frees me to appreciate life today and craft a life I love.

Be gentle with yourself. Trigger feelings can sometimes register as a hollow, nauseated sensation in my stomach. In times like these, I typically go for carbs. Sugar stops that shaky feeling in my stomach and calms my nerves. Unfortunately, the calm only lasts for the moment. It's a bad cycle because sugar is addictive, creating more sugar cravings, which can contribute to bad sleep and even depression. I have to consciously control what I reach for in this mood, and make sure I make healthy choices.

Seek Wisdom: Seeking wise counsel and reading books on making wise choices has been a lifeline for me. Take some time to seek wisdom and understanding. Ultimately, wisdom brings vibrancy to your soul.

You're blessed when you meet Lady Wisdom,
when you make friends with Madame Insight.
She's worth far more than money in the bank;
her friendship is better than a big salary.
Her value exceeds all the trappings of wealth;
nothing you could wish for holds a candle to her.
With one hand she gives long life,
with the other she confers recognition.
Her manner is beautiful,
her life wonderfully complete.
She's the very Tree of Life to those who embrace her.
Hold her tight—and be blessed!
(Proverbs 3:13-18 MSG)

Seek, ask, and knock on your journey. Find a grief support group. Reach out to your friends, talk to a counselor, and pray. I often ask God for wisdom in handling my life as a widowed mom. James 1:5 says, "If any of you lacks wisdom, you should ask God, who gives generously to all without finding fault, and it will be given to you" (NIV). You don't have to meet any criteria to ask God for wisdom. Like a loving parent, God wants to help us live our best life and enjoy our Great Adventure, but it's our choice. It's our free will to pursue wisdom. Give the book of Proverbs a shot. It's full of wisdom.

Have Fun. Slow down a bit. Take time for a walk in the sunshine. Give yourself permission to do something fun. Schedule an adventure with a friend. What is fun for you? Try something new! What about salsa dancing or going on a hike? Be purposeful about moving forward. Do something that makes you laugh.

Make the Next Best Decision. Been in the grief dumps? Get refreshed. Eat something good for you. Make the next best decision, and then make the next best decision after that. In time, you will learn to navigate this trigger stuff. You will learn to be mindful of what sets you off and how to diffuse the triggers. It's not going to be resolved in a day. It's a journey. You may as well take a break from grief and do something that makes you feel refreshed.

Good decisions are like training for a race. It's a continual choice. It takes time and consistency to build up muscle and stamina. Commit to the training process and you will get stronger. Then one day you'll cross your finish line and enjoy the prize of knowing you can craft a life you love.

**You will feel better after you make wise choices,
even if you feel sad right now.
Be willing to work with a support partner
to positively change negative,
painful, or hurtful responses that you might
default to without reflection.**

The Man Fast: Clearing Your Ground

We have all heard that insanity is doing the same thing over again and expecting a different result. Obviously, to get a different result, you have to do something different. Change is hard. Sometimes, it goes down screaming.

About four years after Jason's passing, I blithely walked into a church service at Buckhead Community Church one Sunday morning, not knowing that God was going to hand me a directive that would take twelve months to carry out. In his sermon that Sunday, the preacher, Andy Stanley, suggested that if you had been through a significant loss, the best thing you could do for yourself was not to date for twelve months.

I instinctively knew that this was the equivalent of God elbowing me in the ribs, nudging me with, "This means you, Sweetie." I walked out of church that Sunday with a definite feeling that God was letting me know that this was the healthiest decision I could make for myself.

I will admit, I thought God might have been overreacting. I had begun dating a bit, but had never gotten serious about anyone. There might have been a few inadvertent dating misfires, but there seemed no need to scrap the project entirely. So, I put the idea on a back burner.

Eventually, I got that whisper in my thoughts that meant God had something to convey. I was working in my garden, and a thought crossed my mind, "How can I give you a husband if your heart is not ready to receive him? Just like planting a valuable tree in compacted clay soil, it will not thrive. Even if it doesn't die, it will always give meager fruit. You have to break up the ground, remove the rocks and stumps, and amend the soil first. Then, over time, the soil will be ready to healthfully support whatever you put in it."

I took a deep breath. I understood. I knew that something needed to change in me. I needed to deal with my own stuff for a while. Be happy just being with myself and my girls. That's how the twelve-month "Man Fast" started.

The first benefit of not dating was that I no longer would put my girls to sleep and then talk on the phone with a guy friend far into the night. Sometimes I would have a late-night conversation with one of my single guy friends to stave off loneliness and get a male perspective about something. Then I would wake up exhausted the next morning because I had gone to bed so late. It had a cascade effect; I couldn't catch up on my rest and was too tired to play around with my girls.

I discovered that it was okay to be alone. The solitude wasn't actually lonely. It became replenishing. Learning to enjoy your own company is an art, and it takes time to get there. Once you get comfortable, your own solitude actually grounds you. Later, you can be more selective about the men you let into your life, because you are approaching dating from a place of contentment, not fear of loneliness.

Take time and gift yourself with optimum health and wellness before you look into dating. You will feel centered and at peace, and then your life will open up, a life you enjoy, which may also include someone special to share it with. When you take the time to bring order and stability to your life, you will attract a person who is doing the same.

That twelve-month period became my catalyst to finding my own wingspan and having an adventure with God rather than trying to make myself fit with a man.

It was a great time of self-discovery, and actually, the time when the majority of Team Lady 180 and the concepts for this book were born. I firmly believe that you have to make time to discover and empower your life, honor what inspires you, and enjoy the life you have been given, today, before you can invite someone to share it with you.

Journey to the Sunrise

Discover that little things and big things trigger grief. Triggers can be anywhere.

Realize that it takes conscious work to reclaim your territory and de-sensitize emotional triggers.

Understand that consulting with a professional counselor will help you move forward to reclaim emotional trigger zones.

Steps on the Path

Ask yourself:

- *What triggers and subconscious thoughts, feelings, and behavioral responses are coming out in my present relationships that may cause me and/or others pain?*
- *Do I have a mate, friend, or accountability partner who can help me identify the roots and reprogram my mind—conscious and subconscious?*
- *Will I begin to work on these so that my mind can change and renew?*

Train Your Body

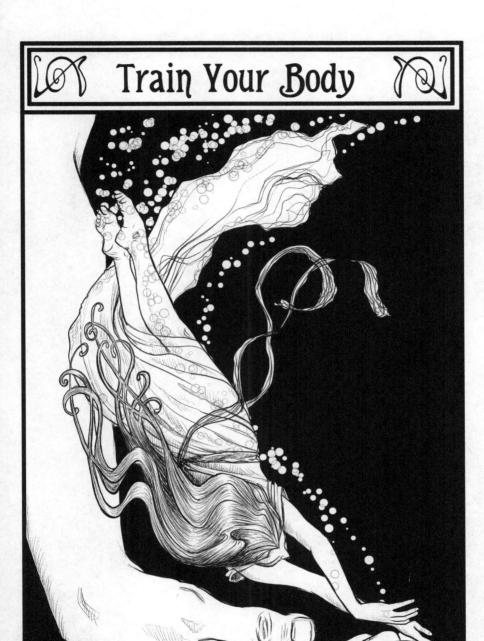

Step 4:

Train Your Body

—⟋⟍⟋⟍⟋⟍—

All good athletes train hard. They do it for a gold medal that tarnishes and fades. You're after one that's gold eternally. I don't know about you, but I'm running hard for the finish line. I'm giving it everything I've got. No sloppy living for me! I'm staying alert and in top condition. I'm not going to get caught napping, telling everyone else all about it and then missing out myself.
(1 Corinthians 9:24-27 MSG)

If I say, "Surely the darkness will overwhelm me, and the light around me will be night." Even the darkness is not dark to You, and the night is as bright as the day. Darkness and light are alike to You.
(Psalm 139:11-12 NASB)

God as Coach

For me, the most traumatic aspect of training for a triathlon—besides jumping into a chilly swimming pool at 5:30 in the morning—has been the swim portion. Almost everyone freaks out about that section of the race. I am not a pretty swimmer. I know how to swim. Well, it might be more accurate to say that I know relatively well how to keep from drowning. Without any swim coaching, I was an aqua-disaster. I usually did a frantic combination of all the swim strokes, and then when I was tired, I'd flip on my back and backstroke until I hit a buoy on the outskirts of the course. Then I'd reposition myself and head to the next buoy. So, like a wet human pinball, I would somehow survive the swim portion of a triathlon.

Then I signed up for an Olympic triathlon—with a .9-mile swim! The sheer need to survive the swim portion in order to parent my

177

daughters into the future compelled me to improve my technique and meet with a swim coach. The first time I went to a coaching session, I didn't know any of the drills, or basically anything about swimming except the part about not drowning. Assessing my skill level, the coach put me in a special lane exclusively for me and gave me the most basic instruction.

The swim coach taught us a certain form that would protect us, especially our faces, during a race situation, when everyone's legs and arms were thrashing about (you can mostly avoid that by swimming in the back of the pack). We ran swim drills to help us focus on the most efficient form of cutting through the water. We worked on breathing techniques so we wouldn't get worn out—or worse, panicked—during the swim course. Eventually, I learned to move through the water with more power and efficiency. I was able to move up from my own special lane to the second-slowest lane—a great victory for me!

Even with the incentive of that visible progress, my mind tended to wander while I was swimming. Somehow, the rhythmic splash-breathe-kick would pull up anxieties from my everyday life. When I've had certain big decisions to make, I felt stress more intensely because I couldn't turn to my late husband for advice.

During one of my swim training sessions, I noticed how my restlessness affected my performance. When I was stressed and rushing, my form and breathing went all to pieces. I was gasping for breath, pushing myself to keep a fast pace, and mostly gulping water, which didn't help matters.

Coach Larry taught us that when you feel your form falling apart, you needed to pause, purpose to relax, find your beginning form again, get a rhythm, take time to breathe, and start over.

That advice became important for me in my everyday life as well. As soon as I calmed down, found my form, stopped rushing to find the end, and took time to breathe, I could feel a belonging and a flow. I stopped flailing about and felt my body cutting through the water, working in harmony with the elements. Sometimes, in that moment of peace, my anxieties felt lifted away, and my problems achieved the clarity of perspective or acceptance. Of course, the answers to my life decisions didn't magically appear, but the process of getting back to the basics, taking time to relax, honoring the speed that worked for me, and purposing to calmly breathe went a long way.

**Sometimes the answers we are searching for don't come right away,
but with the proper technique, you can actually enjoy the swim while you are in the water.**

My swim coach was there to help me achieve success. He loved his job and took joy in my progress. All that was required from me was to show up and be willing to do what he instructed.

I had figured that, in writing this book, I could make it so generic that many people could use it. So, I first determined to focus on the health and exercise components for grief recovery. However, I discovered that unless I also sought to connect with God through honest prayer and reading the Word, total and vibrant healing wasn't happening for me. Yes, I felt strong, but I was still secretly anxious.

When I watched our swim coach instructing, encouraging, and challenging us for our own success, I could feel God whispering in my heart, "Will you let Me coach you?"

Exercise and Healthy Eating

I really struggled with depression after Jason's death. Two significant discoveries for me were that *what* I ate and adding exercise *with a finish line* helped me take major leaps forward in my grief journey. I felt stronger, my body felt calmer, and as a result, my life became exponentially better. I felt so much energy, and that feeling of strength permeated every aspect of my life.

I watched this happen with my first Team of widows as we committed to train for a sprint triathlon together in less than five months. We accomplished this task with the volunteer expertise and leadership of a friend of mine, Tara McLain, who is a personal trainer. In the span of four months, not only did the bodies of my widow Teammates change dramatically, but more importantly, their perspective on life changed as well.[33]

That's what I want for you. I want that sense of strength, renewal, and re-claiming your life.

I *never* thought after I lost my husband, "Wow, this is a great time to train for a race." Grief is overwhelming. There are no words for the pain. I suggest, however, that you simply start the process of moving your body. Consider crossing just one finish line, a simple 5K, which is a 3.1-mile course. It doesn't matter if you finish last. Walk the whole course if you like. I do. I am not a fast racer. I have never placed in a triathlon. I usually finish towards the back, even in a 5K, and especially in a 10K. Over time, I have learned to enjoy building up my distance. I love to bike ride, I now like to swim, and I can tolerate the run/power walk portion of a race.

I started when my young daughter made me walk my cul-de-sac in my pajama pants. Take a year to ramp up to a 5K. Just try for one finish line. If your health does not allow it, you can still work these steps. You can still educate yourself about healthy eating choices and make one positive change in your eating, get used to that, and then make another. You don't have to get this all perfectly done in a year's time. These steps work like a spiral staircase, taking you ever higher in your life. Just take the next step.

Chapter 11:

Stepping out of the Well

Ever notice that when caring friends bring meals to help out when there's been a sickness or death, the food generally comes in a deep-walled dish and falls into the category of "comfort food"? Maybe it's called "comfort food" because it's supposed to make us feel nurtured, like when my Grandma Nelly fed us *arroz con pollo* and *Papas a la Huancaina* (a delicious Peruvian potato dish) for Sunday dinner. Either that, or it's supposed to make us feel comfortable like a piece of furniture—well-padded and hard to move.

"Comfort" in this form started with the funeral, with loving neighbors bringing starchy, fatty meals that were easy to reheat. After many weeks passed, I began to emerge from the initial grief fog. I caught sight of a recent photo and beheld a startlingly well-padded version of myself. In time, I flung myself into another project: lose the grief weight.

Over the years, I have wavered wildly between various diets and comfort-food comas. The problem is, plunging into these weight-loss schemes was akin to buying the latest storage system for my clutter. Until I actually got rid of the junk, it would eventually return to overwhelm me. Most of my diet attempts would work for a while and then stop working.

It took me years before I finally realized that my state of mind was influenced not only by those things and people around me, but also by how I treated my body. There are a series of mental steps I had to take in order to "180 My Life":

- Realize that outer organization in my life contributed to my inner calm.

- Acknowledge that releasing offenses would minimize unnecessary stress in my life.
- Recognize that surrounding myself with more "things" would not create a shield between me and my grief; it would only multiply my chaos and concerns.
- Accept that when I asked friends, neighbors, strangers, and my own children to help on my journey, I was honoring and empowering the transformative power of grief in their lives, too.
- Understand that part of the empowerment and peace I sought was connected to my diet and exercise routine as well.
- Taking time to pray and read my Bible, even if it was frustrated prayer, was a way of beginning to trust God and allowing Him to coach me.

We know that we can reach the mind through the body. On the level of our muscles, we can purposely alter our moods by changing our posture or expression. If we smile, just forcing the face muscles into the smile position helps us feel more positive and less stressed. If we stand up straight, we will automatically feel more confident and less discouraged. The author of *Sink Reflections*, Marla Cilley, hosts a blog helping people beautify their lives by de-cluttering their homes. She encourages us to rejoice in even small measures of progress rather than torture ourselves when our efforts fall short of perfection. The first step that she always insists on: putting on lace-up shoes in the morning. Wearing shoes signals our psyches that we're ready for the adventures of the day, wherever they take us.

My Peruvian grandmother used to offer another helpful bit of advice. It was simple but profound: **When You Feel Bad, Look Good.** Make the effort to take care of yourself. I know it's counterintuitive to look good when you feel bad, but the effort makes all the difference.

I would also add to her wisdom: **When you feel bad, *do* good.** Doing good may only include adding your bit of beauty to the world. It can also include a positive decision, a baby step towards improvement that can build up to great changes. It's not just about having a good hair day when times are tough. There's an art to it.

When times are tough, make good decisions.
Even when that's the last thing you feel like doing.

Good decisions have a cumulative effect. After a while, your good decisions start to snowball, and a host of positive changes comes into your life.

A friend once told me an allegorical story about a stubborn donkey that had been thrown down a well by his nasty owner. To add insult to injury, the owner proceeded to throw trash on top of the donkey in the well. Each time trash rained down on the donkey, she stepped *on top of the trash*. The cruel owner didn't realize that with every piece of garbage, the donkey was getting closer to the opening of the well. Finally, the donkey stepped on top of the last piece of trash and then simply stepped out of the well.

The good decisions you make while you are in the well
are the stepping stones for getting out of a bad situation.
The bad circumstances of life do not need to define you.
Your decisions within those circumstances define
you and your character.
Your character becomes your legacy.
Your legacy is what your children model.

Making good decisions won't erase the loss. You can, however, find your passion again and your zest for living. Your good decisions have the power to craft your current life into something you love. It doesn't happen overnight, but in time, you come out of the well of despair with a renewed strength and purpose. Your good decisions give hope to your family and those around you. The trash that is thrown on you, and the positive decisions you make in response, are your pathway out.

When we nourish our bodies for optimal performance, and then exercise with a goal in mind, we can set a new course in our lives. Our efforts towards "looking good," coupled with wise decisions, will inevitably lead to our *feeling* good.

I will share with you what worked for me, the people who helped me succeed, and some books that provided essential insights. Our health experts will share nutritional strategies for fueling your body for optimal performance. When your body is working and resting well, you will feel happier and more balanced. When your body feels in balance, it's easier to make wise, life-affirming decisions during times of grief.

Bethany Rutledge, a USA Triathlon Certified Coach and part owner of Atlanta Triathlon Club, helped me achieve my first Olympic-length triathlon. Bethany will share practical step-by-step strategies for training and preparing for a 5K, 10K, and sprint triathlon, as well as training plans for each event.[34]

- *Couch to 5K*
- *Couch to 10K*
- *Couch to Sprint Triathlon*

For me, the result was surprising. Not only did I feel stronger, I also felt happier. When I made good food choices, I could train more effectively, had more energy, and slept better. I chose to be outside more, my kids and I were playing together more, and I didn't battle depression as much. I felt joyful. After a few years, my daughters started training for their own races, starting with an Ironkids triathlon. They felt confidence from crossing their own finish lines. Arie completed her first Ironkids triathlon at seven years old, and Sophia completed her first triathlon at eight years of age. Those accomplishments created a healthy community for us and gave my children a sense of strength and pride in who they are.

Choosing to get healthy will look different for every person even if you are not into triathlons. The idea in this section is to give you plans that you and your Team of supportive friends or support group members can activate together.

**Achieving success in the physical realm
is a great step in claiming your life as it is today.**

If you can strengthen your body, you feel more empowered to face whatever challenges are thrown your way. We are all at different places physically, so check with your doctor before you make any changes to your diet or exercise plans.

De-Clutter Your Diet

Grief creates stress in our bodies that results in chemical and digestive imbalances, which can also create an absence of the hormones that help us feel good. According to the article, "The Science of Breaking Up: How Heartbreak Hurts Your Physical and Mental Health," by Lizette Borreli, when we are in a relationship, our brains get a continual dose of positive hormones, like dopamine and oxytocin—hormones that inspire bonding and good feelings in people. When we go through a break-up in a romantic relationship, those positive interactions are then absent. Our brains are literally in withdrawal from the constant stream of those positive hormones.[35]

After reading this article, it occurred to me that if our brains go through feel-good hormone withdrawals during a romantic relationship breakup, it's logical to think that such a withdrawal process would be even more intense with the loss of a loved one. So, it seems natural to want to stimulate those pleasure centers in our brains with an easy fix, like sugar, alcohol, drugs, or smoking. Maybe that's why we all reach for comfort foods in a grief situation. These toxins stimulate the same pleasure centers of the brain, but they do so only temporarily, and with bad side effects.

Instead of reaching for toxins, we can opt for a cleaner, more efficient way to re-balance the chemicals that have been knocked awry by the stress of our loss. Properly nourishing our bodies while grieving can help us feel stronger, calmer, and better able to manage our circumstances. The body, mind, and spirit are closely intertwined, so we have to intentionally heal each area in order to live vibrantly, especially during grief.

In this section we will address what foods are helpful and harmful to your body, especially during times of grief.

First, we have to de-clutter our diets in the same way we de-cluttered our house. Like all of the junk that does not bring us joy and peace of mind in our homes, many of the foods we crave only work to keep us muddled and fatigued. In fact, the foods we crave are often foods we cannot metabolize properly because we have an intolerance or allergy. Dr. Mathews-Larson says that we crave foods that are bad for us—meaning our bodies aren't able to get necessary nutrients from them, or they block our ability to get nutrients from other sources. In other words, I crave chocolate because it doesn't work with my body, and I get a "mild high" when my body has to deal with the leftover junk in my system.[36]

Of course, the "high" is not actually the problem; the problem is the cost to my system when it has to process harmful substances. I recently discovered something I wished I had known for years. I stumbled on it quite by accident. As I have matured, I want my body to work at its optimal levels so I can keep running around with my young children and competing in races. When I ate cheese, my nose became congested. When I had chocolate, I got dizzy. These foods made training uncomfortable. A friend of mine recommended that I have my blood tested for food allergies and sensitivities. I took an allergy test, which conducts a blood panel showing the specific foods my body was especially sensitive to. You can ask your doctor or visit the website 180YourLife.com for a recommended allergy test kit.

I ordered the test kit and had my blood drawn at one of those walk-in labs for any test, and then overnighted the sample to the recommended lab. In about a week, they came back with the results. I was surprised to learn that my body was allergic to tomatoes, dairy, quinoa, cocoa, and wheat, among other things. They also provided a detailed diet plan with the optimal foods customized for my body according to my blood panel. When I customized my food choices for my specific blood chemistry, my body felt even better and more energetic. Training was easier, and I felt healthier. Check with your health care practitioner for allergy testing options.

According to Dr. Mathews-Larson, my body's responses were fairly common: "cow's milk, wheat, eggs, cane sugar, corn, and chocolate" are the most common foods causing these "maladaptive responses" for people.[37] So, as we move towards making our lives and bodies healthy, we should note the foods that are working against our efforts. The most common culprits are probably not surprising. In the first chapter, I mentioned the bad types of sugars and fats that we encounter in our friends' well-meaning funeral-day food offerings. I asked sports nutritionist, Ilana Katz, to expand the list so that we could make a clean sweep of foods to avoid:

As noted, sugar is used as energy fuel, which is needed by the brain. The downside is that it causes blood sugar to rise, and as quickly as it rises, it plummets back down, resulting in the physiological need for more sugar to get it back up, and the vicious cycle of craving sugar begins. It is like a rollercoaster set in motion, swinging from hyper- to hypoglycemic reactions (a pendulum of high to low blood sugar levels). This is the body's homeostatic response to stable blood sugar—in other words, trying to keep the body in balance. Unfortunately, the physiological *over*compensation is what causes our uncontrollable cravings.

This does not mean that you should be on a low carbohydrate plan to avoid cravings; in fact, it is quite the opposite. For one thing, it has already been stated that the required fuel for the brain is carbohydrates in the form of glycogen, so avoidance of carbs is unhealthy in itself. It is the amount of carbs that is relevant, as well as the type of carbohydrates eaten, that will reduce sugar cravings.

Trying to cut calories by reducing carbohydrates tends to increase sugar cravings. Sugar substitutes like Splenda and sugar alcohols are used by manufacturers to enable them to market lower sugar or lower net carbs on the label, seemingly offering a more attractive product for dieters. Be wary – firstly, the jury is still out on the long term safety of these substitutes. And secondly, sugar alcohols have been found to actually have a negative effect on blood sugars. We are then back to square one; the pendulum swing in blood sugar in a day is what leads to the vicious cycle of cravings, trying to satisfy them with foods that trigger and result in more cravings. In other words, sweet things make you want to eat more sweet things, and although artificial sweeteners are calorie free, they are not helping with reduction in cravings whatsoever. Furthermore, sugar alcohols have a tendency to cause gastrointestinal distress, in that they induce diarrhea and flatulence.

Net carbs is also a marketing "con," so to speak. Supposedly, net carbs, a term coined by Atkins Nutritionals, is defined as the net value of carbs once fiber has been removed. According to the Food and Drug Administration, there is no such value: carbohydrates are carbohydrates, whether they are made up of refined sugar, starch, or fiber, and every gram of carb has four calories. So do not let low carbohydrates fool you in your endeavor to reduce cravings. Manufacturers have simply replaced regular carbs with sugar alcohols and sweeteners.

Craving sweets is often an indication of a deficiency in certain nutrients. Chromium, carbon, phosphorus, sulfur, and tryptophan are often the culprits, and eating a rainbow of color is a simple solution. Broccoli, grapes, legumes, and chicken (chromium); fresh fruit (carbon); fish, eggs, legumes and chicken (phosphorous); cranberries, cauliflower, kale and cabbage (sulfur); and turkey, liver, lamb, sweet potato and spinach (tryptophan).

One last point on preventing the energy swing that is the main culprit of sugar cravings has to do with timing of intake. Waiting too long to eat or grazing all day (not waiting long enough to eat) has a similar effect to that hyper- and hypoglycemic response mentioned earlier. It is during the steep peaks and valleys in energy that one feels lethargic and emotional. At these times, the physiological response is to eat sweet things. Furthermore, we justify allowing ourselves to eat the treats and sweets that stimulate a pleasurable response by blaming our stress and emotions (as if we deserve the pleasure). This only leads to guilt and depression. Leveling out the peaks and valleys is the solution to curbing those debilitating cravings.

In summary, the details thus far reflect on the amount of carbs, sources of carbs, and timing of meals in combination as a solution for erasing sugar cravings. Practically worded, eat fresh fruits to satisfy a sweet tooth, get the refined sugars out of the body to aid in stable blood sugars, avoid high sugar or processed products like candy, soda, fruit drinks, pastries, etc., replace the "processed" products with foods that come from the earth (grains, legumes, potatoes), and avoid artificial sweeteners. Make sure you get a rainbow of color in your daily intake. All the colors found in fruits and vegetables represent the vital vitamins and minerals that, if lacking, will stimulate cravings.

Dr. Mathews-Larson adds a few other health thieves to the list: alcohol, nicotine, caffeine, dairy, and gluten. Addressing the more widely-known dangers, she explains, "Alcohol, street drugs, and prescription drugs all have one thing in common: They deplete your body and brain of essential natural chemicals, many of which keep you emotionally stable. They fire off excessive amounts of your brain's neurotransmitters and endorphins, leaving near-empty sites in the brain."[38]

Caffeine is harmful because it gives our bodies an unnatural energy boost—but that energy has to be fueled by our own store of nutrients. It produces an energy burst "by stimulating your (overworked) adrenals to release adrenaline—and thereby emergency sugar—into your bloodstream. Never mind that your real level of energy is nil. Continually doing this to your adrenals is akin to beating a dying horse. Adrenaline circulating in your bloodstream makes you irritable, anxious, shaky, and restless. Your heart may pound, and you may even have panic attacks. Eventually the surge of energy is reduced to temporarily alleviating your ongoing fatigue." She recommends, however, that giving up caffeine should be a gradual process: you shouldn't stop drinking caffeine cold turkey, because withdrawal effects could include headaches and jitteriness. Instead, decrease your caffeine intake over the course of a week, and gradually replace coffee with less-caffeinated drinks. She says, "Your reward for dumping caffeine will be evident in your increased energy levels and reduced sugar cravings."[39]

Dairy and gluten are, according to Dr. Mathews-Larson, "the most common allergy foods in the United States today." An allergic reaction to these substances, however, might not be easily recognized. Dr. Mathews-Larson explains: "Today, science is aware that peptides formed from digested proteins are identical to certain brain endorphins that are linked to panic attacks and other 'mental' conditions. The first two discoveries in this area were peptides that came from poorly digested casein (milk protein) and gluten (wheat protein)." She reminds us that a clue that we have such a food allergy is our craving for it.[40]

At this point in my de-cluttering process, I learned that when it came to food, the cleaner I ate, the more amazing I felt. I have offered the scientific explanations because that is what I required: I knew that if I was going to give up certain foods I enjoyed, I needed to know why they weren't good for me. My research, along with Ilana Katz's explanations, helped me to understand what my body was trying to communicate when I felt the urge to scarf a chocolate chip muffin. I felt able to view my body, and its cravings, as a tool, one that could either help or hinder me on my journey towards peace of mind. Somehow, I felt better able to respond to its cries for help—by not giving it a harmful food—than I would have felt responding to its cry for treats.

Fueling a Ferrari

There are some days I want to train more than others. I recall one specific Monday night that was not one of them. Before jumping into the cold pool, I stood in the warm shower at the Cobb County Aquatic Center, where the swim coaching session through Atlanta Tri Club was about to take place.

I don't want to do this, I don't want to do this, kept rebounding through my head.

It's always a shock to jump into cold water, and I do a little underwater yelp every time I have to go in.

I had stressed during the past weekend. I had then tried to douse the pain with my old food standbys. I had thrown caution to the wind and activated almost every known allergy in my body. Chocolate? Bring it on. Gluten? Order up! Milk? Yes, please!

With the weekend over, it was time to get in the pool and swim. I had a dull headache. I felt tired and sluggish. My sinuses were stopped up, so breathing while swimming became a real challenge. In short, I was a disaster.

As I was gasping for breath during my swim workout, I noticed that I could not go as far and fast in the pool as I had in the past.

"You have to nourish yourself for success," I told myself while I was dragging through the water.

"Remember this moment when you are tempted again," I thought, and I will. The brief pleasure of those snacks was not worth feeling sluggish and fatigued.

Whether you are training for a 5K, 10K, triathlon, or crafting the life you love in a different way, you have to nourish your body for success. If you put sugar in the tank of a Ferrari, it won't go very far. You must give yourself the proper high-octane fuel.

I have learned to work with my body's chemistry and how to nourish it as part of living the life I love. Each person's body chemistry is different, and you should consult your doctor to see what works best for you.

Journey to the Sunrise

Discover that your state of mind is influenced not only by those things and people around you, but also by what's inside you. Your body consumption and chemistry are an integral part of your healing.
Realize that outer calm is a necessary component for inner peace. Purpose to make wise eating choices.
Understand that achieving success in the physical realm is a great step in claiming your life as it is today.

Steps on the Path

- Take the Nutrition Challenge
  Nourishing your body, especially during times of grief, empowers you to feel stronger faster.
  Try it for twenty-one days by taking away one food that is bad for you every three days, such as refined sugar, alcohol, artificial sweeteners, soda, caffeine, dairy, and gluten and see how you feel. Want to get more strategies for a healthful detox? Check out the book *The Hormone Cure* by Sara Gottfried, MD.
- Let your body "reset" nutritionally by making conscious choices to eliminate destructive foods that disrupt your digestion and your body's ability to nourish itself. Instead, take wise steps to strengthen your body for the adventure that lies ahead.

A healthy lifestyle is not just about avoiding certain toxins, it's about making good choices.

Chapter 12

Eating for Optimal Health

It became possible for the donkey to take a glorious breath of fresh air when she finally finished tramping down the garbage and took her last step out of the well. I could finally breathe easy when I succeeded in unwrapping Kathy the Python from around my torso. Similarly, after we have cleared the clutter from our systems, we can begin to nourish ourselves with what will strengthen and replenish us. The next step after de-cluttering our diets is introducing good foods to take the place of the toxins. These foods will act like high-octane fuel in your body, nourishing and strengthening you to empower your best life. Again, nutritionist Ilana Katz has lent her expertise:

Optimal Nutrition Daily means ….
   Balance your caloric intake (what you eat) **and caloric expenditure** (what you burn e.g. exercise) to attain and maintain your desired body weight. Overeating or lack of exercise will upset caloric balance and may result in weight gain.
   Use recommended standard serving sizes for portion control. A "portion" is how much food you choose to eat, whether in a restaurant, from a package, or in your own kitchen. A "serving" is a standard amount set by the U.S. Government, or sometimes by others for recipes, cookbooks, or diet plans. Use the Food Guide Pyramid as a guide to see how many *standard serving sizes* you should eat from each food group.

Establish consistent eating patterns. Eat at least 3 meals per day with one healthy snack between each meal (totaling 5–6 smaller meals per day). Eating on a regular basis promotes sound nutrition, reduces stress, increases energy, prevents overeating, and helps control eating patterns. Never skip meals, especially breakfast. Eating every 3–4 hours aids in keeping your blood sugar normal and will raise your metabolism, allowing you to burn fat more efficiently.

Choose a variety of foods at each meal to maximize your nutrient intake. Color variety generally makes a meal more nutritious and psychologically satisfying.

Choose whole, fresh, and unprocessed foods. Fresh fruit, vegetables, and whole-wheat or wholegrain breads and cereals are always a good idea. These contain more nutrients and fiber and less sugar and salt.

Choose more dietary fiber. Fiber results in good digestion, regulation of blood sugar and cholesterol levels, and reduces the risk of digestive problems and colon cancer. Fiber also makes you feel full and prevents overeating. (Good sources: bran, whole grains, fruits and vegetables, nuts, seeds, beans, peas, brown rice, oatmeal, and corn).

Choose unsaturated fats in place of saturated fats. Saturated fats are usually solid at room temperature (animal fats: butter, lard, etc.). Poly*unsaturated* fats are usually found in vegetable oils, margarine*, peanut butter, and fish (specially salmon and tuna). Mono*unsaturated* fats are olives, peanuts, olive oil, canola oil, and avocados.

* Margarine may contain trans-fats: read food labels and avoid trans-fats, as they behave like saturated fats.

Increase fluid intake. Drink 8 -10 glasses of fluid, preferably water, per day (at least 4 should be water). Proper hydration will prevent hunger and thirst.

Daily Hydration. Fluids help the body maintain acceptable body temperatures and thus prevent heat-related illness. As your metabolism is the natural rate at which your body burns fat; dehydration has the unwelcome side effect of slowing that fat-burning capacity down. The more water in your system, the more your fat-burning function operates properly. This means drinking 8 – 10 8oz glasses of fluid per day, (total of 64 – 80 fl oz; with 50–60 fl oz of pure water).

Other tips

Cut out processed food (there is hidden sugar in everything. If you stay with foods close to the earth—fruits, veggies, whole grains—you will have the chance of much better results).

Use herbs and spices and seasonings instead of high-fat sauces (remember to limit the extra fats: condiments, marinades, dressings, nut butters, etc.).

Planning is your best route to success. Grill fish and chicken over the weekend, freeze 4-ounce portions for future use. Get in the habit of packing a cooler for the day. Load up with premade mini-meals, protein bars, shakes, fruit, and vegges.

Eat less sodium	**Limit caffeine**
Eat less cholesterol	**Limit alcohol**
Eat less high-fat foods	**Eat less sugar foods**

Eating out:

Most restaurants want you to come back, so even their basic grilling and baking is loaded in fat – it's the fat that adds the satisfying flavors to food. Be high maintenance in restaurants, they are there to please you – ask for sauces and dressings on the side, take half your meal home (restaurants serve on average 2 – 3 times the size of appropriate portions)

If you don't see a healthy choice on the menu, ask for grilled or baked chicken breast or fish with steamed veggies.

Finally, I asked Ilana Katz for some suggestions on what to include in my kitchen, now that I have cleansed it of known threats, and she provided me with a Top Eleven List:

For starters, to include some of the healthiest foods, you can look and feel your absolute best, slow down aging, and help protect yourself from illnesses and degenerative diseases more for daily.

1. Water

Surprised? Water is the most essential nutrient in your diet. It's needed for digestion, assimilation, metabolism, elimination, weight control, and more. Unlike coffee, colas and alcohol, eight glasses of pure water a day has no calories or negative side effects.

2. Vegetables

Five or more servings a day of broccoli, carrots, tomatoes, cauliflower, Brussels sprouts, spinach, kale or other green leafy vegetables are excellent choices. They're rich in fiber, vitamins A and C, calcium, iron, magnesium, and phytonutrient antioxidants that help prevent cancer and heart disease.

3. Fish

Eating fatty fish, particularly salmon, at least three times a week is one of the healthiest things you can do. The omega 3 oils lower the risk of heart disease, as well as improving nerves, eyes, and brain. Fish oil also helps reduce inflammation and makes an excellent natural alternative to anti-inflammatory drugs.

4. Fruit

Two to four daily servings of fresh or frozen fruit are recommended. Strawberries, blueberries, raspberries, oranges, red grapes, plums, apricots, peaches, and papaya are some of the best. They're rich in fiber, vitamins, minerals, carotenoids, and flavonoids.

5. Whole Grains

Brown rice, oatmeal, sprouted breads, and other whole grains are great sources of fiber, vitamins B and E, protein, minerals, and essential fatty acids. The fiber helps prevent colon cancer, high cholesterol, and constipation. Beware of gluten, however, if you have an intolerance for it.

6. Garlic and Onions

Garlic is a powerful natural antibiotic that boosts immunity, protects against bacteria, parasites and viruses, and helps prevent heart disease, stroke, and cancer. Onions are antibiotic, anti-inflammatory, and antiviral and have been shown to help improve LDL / HDL cholesterol balance and fight off bronchitis, asthma, hay fever, and infection.

7. Yogurt

Plain, unsweetened, low-fat, nondairy yogurts are excellent sources of complete protein, calcium, and lactobacillus. There are many nondairy options available for yogurts, such as almond milk and coconut milk yogurt, and they still offer the benefits of protein and good bacteria. They help protect against osteoporosis, cavities, high blood pressure, high cholesterol, and intestinal disorders. Yogurt's beneficial bacteria also make it a natural antibiotic and anticancer agent.

8. Poultry

Skinless chicken and turkey are valuable sources of complete protein and B vitamins. Chicken soup is good for colds and flu. Its high cysteine content helps break down mucus. Turkey is leaner, low in calories and high in selenium, which strengthens the immune system. White meat is easier to digest than fattier dark meat.

9. Beans
Lentils, peas, and other beans are good sources of fiber and B vitamins. Combined with whole grains, especially rice, they become an excellent source of complete protein. Beans have also been found to help lower cholesterol, regulate blood sugar, and reduce cancer rates.

10. Nuts
Raw nuts are rich in protein, vitamins B and E, minerals, and essential fatty acids. They've been found to have both anti-cancer and anti-heart disease properties. Almonds, for example, help lower cholesterol.

11. Super Foods
Try including foods that are especially high in nutrients like Spirulina, Chlorella, Chia Seeds, and Green Algae in your green smoothie for a boost of "high octane" fuel.

Create Art Out of Your Life Today
Though I have never been the chef in our family, a friend helped me consider cooking for my family as an art, much more than just defrosting pre-packaged foods. I want to encourage you to take your time to savor the experience of nourishing your body and your family. We can savor the family around us, and we can choose to find the beauty in the midst of pain.

Several years ago, I was doing my normal shopping at Trader Joe's. Usually, as I loaded my cart with frozen meals, I silently promised myself that next week I would start cooking. This had been my modus operandi for five years following Jason's death.

While cruising the aisles, I often saw Bill, a friendly Cuban man who worked at the store. I would practice my Spanish with him while he gave me fun Latino food suggestions to try.

One Sunday night, as I loaded up my cart in my last lap through the frozen food section, I rounded the corner and bumped into Bill. I asked him if he had any new sauce suggestions.

"What are you cooking this week?" he asked as he looked at my cart full of frozen meals.

Acknowledging his silent assessment of my food choices, I confessed, "I'm still learning to cook."

His quiet, questioning look spoke volumes. How had I gotten this far in my life without cooking?

In answer to his look, I offered, "My late husband was the gourmet cook."

I could tell he hadn't known I was a widow, so with a smile, I tried to lighten things up, "I've just been defrosting since I became a single parent."

He didn't laugh. Sometimes that line got a laugh.

"How long ago did he pass?" Bill asked, looking at my five-year-old youngest daughter.

"About five and a half years ago," I replied matter-of-factly.

By now his silence and obvious sadness was becoming uncomfortable.

Trying to redirect Bill and resume my shopping, I said, "I don't know what I'm doing in the kitchen. I always like your food combination suggestions. Any ideas for me?"

Brows unfurrowing, he took a deep breath and said, "Cooking is not a duty. It is my passion!"

He then offered me some ideas and moved back to work the cash register.

Once I was done shopping, I ended up in Bill's line, and as he scanned my frozen meals, he said, "I am going to step over a line here."

He looked at me, eyes brimming with tears, "If your late husband was such a good cook, you must enjoy cooking, not run from it. *Para honrar a su esposo y sus hijas*. To honor your husband and daughters."

He spoke in Spanish to emphasize his point. I just stood there, stone cold.

I wanted to say, "But he left and died. Sometimes, I still get angry."

"I'm sorry, I am a passionate man. I am too emotional," he said as he lifted his wire-rim glasses to wipe his eyes.

His sadness for us was touching.

I said quietly, "When I cook, I feel sad because I miss him, so I don't."

Right there in the checkout line, my eyes welled up, and then I was wiping my cheeks, too. The truth had been spoken, and Bill smiled.

"But you have to!" Bill encouraged me. "Are you a creative person? Cooking is an art! The staples are your black and white, like rice and fish, and the sauces and flavorings are your colors. Do something unexpected! Have fun with it!"

197

He smiled again. Now that he had moved into the realm of creativity and fashion, he was speaking my language. I wiped my eyes and smiled back.

"Okay, I'll try. *Gracias por ayudar a mi corazón sanar,*" I said in Spanish. Thank you for helping my heart to heal.

He hugged me, and I walked out of Trader Joe's into the cool Sunday evening. I silently cried as I loaded my groceries. Not from sadness—mostly just from the unexpected gift of being truthfully seen by a friend. I felt something shift in me.

When I got home, I put on flamenco music. Instead of heating up another pre-packaged frozen meal, I made some brown rice, added lentil beans, chopped in some veggies and avocado, and added Marsala sauce.

My dad and girls set the table, and we all sat down to lovely dinner.

We laughed, and then my younger daughter asked me, "Can we eat this again?"

An artistic experience. I can do that. Thanks, Bill, for your encouragement, and thanks, Jason, for the years of delicious meals you gave us. Now it's our turn.

Journey to the Sunrise

Discover that a healthy lifestyle is not only about avoiding certain bad foods; it's about making good choices.
Realize that you must plan for success.
Understand that when you eat "clean and green," you will feel strong, balanced, and energetic.

Steps on the Path

- Since you cannot fight chemistry with will power, you must work with your body's chemistry and learn how to nourish it as part of living the life you love. Each person's body chemistry is different, and you will need to consult your doctor to see what works best for you.
- Check out our Taste of Triumph Recipes in the Appendix 2 for health food plans.

Chapter 13:

Training Plan

W hen I started giving my body the nutrients it needed, my "comfort" weight began to come off. I had been in sprint triathlons in the past. In time, once I had built my Team, I found that it was even more fun to train in a supportive community that I knew would hold each of us accountable.

Am I ever going to think at 5:30 a.m. that I can't wait to get out of my warm bed and exercise? Probably not, but I know that after I exercise, I feel relaxed and alert.

The reason I strongly encourage signing up for a race, like a 5K, 10K or sprint triathlon, rather than just deciding to start exercising without a finish line, is that the date of the race gives you a specific goal. You commit to exercises that will prepare you for the race (instead of simply trying to burn calories). There is a definite deadline to work towards, so that the cost of procrastination becomes real. You know you will be racing in public (wearing carefully orchestrated exercise gear, of course). When you run your race, crowds of people will be there to cheer you on.

After participating in sprint triathlons for five years, I decided it was time to kick things up a notch. So I called on Bethany Rutledge to help me train for my first Olympic-length triathlon in 2014. Bethany Rutledge is part owner of the Atlanta Triathlon Club and USA Triathlon Certified Coach and trainer. Atlanta Tri Club partners with my non-profit Team Lady 180 to offer discounted memberships to widows and single moms and training scholarships for grieving families in need. Check in your area if a tri team might be willing to partner with your active Team Lady 180 support group as you train for your finish line. You don't have to be a group of widows. It can be any Team of women supporting each other. If you have a mixed support group of men and women, you can start a 180 Your Life group using these same principles. Check out 180YourLife.com to learn more about starting your own area Team.

I asked Bethany to contribute her helpful steps to start training, and more specifically, train with a finish line in mind, such as a 5K, 10K, and sprint triathlon. Bethany outlines how we can "stack the deck" for our success in the area of exercise by:

- Planning ahead
- Committing to a schedule
- Creating accountability and
- Preparing for our race

When I make a positive decision for my life such as exercise, then consistently make those positive decisions, eventually, I've changed the landscape of my life.

Bethany's Training Plan

Couch to 5K, Couch to 10K, and Couch to Sprint Triathlon
One of the first things you need to do is make space in your life to accommodate this new level of activity. It's easy (and usually true) to say, "I'm too busy to do that." If you're like most busy people, you're already using your available hours, and you don't have "extra" time to spare. The answer is to eliminate some activities you're already doing to make room for this new level of activity.

Here are a few preliminary steps:
- Make a list of your non-negotiable activities for a week. For example, you can't drop eating, sleeping, getting kids ready for school, family time, or work. Count up the hours.
- Make a list of the ways you spend your time on things you do for relaxation (watching favorite TV shows or movies). Count up the hours.

- Make a list of things on list #1 that could be done more efficiently. For example, if you can't figure out how to get in training because of lack of childcare, perhaps you could consider trading off with a neighbor on Saturday mornings. She gets an hour while you watch all the kids, then you switch. If a gym membership is a possibility for you, then join one with childcare.
- Determine where you're willing to cut and where you're not. Everyone has different time management challenges. Kids add a whole new challenge to the mix.
- Whether your biggest limiter is time, money or a combination of both, try to find shortcuts to make things possible for you. If your primary limiter is time, you might hire out some chores and duties to create more space on your schedule. Some examples might include hiring someone to mow the lawn or clean your house, or having groceries delivered instead of going to the store. If your primary limiter is money, there are also many ways to make this lifestyle more affordable. Think of ways you can incorporate training into your life. For example, if you work in a high rise, walking up fifteen flights of stairs several times a week might be just as good as a short jog.

Getting Started

If you're brand new to regular exercise, it's easy to get overwhelmed and intimidated when you look at all of the gear involved. From fancy watches, to special tech gear, high priced shoes, special nutrition and bottles—and that's just to run. Then you have to track it with fancy apps and programs, scales that connect wirelessly to your tracking software, and on it goes. The good news is that you don't actually need all of that paraphernalia. Whether your venture of choice is walking, running, or even a triathlon, you actually need very few things to get started.

Running: Even if your "running" clothes haven't seen the light of day since gym class 1986, you probably already own something that will work. Eventually, you will likely want to upgrade to some sort of wicking material (cotton tends to stick and chafe), but it's not mandatory. The one thing you need to purchase is running shoes—good ones. I would highly recommend you start out, at the beginning, with new shoes that are fit for you. In order to do this right, you should go to any specialty running store where they can look at your gait and choose shoes for you that will support your feet properly and better protect you from injury. You shouldn't feel intimidated about going in for the first time because there are other new people going in every day to the same store who feel the same way. There is probably no question you're thinking of asking that hasn't been asked dozens of times before.

Triathlon: For a triathlon, the gear can get intimidating. From fancy bikes and kits, to strange aero attachments and supplements, there is a lot for sale in the world of tri. As with the running category, there is very little you actually need in the beginning.

* Attire: You will need clothes for running, swimming, and biking. You will also need good running shoes. For the bike ride, ultimately, you will want a pair of bike or triathlon shorts, for comfort reasons. For the swim, you'll want some sort of swimsuit, but you may already have something that will work for training.

* Gear: Eventually you'll need a bike, or at least a bike to ride during the event. In the meantime, you can train at a gym on a spin bike if you have to, or an indoor cycling class at a studio. If your first mission is a sprint triathlon, any type of bike is accepted for these types of races. (Note: races require that bikes have bar end plugs for safety reasons).

You may already have a bike that will work just fine, whether it be a commuter bike, mountain bike, or beach cruiser. You can even borrow or rent a bike for the event, although it would be in your best interest to practice on your borrowed steed prior to the event day. When biking outdoors, you'll also need a helmet and some sunglasses. It is never acceptable to cycle without a helmet.

* For the swim, you will also need a swim cap (at least for the ladies) and a pair of goggles. These can be purchased at any triathlon store or at most sporting goods stores.

Getting Up Early

If you went through the steps above and looked for time you could re-appropriate as training time, you might have honed in on the early morning hours. Here is a little more color around adjusting to training in the early morning hours.

There are very few people in this world, who, upon hearing the shrill cry of the alarm clock, awaken with gusto and jump out of bed excited to face the world. I say this because, as someone who runs a cycling studio in which half of our classes start at 6 a.m., I often hear the reasons why people can't make the classes. Phrases such as, "I can't get up that early," or, "Doing that is for the motivated people," or even, "I absolutely cannot do anything before 8:00 a.m."

The thing that stands out in those three phrases is that these people are claiming to lack any choice in the matter. They *cannot*. They are literally missing some sort of gene that would enable them to be as enthusiastic and peppy as Richard Simmons at 6 a.m.

Let me assure you, no one is thrilled when the alarm goes off. If she says she is, she is probably lying. Thus, there is no need to wait until it sounds like a fun prospect, because it's likely that day will never come. It's okay if you don't feel like doing it, or you can think of other important obligations that could potentially fill that time slot.

It's all about just doing it anyways, and there are a number of actions you can take that can help you get to that step. For most of us, the way to find more time in your day is often to get up earlier than usual a few days a week. Since when the alarm goes off, the prospect of a warm bed will almost always seem better at the time than getting up to exercise, let's explore some ways to best set ourselves up for success.

Bedtime Routine
- Lay out everything you will need in the morning. If you're running, find your running shoes, watch, and, for extra credit, wear your running clothes to bed.
- Set up equipment: If you're planning on cycling indoors, make sure your bike is already set up on the trainer. If you're riding outside, fill up bottles and lay everything by the door and ready to go.
- Driving and traffic plans: If your plans involve driving somewhere to work out, then plan traffic patterns accordingly. For instance, I train someone who, we realized, could save a lot

of time by changing up his routine from the norm. Instead of getting up, prepping for a workout, training, showering, then driving to work, he could save nearly thirty minutes of commute time and fifteen minutes of prep time by getting up and immediately driving to a gym close to his work (using the drive time to "prep" with coffee and breakfast), and then getting ready for work at the gym.

• Another tip is planning a walk or group training session with one or more friends. I find that if I mention to someone that I will attend a group ride or swim, even if they won't miss me at all or even notice if my plans change, then I can't stand to cancel on the plans I've made. We'll talk more about creating accountability in the next section.

Buddy Up: Creating Accountability

Success can often hinge on the simple factor of whether or not you have accountability. When I say simple, I mean it. Simple bits of support include meeting a friend at a training session, having regular communications with friends also exercising, or even just knowing that a friend is out there somewhere in the world going through what you're going through. Yes, accountability is a major motivator and can help you stick to your plan long-term.

If you've completed a 5K or 10K, you're a great candidate to train for a sprint triathlon. Though it can sound intimidating, a triathlon is great because it's really a sport that's for everyone.

To keep things fun, you might want to venture a little farther afield. An obstacle course event, such as a Spartan race or Tough Mudder, is a fun way to mix in cross training without the danger of taking oneself too seriously. If you want to stick to running, a twist on a 5k such as a color run can be a great way to recruit others into the sport who may be turned off by the thought of "just running."

The ideal situation is to find a helpful community of like-minded individuals, where you all can form a Team of sorts and offer ongoing support, have multiple friends training at any given time, and offer each other motivation and encouragement.

Check into teams or groups affiliated with Team Lady 180—links can be found at 180YourLife.com. If that isn't available, there are other community resources available as well. Search online for running or triathlon groups in your area. Many times, it can be intimidating to join a group for the first time because the assumption is that everyone is more experienced and faster. Chances are, that is not necessarily the case.

For example, in Atlanta Triathlon Club, members run the gamut from very new to very experienced. People join who are running or walking one mile and who do not yet know how to swim. Many members join at that level who then go on to complete all distances of running races and triathlons.

If your schedule doesn't allow you to meet up with a group or if there are no suitable groups in your area, then online accountability can work as well. Through the resources of Team Lady 180, you can find women from all over the world who have similar goals and struggles. There are also all kinds of beginners' groups on sites ranging from Meetup to Facebook, geared specifically towards running, triathlon, or whatever your goal is.

It's always nice to have some in-person camaraderie as well. If you are the first in your network of friends to pursue a more active lifestyle, then a good option for you may be getting more friends involved. In order to get them on board, you can use some of the tips we've already talked about. I have found that getting someone to sign up for a race event is a huge motivator. After that, they won't want to back out.

Creating Your Own 180 Team

If you end up deciding your best course of action is to create your own Team, then there are a few steps you should take.

- Communication Forum: Sometimes the simplest solution is the best. A closed or private Facebook group is an easy, free way to get everyone excited and to communicate on a regular basis. As the leader/group administrator, your job will be to get everyone engaged and excited about the culminating event.
- Regular Check-Ins: Posting frequent Meetups, asking questions about how others' training is going, and commiserating over any hurdles or setbacks, will set the tone for everyone to share openly.

- Setting a Deadline: If you choose to use a Facebook group, you can create your own group-specific events to start to flesh-out details and amp up the enthusiasm. For example, if your culminating event is a specific 5k, set up an event so that others can RSVP, talk about pre- and post-plans, and plan other logistics.
- Regular Training: You can also use your group to plan group training, whether it's in-person training or virtual training.

Challenges: Getting over a Training Hump

If only training were as easy as following a prescribed path that goes in a perfectly straight line. There's a reason we have coaches, training groups, and support groups. Nothing in life is ever as straightforward as everyone's following the same set formula to achieve a desired result. Therefore, do not become discouraged when inevitable setbacks occur. The following things happen to everyone. It's how you deal with them that matters.

- *Something hurts*
- *Work, family, life gets in the way*
- *You or a family member gets sick*
- *You temporarily lose motivation*

The challenges listed above happen to the best of us. It's what you do next that determines your ultimate success. When your circumstances allow, try to rekindle your motivation by remembering what inspired you in the first place.

The most important thing you can do is not to get discouraged
and try to pick up as close to where you left off as you can.

What happens if I miss a few days?
- If you miss a couple of days to one week of training, then take a few easy ramp up days and continue into the current week on the plan
- If you miss more than five days of training, then you may need a longer period of reduced training/ramp-up to get back on track
- Whatever you do, do not try to make up missed training sessions. You can rearrange future sessions if you miss a few priority

workouts, but don't try to cram everything in, or you could possibly injure yourself.

Preparing to Cross Your Finish Line

You can find "Couch to 5K," "Couch to 10K," and "Couch to Sprint Triathlon" plans as free downloads at 180YourLife.com. If you're following an organized plan, then you should be reducing your training as the race date approaches. This allows your body to rest and heal as you prepare to put all that training to good use on race day.

Here is a timeline of the extra stuff that needs to be accomplished in the weeks leading up to your race:

- **4-6 weeks prior:** You should have practiced all your race day details. This includes training in the attire that you will wear on the day, practicing your hydration and nutrition plan several times in training, and making any last-minute purchases you will need. Most importantly, do not make the mistake of running in new shoes. If you are staying in a hotel, your reservations and travel plans should already be made. Try to wrap up any other logistics so you won't have to stress about them at the last minute.
- **2 weeks prior:** Depending on the length and type of event, you probably have started to reduce your training in preparation for a great race day performance.
- **1 week prior:** You may be starting to feel the effects of your taper. Interestingly, this can include feeling great or feeling terrible. Do not worry if you feel a little extra grumpy, hungry, or anxious. It is totally normal. Do not make the mistake of doing too much. Do only what your plan calls for and nothing else. Doing too much this close to race day will only hurt you and not help you. If you are doing any cross-training such as strength training, consider dropping it the last week and a half prior to your race.
- Also, don't go to the other extreme and do absolutely nothing in the week prior to your race. You will not feel good if you have had zero exercise. Ideally, your taper will include close to the same frequency of workouts, with a reduction in volume and a sprinkling of intensity at race pace.
- **2 days prior:** Be sure to get as much rest as possible in the last few days before the race. If possible, try to avoid spending a lot

of time walking around a crowded expo. If you're traveling to an out-of-town race, try to limit how much walking you are doing in general. Also, be cognizant of sleep. The sleep two nights before the race is the most important. It is totally normal to have trouble sleeping the night before the race, so don't worry if it happens to you. Be sure to eat something you are used to eating.

- **1 day prior:** Lay out everything you will need the morning of the race. Make sure you have your number and timing chip if your race includes one. Relax, and try to get off your feet.
- **Race Day:** All the work is done! Although it's normal to be nervous, a little anxiety is okay. It just means that you care. Have fun crossing your first finish line!

Training Plan Questions

1. **Why is some of the plan organized by time and some by distance?** The first two workouts of each week are organized by time, since runners of many different speeds will be using the plan. For the weekly long run workout, the plan is by distance, since it's important to build up to the distance of the race.

2. **What type of person will be able to use this plan?** This plan can be used by someone who is already used to exercising three times a week for thirty minutes each session. You should be in generally good health and cleared for physical activity by your physician. If you can run half a mile and walk a few miles as a regular part of your activity level, then you should use this plan.

3. **What if I am doing less than the recommended activity level?** You should start with more than eight weeks to your first 5k. You can start, say, twelve weeks prior to your goal race, and use the first four weeks to gradually build up to the distances in Week One of the plan.

4. **What do I need in order to start this plan?** All you need to start this plan is a safe place to run and walk, and a good pair of shoes.

5. **What do I do on the other days?** On the other days of the week, you can rest or cross-train, depending on your activity level prior to starting.

> **6. Can I use a treadmill for this plan?** Using a treadmill is fine, though if you are targeting a 5K that takes place outdoors, it is good to get in at least some runs and walks outside. To better equalize your treadmill running to outdoors, it is recommended that you set the treadmill to an incline of at least 1 percent.

From Mishael: Here to Complete, not Compete

Personally, I have never considered races to be a defining part of my life. I am not a former college athlete. I'm a former college drama geek, not known at all for my athletic capabilities. If I can do this, so can you!

When I am encouraging the widows and single moms of our Team Lady 180 group to train for a sprint triathlon, I always say, "You don't have to compete, just complete." I set the example. I was number 994 out of 1,000 participants to get across the finish line of my first Olympic triathlon. One time, when a local news station was filming my triathlon training as part of an inspirational widow story, the cameraman stopped shooting and squatted by the pool to give me swimming tips so that I wouldn't look like such an aqua-geek on television.

Do you have to run the whole 5K or 10K portion of the race? I don't, because my knees complain too loudly. However, I can powerwalk and get across the finish line. Finishing, accomplishing what you set out to do, moving forward, and getting healthy are all that really matter.

Finishing a triathlon might sound too challenging, especially while you are mired in grief. In that case, start with a 5K run, work up to a 10K run, and then try a sprint triathlon. A sprint triathlon is, by definition, a short triathlon: usually about 400 yards swimming, 13 miles biking, and 3 miles running.

Possibly, the prospect of swimming any distance in open water feels intimidating. I know it was for me. There are other options: some triathlons are held in lakes or open water, but others take place in an Olympic pool setting. The sprint triathlon that I prefer for my Team Lady 180 widows and single moms is the Calloway Sprint Triathlon. It's a quarter-mile swim, a nine-mile bike ride on mostly flat terrain, and a two-mile run. One of the great things about the Calloway Sprint Triathlon is that the swim is in only five feet of lake water, and they don't mind if you stand up and walk the swim portion. This is the race my older daughter, Arie, participated in with our widow Team when she was eight years old. It's a very family-friendly environment. The main point is to get through it. If any portion of the race seems too challenging, you can also opt to be part of a triathlon relay team and let someone else race that portion for you.

I suggest working up to a triathlon.
The act of facing your fears and physically overcoming them
will do wonderful things for your mind and spirit.

Stack the Deck for Your Success

When I began to exercise, I didn't feel fabulous at first. I felt the creaks and soreness of body parts that weren't used to being worked. At the beginning, your body is like a toddler throwing a tantrum. It wants what it wants, and it's not having a pretty reaction to discipline. I don't know about you, but I cannot yield to tantrums when my children have them, because I know that there is a higher good that we are striving to achieve.

One of my wise friends, Elaine, once told me when I first became a parent, "Harder now, easier later. Easier now, harder later." Meaning, stick with kind, consistent, thoughtful discipline now, and though it will be harder in the relative short term, your life will be much easier in the long term. Or you can opt for easier in the short term and harder for the long term. I can attest that I like easier in the long term.

That principle applies to health, too. Lots of sweets now, health problems later. The same applies to active grief recovery. You will not feel like making these decisions now, and there will be times that your body will cry out like a toddler having a tantrum. Keep on track anyway. In time, it will become easier, and the health and community you achieve will ripple out in so many positive ways in your life over the long term.

Here are some strategies that helped jump-start my exercise routine:

Create accountability. I make appointments with my friends to meet me at the gym. I am less likely to ditch a training session at the gym if I know that someone is waiting to meet me there.

Hire a certified trainer to help guide your exercise routine. If that's not in your budget, then join an exercise class with a friend at your local gym. For example, my gym has great spin classes.

Announce your race on social media. If I am committing to a race, I post it on my Facebook page. Once I have publicly committed to a specific finish line, I am far less likely to back out.

Gather the needed items for your exercise the night before. Lay out your sneakers, exercise clothing, and so forth so they are ready to go.

Plan your exercise schedule a week in advance. Commit to certain training times on your calendar. Using an online program like TrainingPeaks.com is a great way to keep accountable to a training schedule. You can even purchase customized training plans to populate within Training Peaks for specific race distance and length of training time that interest you, from a 5K, to 10K, to an IRONMAN triathlon.

Take a picture of yourself. Sometimes seeing yourself in a photo gives you the needed perspective as to how healthy your body is and where you can improve. I'm not saying that you need to compare your body to some swimsuit model. We are each fearfully and wonderfully made, and we all come in unique packages. Take a photo of yourself to see if you look well rested and energetic. It's always a great motivation to me to make healthy choices in my life so I can be the most vibrant version of what I am created to be.

And, once you have committed to a race and you are staring down the barrel of actually putting on the swimsuit or running shoes and lining up with countless others at the starting line, you can top off your optimum training with a pre-race menu—which, in this case, includes a blessing of carbs. Nutritionist Ilana Katz, who has successfully counseled numerous elite triathletes regarding their training nutrition offers these suggestions:

An eating plan for the day before a race and for race day:

The macronutrient breakdown leading up to an event starts to transition from moderate carbs, protein, and fat to higher carbs, lower protein, and almost none to minimal fat and fiber. The reason behind this is to make more room in the storage capacity of glycogen (main source of immediate fuel for muscles to operate at full capacity) with the most efficient digestion to reduce risk of gastrointestinal distress (which tends to happen during high stress, race day anxiety, increased intensity of aerobics, as well as sports nutrition added in the mix).

A sample menu the day before the race will thus look like this:

(Avoid: animal proteins such as poultry, beef, pork, protein powders, Greek yogurts, eggs, nuts, avocado, oils, milk, cheese, sauces and dressings)

Include: fruit, grains, oats, breads, pastas, potatoes, legumes, and regular non-dairy yogurts.

Neutral: vegetables (do not overeat vegetables the day before, because of their high fiber content, but a few good ones are great based on their carb content and antioxidant qualities).

Breakfast: Make a smoothie with regular non-dairy yogurt, fruit, almond milk, some greens (spinach or kale) OR a plain bagel with smear of almond or peanut butter

Mid-morning: Oatmeal and fruit

Lunch: Baked potato with regular plain non-dairy yogurt as a topping, small side salad (optional based on reaction to fiber), and some fruit salad for dessert

OR PBJ Ezekiel sandwich, baked chips or pretzels on the side, and fruit for dessert

Mid-afternoon: Lara or Quest bar

Dinner: Small salad for starters, a slice of bread, a small bowl of pasta with marinara, and some vegetables as an option, with fruit for dessert

Before bed: A piece of fruit, or a couple of small cookies as a pre-race treat (do not overdo the sugary carbs on a daily basis; however pre-race, it is a good treat to finish off the carbo-loading concept).

The meal two nights before the race is probably the most important one for carb loading, and can also be something like bread, potatoes, and fruit, OR bread, pasta and marinara, and fruit.

PTSD, Grief, and Exercise

Pretty much everyone agrees that healthy eating and exercise will make your life better. I like to know specifics, though. With my background and training in news journalism, I always like to know *why*. If I'm going to turn off the TV, leave my comfort zone, and put away the chocolate and ice cream, there had better be some good reasons to propel me forward. Most exercise does not feel fabulous when you start, but you may feel much better when you get in the groove. Exercising with a Team creates accountability and much-needed social support. Exercising with a deadline in mind will keep you motivated and focusing on the future.

**When you cross that finish line,
your feeling of accomplishment can inspire
new dreams and goals for your life moving forward.**

"You know, this [exercise] is a form of PTSD therapy," Lauri Hooker, a grief counselor in Atlanta, once told me. She suggested this as I shared with her my idea for starting a Team of widows to train for the Iron Girl triathlon as a form of grief recovery, since the process had worked so well in my life. I thought the connection she had made was interesting, but it was only later that I recognized the connections between PTSD and my own grief experience.

Whenever I heard about Post Traumatic Stress Disorder, otherwise known as PSTD, I always thought of it as a problem suffered by soldiers coming back from a war zone, victims of disaster, or assault victims. I didn't think of PTSD as being associated with grief, but that oversight left me with lots of symptoms and little understanding of how to handle them.

M. Katherine Shear, M.D., and Krissa Smith-Caroff, B.S., researchers at the Department of Psychiatry Western Psychiatric Institute and Clinic University of Pittsburgh, report, "Learning about the death of a close relative or friend from any cause, including natural causes, qualifies as a stressor for PTSD, as long as the death was sudden and unexpected." There are, however, "no operationalized criteria for 'sudden and unexpected,' leaving this to subjective judgment."[41]

**Experts are beginning to recognize that an increasingly valid
form of PTSD recovery includes getting healthy and exercising.**

In an online article entitled "'Working out' PTSD – Exercise is a
vital part of treatment," Simon Rodenbaum states, "For the first time,
this research shows that individualized and targeted exercise programs
can improve the physical and mental health of PTSD patients." He
concludes by saying, "While it is true that without mental health there
can be no true physical health, exercise appears to be vital for both."
Studies conducted with mainly former soldiers and police officers
suffering from PTSD at the St. John of God Hospital in Richmond,
Australia showed a marked improvement among those participating
in an exercise program in addition to their other therapy, when compared to those doing only traditional cognitive therapy. Research in the
United Kingdom has shown the benefits of surfing for combat veterans,
and several veterans' charities promote exercise therapy as well.[42]

I was surprised to note that some of the markers of PTSD so closely
mirrored the symptoms I experienced during grief, such as difficulty
falling asleep, short temper, hyper-vigilance, and wanting to avoid
triggers that stimulated my trauma, just to name a few. I've included a
comprehensive list on PTSD symptoms in Appendix 3.

**After years of struggle, I was finally able to put it all together.
Getting healthy and crossing finish lines *with* a grief support
group—in my case, a Team of widows who understood my grief—
finally helped me to thrive, not just survive after loss.
I felt strong and empowered, I had my Team of friends,
and I was moving forward with my life.**

When I crossed my first triathlon finish line, I thought to myself,
"If I can do this, I can do anything!"

Another widow with Team Lady 180 exclaimed when crossing her
finish line, "I got my life back! How awesome is that?"

That is the goal I desire for you through this book. We do not
have to stay in the darkness. We have the tools, team, and training—to
journey to the sunlight.

Journey to the Sunrise

Discover God whispering in your heart, "Won't you let Me coach you?"
Realize when you make a positive decision for your life like exercise, and then consistently make those positive decisions, before you know it, you will have changed the landscape of your life.
Understand that you can "stack the deck" for success in the area of exercise by planning ahead, committing to a schedule, creating accountability, and preparing for your race.

Steps on the Path

Here are some strategies that helped jump-start my exercise routine. Use them as your checklist and begin to implement them in your life.

- ☐ **Create accountability.** Make appointments with friends to meet you at the gym.
- ☐ **Hire a certified trainer** or join an exercise class with a friend at your local gym.
- ☐ **Announce the specific race you will be participating in on social media.**
- ☐ **Gather the needed items for your exercise the night before.**
- ☐ **Plan your exercise schedule a week in advance.**
- ☐ **Take a picture of yourself.**
- ☐ **Ask yourself:**
  Do I look tired?
  Do I look happy?
  Do I feel healthy?
  Does my body have lots of energy?
- ☐ **Ask God to be your coach.**

Speak Life: Train Your Body
(Please Say Out Loud)

Even when the sands were hot, I have purposed to strengthen my body through conscious, healthy choices in what I eat and drink. I commit to an exercise schedule in a supportive, accountable Team, with a definite finish line, in order to accomplish my health goals. I will be open to asking God to be my coach.

Train Your Spirit

Step 5:

Train Your Spirit

And the Lord will continually guide you, and satisfy your desire in scorched places, and give strength to your bones; and you will be like a watered garden, and like a spring of water whose waters do not fail. (Isaiah 58:11 NASB)

"For the mountains may be removed and the hills may shake, but My lovingkindness will not be removed from you, and My covenant of peace will not be shaken," says the Lord who has compassion on you. (Isaiah 54:10 NASB)

The Kitten Pillow

I have a pillow made by my Polish grandmother, Julia Porebska, that I have kept with me since childhood. I called her Babcia (pronounced bapcha), the Polish word for grandmother. She sent me the pillow when I was nine years old. It has traveled with me through grade school, high school, college, multiple moves—it even went with me to Costa Rica when Jason and I lived there for a time—and then to Florida and back to Atlanta.

The reason I keep it is not because I was so close to with my paternal grandmother; in fact, I didn't spend much time with her when I was young. She was a Polish Catholic from Warsaw who didn't speak much English. She was rough around the edges, and with good reason. She mothered two children through World War II and the Warsaw Uprising in 1944. She was there when Nazi soldiers ripped her husband from their family one night in war-torn Warsaw. With only moments to kiss his family good-bye, my grandfather Henryk, her husband, was never heard from again.

My father was ten at the time, and he, his mother, and his seventeen-year-old sister were then loaded onto cattle cars to be processed as Polish Catholics at Auschwitz. They traveled in standing-room-only conditions for three days on that train. Soon afterwards, they were moved to the Bergan Belsen Nazi concentration camp. Miraculously, my father, aunt, and grandmother were moved out of the concentration camp and survived the war as slave labor on a German farm with a kind German family.

In her later years, my Babcia was bedridden with rheumatoid arthritis, which hobbled her body and gnarled both of her hands, making everyday activities incredibly painful.

This story, if I ended it there, would be enough, but not for Babcia.

From her bed in her winter years, she made me a pillow with an intricately embroidered kitten on it. Each larger stitch is comprised of six small stitches. Each stitch, painfully made with her disfigured hands, demonstrated her determination to create beauty out of pain.

When I first told my father about my husband's death, he immediately drove fourteen hours straight, from Florida to Atlanta, in order to be with me. My mom couldn't travel because she had stage-four breast cancer and was confined to her bed.

After the memorial service was over, my dad came back to my house with me. While Arie played with family members in the living room, I retreated to my room with some food from my now-packed fridge. I felt like a lone speck in the wide world. My second child lay heavy in my belly, and my toddler usually stuck so close to me she showed signs of wanting to crawl back in utero, herself. I suddenly felt the pressure of caring for these little ones, *alone,* for the vast unforeseeable future. Jason had been the "baby master," not me. I was trained by my father to work in network news. How on earth would I do this?

My father found me sitting on my bed, staring out the window with thoughts crushing in on me, and I turned to him as a source of strength.

"Daddy, I don't think I can do this," I said quietly.

I should say that my father is a dignified, kind, patient man. He doesn't yell or raise his voice unless it's absolutely necessary.

But at this moment, he looked at me with fire in his eyes, and sternly but calmly replied, "Your grandmother went to a concentration camp. You…Will…Do…This."

That was the end of it. How can you argue with such a statement? He had pulled the Babcia card.

Later on, I thought about my grandmother and her suffering. I wondered if she ever questioned God as she heard screams in the night of Jews being gassed in the ovens near her bunker, "Why me? Why now? Where are you, God?" I can guarantee that losing her husband, home, and extended family, sleeping on the hard wooden bunk beds of the concentration camp, with Nazis as landlords and mass graves on the premises, was a universe harder than what I was enduring. By dogged faith and the grace of God, she did it. We are here as a family, today, because of her determination and unwavering faith then.

It dawned on me: her suffering was not just about her. How could she have known that the perseverance and hope in God that she showed would inspire me in my moment of need years after she had passed on? In that moment, I realized that the way we live matters beyond our time on earth.

**Our suffering and the choices we make in our tragedy are not only about us, or even about survival of our immediate family— although that is certainly part of the process.
From a larger perspective, our choice to have hope, faith, and strength in desperate times may be the example needed by those who will go after us. Those we have never met.
That is our living legacy:
Creating beauty through our pain and determining
to find hope in excruciating circumstances.**

That is our own intricately embroidered kitten pillow that we pass on to those we love. My Babcia was the grandmother elephant who led her family through the desert to find water, and in doing so, left a path for others to follow. I came from her, and I would follow her steps of determination, not just for myself, but for my children and their children and those around me.

Once I stopped asking, *"Why did this happen to me?"* and instead asked, *"How will I live my life?"* I gained hope that there was a light at the end of the tunnel.

Until then, I was not in a tunnel but a mineshaft. With the help of his mother, my father pointed me away from my pain and forced me instead to confront my strength. I took from Babcia's kitten pillow a message of solidarity: each stitch that she had labored over became a gesture of support by a widow who pushed through her own despair. I realized that I could find strength for myself by tapping into the inspirational strength of those around me. Just as Babcia had not been aware that her legacy was answering my need in the future as she struggled to help her family survive in Nazi Germany, in the same manner, how we live through trauma can inspire our families and loved ones in the future. The perseverance, faith, and wise choices we make now become our tapestry of beauty through pain, and can become a lifeline to those we love when they need it most.

Chapter 14:

Learning to Trust Again

J ason's death was so shocking and emotionally ripping for me that the memorial service, only a few days later, was agonizing rather than comforting. The news of his death was so sudden, the funeral so immediate, and the trauma so severe, that I stumbled away from it feeling shell-shocked rather than ready to begin processing my grief.

Later, I learned from a friend, David, about a Jewish tradition called a *"Matzevah" (Headstone* or *Monument)*. In most Jewish customs, a burial will typically happen within seventy-two hours of death. Then, depending on their relation to the loved one, for up to eleven months, those who are mourning say the Kaddish, a prayer that affirms life and praises God. On the one-year anniversary of the loved one's passing, there is a service in which the headstone is installed and "unveiled" at the gravesite. This service focuses on honoring and celebrating the life of the person who has passed.

This seemed to me a more realistic timeframe for my own grief process. I had been too shocked at Jason's passing to get my heart to the place of truly celebrating his life at his first memorial service. After I had begun to heal, I wanted to honor his life more fittingly. So, I borrowed from that Jewish tradition and had my own headstone service, although it wasn't until two years after his death that I felt ready to commemorate Jason's life with the clarity and joy it deserved. His body had been cremated and the ashes placed in a decorative box. So, for the intervening time, his ashes were resting peacefully in my house—first on my living room shelf, then in my bedroom, and then in my master closet. There was no rush.

On the second anniversary of his passing, I arranged a genuine celebration of Jason's life in a service at the memorial gardens where I interned his ashes. I invited our family and all our dear friends. A good friend from our married class softly played Jason's favorite songs on his guitar. I decorated with Jason's favorite flowers — sunflowers — and scattered red rose petals on the ground (which was the flower we had at our wedding) up and down the aisles. At this memorial garden, we were able to have the service at a replica of the tomb of Jesus. There was a two-story natural stone wall covered by moss with naturally cascading water, and a cathedral of trees surrounding us. For a few days before the service, family members painted words of love on the decorative box that housed Jason's ashes. I helped Arie and Sophia make butterfly pictures on the wooden box using their handprints.

It was a quiet service, filled with love. I could feel him there. It was beautiful and natural, an extension of our love shared with our closest family and friends. It felt right. I re-inhabited that space of grief and made it mine. No roar of grief-stricken rage. There was only peace and love, joy in who Jason was on earth and celebration that he is in heaven. This ceremony was for us, to celebrate Jason and our love for him. There was such a sense of restoration. The ceremony was so healing for me that I have a hard time describing it. This was another major step in crafting a life we loved, trekking toward the floodwaters of renewal, by honoring our love and memories of Jason. After the ceremony, we served Jason's favorite foods and released balloons in his honor.

Our friend and former neighbor Kristi later wrote me her impressions from the service. I think she said it best.

Dear Mishael,

When I'm driving, I'm usually making the best of my time by returning phone calls. Today, after the beautiful service, I found myself wanting to be alone with my thoughts of what I had just experienced…

It was such a messy, rainy afternoon that I couldn't imagine how things would work out at the cemetery. I was running close on time, thought I remembered my way to the cemetery, made a wrong turn, finally figured it out, but didn't know how to find the Grotto once I got there. I drove to the back, past the construction, and thought, "This CAN'T be the right way," and then I saw the cars and one of the most beautiful places I've seen in a while.

As the service started, the rain on the tent was very calming and gave me a huge sense of peace that immediately washed away my stress. The service was so perfectly "Jason." The strong breezes that would occasionally come from "out of nowhere" and the bells that rang just as you stood to speak. Your words were so special to me.

I loved the red rose petals on the ground beneath my feet with raindrops beading up on each one. I watched a man at the end of my row pick up one of the petals — oh, so carefully so that the rain wouldn't roll off, as he cupped both hands to gently hold it.

I loved watching the little girl stomping her feet in a puddle of water, turning round and round with her hands in the air, smiling and looking upward toward heaven.

I loved watching Arie running from front to back, and front again, reminding everyone that we were there to celebrate life, just as she was doing.

I don't know if anything could have been more special than the songs you played, especially the last one with Jason's words. How special that you and the children have that to cherish forever.

While driving home in the quiet of my car, I felt washed with love. Then I remembered your wedding, and I don't recall ever having felt more love at a wedding than I felt at yours and Jason's. What a wonderful day that was.

I know you miss him terribly each and every day, but you are SO blessed to have had someone so very extraordinary in your life. And I am so thankful that I got to be a part of it all — then and now.

I love you very much. Thank you for being my friend.

Love,
Kristi

Although I adopted only what I most needed from the tradition of the unveiling and its memorial service, I was also compelled by the logic and the reasoning behind this ritual. This Jewish custom shows a great understanding of grief as a long process. What I felt about my husband and my widowhood a few days after his death was vastly different from how grief would transform me in the coming months, and then years.

The Kaddish prayer is an affirmation of faith and of praise for God's name, which mourners say each day for up to twelve months after a loved one has died. Saying this prayer every day as a way of honoring your loved one also becomes a way to remind yourself of God's greatness, even if you are angry about your loss.

Mourner's Kaddish Translation:

*Glorified and sanctified be God's great name throughout the world which He has created according to His will. May He establish His kingdom in your lifetime and during your days, and within the life of the entire House of Israel, speedily and soon; and say, Amen.
May His great name be blessed forever and to all eternity. Blessed and praised, glorified and exalted, extolled and honored, adored and lauded be the name of the Holy One, blessed be He, beyond all the blessings and hymns, praises, and consolations that are ever spoken in the world; and say, Amen.
May there be abundant peace from heaven, and life, for us and for all Israel; and say, Amen.
He who creates peace in His celestial heights, may He create peace for us and for all Israel; and say, Amen.*[43]

For me, the beauty of this ritual is that it tackles head-on one of the most emotionally charged spaces that grief created: my faith. When Jason died, he had our family Bible with him, which meant that whenever I turned to our family Bible in the weeks and months afterwards, I felt his loss. So, I wanted to avoid the Bible, and to be honest, I felt like giving God the silent treatment as well.

If I forced myself to sing these praises to God, then I would also be forced to include my anger at God in my relationship with Him. This was a healthier approach for me than simply allowing my anger over losing Jason to become an obstacle or a reason to turn away from God. The beauty of the Kaddish tradition is that it begins immediately. In the midst of our deepest, most mind-numbing grief, the tradition calls us to exercise those muscles of prayer and praise, which will eventually be able to carry us out of our fog, and then farther than we can imagine. The prayers are ritualized, so that we don't have to consider them beforehand. We might not even believe we are feeling them at the time, but we are returning to God every single day, and training our spirits to praise in spite of whatever our emotions or inclinations demand.

I found that I had to train my spirit as conscientiously as I was training my body, mind, and household. I had to re-teach myself how to incorporate gratitude, forgiveness, reconciliation, and joy into my life. By an act of will, I had to bring myself to the place where I could become stronger, to the edge of the swimming pool early in the morning, to the company of widows who could encourage me with wisdom rather than pity, and to the feet of God where I could submit my anxieties and learn to trust His plan.

Of course, I struggled with my anger and distrust. It has been an ongoing process. As with all my other processes, I didn't immediately grasp the wisdom from tradition or counsel, but instead scrabbled along with my own efforts and gleaned pieces of the process through trial and error, and occasional gifts of insight.

Eventually, I realized that my being mad at God was like a child being angry with a parent.

How far can a child go without food and shelter? Sometimes my kids are mad at me because I am doing things for their own good that they do not understand. They are children; I am an adult. All they need to know is that I've got their best interests at heart and I'd give my life for their safety. They simply need to stay with me, and eventually they will understand that things are working to their benefit. As adults, we can usually manage to supply food and shelter for ourselves, but eventually we will run into needs that we cannot meet on our own, such as the need for internal peace.

So, whether I liked it or not, and whether I understood God's plan or not, I knew that my anger with God should not keep me from moving towards Him. Even if the verses were like chewing dry bark in my mouth, returning to the Bible refreshed my spirit and created a baseline of peace in my soul. Plain and simple, this exercise yields results. Staying connected to God through prayer and Bible study was necessary to my emotional wellbeing.

When my anger against God waned, I found that I still didn't quite trust Him. But as I took time to be alone and looked back over the previous months and years, I could sift through the wreckage strewn over my life and see that God had been there to help me in one form or another at every turn. I discovered that trust must also be exercised like a muscle. Similar to waking up early and jumping into a cold swimming pool, I had to force myself into this exercise over and over again.

Running Wild

This would be a much easier book to write if I could tell you that when I found my community, ate healthy foods, and crossed finish lines, everything in my life came into order and my heart was healed. If I said that, I would not be practicing transparency with you. Certainly, my life moved forward dramatically when I found my Team, trained my body and mind, and felt the triumph of crossing finish lines. If that's as far as you want to take this program, I respect your decision.

However, my spirit was still restless, on guard, and on the lookout for danger. Constantly wanting to protect my heart and my children, I became exhausted. Viewed from the outside, I was still going to church, still reading the Bible, and still praying with my kids. However, I didn't fully trust God again after Jason's death. I held my heart back from Him.

A few years ago, I saw the movie, *The Horse Whisperer*. It struck me immediately that I felt like the injured horse — the one who was hit by a truck, whose closest companion tragically died, who had healed, but never recovered. I've always loved horses; I identify with them. There is a part of me that still feels wild. I love to run free, to explore life, to go on adventures, and to experience other cultures.

Despite my efforts to rehabilitate myself after Jason's death, my spirit still felt like that disfigured horse in the movie. If someone touched the site of my wounds, or if I felt threatened, my spirit would kick and buck, wild-eyed in my dark stable. This instinct to buck and run was certainly related to my dating relationships after my husband's passing. If a good man tried to get too serious with me, I would bolt. I threw myself into mothering my daughters, learning about health, working with widows, and training for triathlons.

I have worked hard to heal and to appear stronger than before. Still, if someone came close enough, it would be obvious that I have been wounded. I have an amputation you cannot see. Rage that I was left in a vulnerable position. I thought I could tuck away that wounded part of me, that distrusting part, behind accomplishments. For many years, my answer was that I would take care of things the best I could. This often left me overwhelmed as I depended solely on myself and my capabilities. I could never fully rest.

I was aware that I kept a part of myself shielded, and that the approach of any romantic relationship with a man would trigger a silent panic reaction for me. I don't think I fully realized that I was also trying to shield my vulnerability from God, and for some of the same reasons. So what if I didn't fully trust God again after the death of my husband? I felt justified in holding back a little of my heart, or even a lot of it. I thought I could hide my sense of Divine distrust deep within myself, and that I could go through the motions and no one would notice.

The truth is that without finding the spiritual rest
that comes from trusting God,
I will always be on the run.
Always on-guard to protect my family.
Always scanning the horizon for danger.
Always spiritually exhausted.

There was a later scene from *The Horse Whisperer* that quietly spoke to me. Everyone is terrified of the injured horse, and then an enigmatic trainer shows up. He is there to reach her and help her heal. In his training process, the trainer doesn't dominate the horse, but rather sets her free from her dark stable. When she is free from her stall, the horse runs away from him into the fields, yet he doesn't demand obedience from her. Instead, the trainer sits and waits all day. He sits still in the hot sun and swaying grasses. Unmovable in his loving commitment to her. The horse watches the trainer from a safe distance. Then, over the course of hours, she incrementally approaches. Until, after a long day of watching and waiting, she comes close enough for him to touch her.

This is the beginning of their training together. The trainer is there to set her free, to give her life *back* to her, and to help her enjoy the sunshine again and live in peace. He wants to offer her healing. He is there to help her build trust again. This is what God does. Jesus said, "The thief comes only in order to steal and kill and destroy. I came that they may have and enjoy life, and have it in abundance (to the full, till it overflows)" (John 10:10 AMP).

It took much longer than a day for me to learn to trust God again. Frankly, it's an ongoing process. There is no predictable journey of the spirit; each journey is customized and unique. While He may reach me through a horse movie, He may reach out to you in a different way, one that resonates especially with your spirit. Just be open to the life lessons, the Divine conversation.

> *The Messiah has set us free so that we may enjoy the benefits of freedom. So keep on standing firm in it, and stop putting yourselves under the yoke of slavery again.* (Galatians 5:1 ISV)

Without trust, there is no vital relationship.
There is polite distance, but no Cosmic Dance.

This part, trusting God again, has been for me the most nuanced portion of the journey. I cannot presume to tell you how to trust God or the freedom and peace that this will bring to your spirit. I can only share my story and hope that some nugget inspires your journey. This has been the simple prayer I have prayed with my daughters for years now: "God, please heal our hearts and minds." We have also added, "Help us to trust You."

> *The LORD will fight for you; you need only to be still.* (Exodus 14:1)

Full Stop

After about five years of running hard from Jason's death, I contracted walking pneumonia. I was physically exhausted. My normally high-energy way of life dropped into low gear, by the sheer fact that it was hard for me to breathe, and I was coughing so deeply that my body shook. I was limited to getting only the absolute basics done for my family.

I had to trust God to help me get even those bare necessities completed. I was in constant dialogue with God, asking Him to provide help at every step. Out of sheer exhaustion, I began coming to God more as I would go to an actual husband. I came to Him sharing concerns I had about my daughters, work I had to do, general chores, and necessities around the house. I also had to humble myself and ask others to help me out.

Out of desperation, I was compelled to start trusting God as, dare I say it, my *Heavenly Husband*.

I found, in my utter dependence, a shift in my relationship with God. An honesty on my part, coupled with budding trust, helped me to consciously come to Him with my raw thoughts and everyday problems. I began waiting on His timing rather than always moving forward in my own strength. Since I had been trained in my news-work to take charge and proactively produce results, I had not wanted to make room for God to accomplish those things for which I had prayed. Instead, I would figure out a way to make them work, afraid I might be let down if He didn't show up. This led to my being in constant motion, exhausted from getting things done, feeling accomplished but empty.

When I had to trust and depend on God, He came through again and again.

During that time, I had a tiny prayer that was so insignificant that I wouldn't dare say it out loud. It was a "want" that was in the back of my mind, and which I didn't think would result in anything.

While I was in the kitchen, cutting up vegetables and making sandwiches for lunch, my inner voice whispered, "God, if you are my Heavenly Husband, then do I come to you for regular husband-stuff? Take for instance, these countertops. Do I come to You like I would a husband and say, 'Honey, when the time is right, I'd really enjoy granite countertops. I think that would really make the kitchen "pop"'?"

About two months earlier, I had brought some pumpkin bread to an older neighbor, Ed, who showed me the amazing kitchen that he had customized for his wife. Every detail of the new kitchen had been designed with the thought of pleasing his bride of over thirty years. He took half an hour explaining to me the kitchen he had built for her as he opened cabinets and pulled out custom drawers that closed with cushioned quiet. It was his act of love. He was so proud of the fact that he had provided this wonderful space for his wife whom he loved so much.

I walked home from his house, thinking, "Now that's a good husband. He takes great pleasure in making his wife happy. I am grateful that during my marriage Jason often did his best to lavish me with thoughtful gifts and sweet memories. He was a good and kind husband."

233

My own wish for granite countertops remained only an unspoken thought. I wouldn't even say it out loud, because praying for granite countertops while my Formica ones were fine felt a little ridiculous, maybe even ungrateful. I figured that, at best, maybe God would help me find a granite company that would let me barter my video production work in exchange for granite countertops. A *"God helps those who help themselves"* type of gift.

Later on that same day of chopping veggies, I heard that there was a $20,000 kitchen makeover contest. It was sponsored by the local ABC News radio station, 750 AM, on their home fix-it show. The rules were to send in a photo of your kitchen and explain in twenty words or fewer why you should have your kitchen renovated. I figured it couldn't hurt to try. I submitted this literary masterpiece just before the contest cut-off date:

Cluttered Kitchen
Flaking Formica
Needs a Facelift!
Platinum Kitchens
Create Culinary Paradise
Serving Beauty
Which makes Cooking
Twice as Nice!

Four days later, on Mother's Day, I was told on the radio that I had *won* a brand new $20,000 kitchen makeover! New cabinets, a backsplash, a custom kitchen design, pull-out spice racks, under-counter lighting and, yes, *granite countertops*! It was way more than I had asked for, more than I could have imagined receiving.

God wants us to come to Him. Not with the idea for lots of stuff, but just to be real with Him. For me, it touched me deeply that God was acting as a husband in a way that spoke to me, with a gift that is at the core of my home, where I daily nourish my family.

All I know is that I secretly came to God like I would have to a real husband, and He gave me more than I asked for. He provided a custom kitchen in just the way my neighbor had shown his husbandly love for his wife. It reminded me of the story of Hagar in the desert, the only woman in the Bible who gives God a name: El Roi "The God Who Sees" (Genesis 16:13).

The gift of a new kitchen was amazing,
but the real gift was feeling *seen* and *heard*.

I am not saying that God typically hands out free kitchen remodels. That was an unexpected response. I am saying that starting to trust God and having an authentic conversation helped me feel seen and even loved. When I started to genuinely believe that God loved me and that God was aware of me, then my spirit could relax. I could relax knowing that God would provide for us and protect my family, though His provision and protection might not come in the form I expected.

I want to encourage you to simply start the Divine conversation. Maybe, Dear Reader, you don't share my faith. That's okay. God is big enough to reach us where we are when we truly and continually search to connect with Him. Remember, my conversation with God after Jason's death started me yelling with, "Fine, if you want to be my Heavenly Husband, I am giving you the Stink Eye!" as I waddled out of my house to my minivan. Not exactly how I envision a Divine Romance starting up, but it was honest, and honesty is the beginning of trust, which gives way to healing, and eventually, love.

Journey to the Sunrise

Discover that without finding the spiritual rest that comes from trusting God, you could be always on the run, trying to protect your family, and always spiritually exhausted.

Realize that you must train your spirit as conscientiously as you train your body, mind, and household.

Understand that God will protect and provide for you and your family, but it might not come in the form you expect.

Steps on the Path

- Be open to the life lessons, and simply start the Divine conversation.
  - Take a step to release Divine distrust, because it will affect everything in your life.
- God is there to help build trust again so He can bring you healing.
  - With your utter dependence on Him, a shift will begin in your relationship with God.
  - Begin to train your spirit to praise in spite of whatever your emotions or inclinations demand each day. Reading a Psalm from the Bible each day is a great place to start.
  - Focus on honesty with God, which is the beginning of trust, and gives way to healing, and eventually love. This has been the simple prayer I have prayed with my daughters for years now: "God, please heal our hearts and minds and help us to trust You."
  - *"You will seek Me and find Me when you search for Me with all your heart."* (Jeremiah 29:13)

The LORD will fight for you; you need only to be still. (Exodus 14:1)

Chapter 15:
Turning Around

"Grateful people are happier, healthier, less stressed, and more fulfilled."
Alan D. Wolfelt, Ph.D. and Kirby J. Duvall, M.D.[44]

As we resolve to train our spirits for the journey ahead, there are a few key practices that strengthen and free our spirits in amazing ways. Gratitude is one of the virtues that bring peace and joy, even if it might be an exercise to find it and hold on to it after tragedy. A recent study reported by Lucy Animus even shows a scientific basis for the power of gratitude. Apparently, the heart "creates an electromagnetic field that expands up to five feet from the body," and "when people cultivate positive feelings, the heart's frequency changes and its waves become smoother and more consistent, while anxiety or stress caused waves to be shorter and less organized."[45]

Feelings of gratitude can create effective, positive change.

Just as importantly, Animus reports that this "gratitude" frequency "can even 'entrain' hearts and brains nearby. So, if you're cultivating gratitude, it's probable that you're changing the feeling state of those around you for the better too." Our decision to choose gratitude can bless not only our spirits, but also our bodies—and just by the electric impulses of our hearts, our families and friends in close proximity can feel more relaxed as well.[46]

I was watching television one day when Oprah was interviewing Amy Grant about her husband, Vince Gil. They were talking about their marriage and blended family. Amy recalled Vince saying to her, "I may not always understand you, but who you are and what you bring to the table is enough. I welcome you, I welcome you."[47] What struck me about his statement was that it conveyed simple gratitude and acceptance. I had been looking for someone to swoop in and save me from my mess. Instead, God had brought around me many people who encouraged and helped me. I had to set aside my expectations and plans, and instead simply welcome the gifts before me. This gratitude freed both me and the other person. For the rest of it, I would have to trust God. He had met my needs up to this point, and the choice to trust in His provision brings me peace.

Don't get me wrong. I make a decision to feel this way, and then sometimes I focus on my circumstances and freak out. Then I have to make the conscious choice for gratitude again.

One of the most powerful lessons in gratitude came when our live-in nanny, Caroline, who had been helping me for about six months after the birth of my second daughter, announced that she would be moving back to Vermont. I knew she was going to leave, and even as I saw her packing her car, I didn't want to think that in a few minutes our family dynamic was about to change again. She had been an amazing help, a faithful friend, and a part in our family's healing.

Earlier in the day, I had told her how much I appreciated her. She had weathered some of my fiercest storms. She had been an angel in our midst. What she had given was enough. I had determined to exercise gratitude, so instead of thinking, "Why can't you stay longer, Caroline?" I thought, "Thank you for coming. Thank you for what you gave us and how you helped us. It is enough, and you are welcome here."

We made it through the rest of that day, my daughters and I, after Caroline left. Arie and I vacuumed out Caroline's room and moved some of Arie's toys in to make it her room again. Before I knew it, Arie was having a tea party with her stuffed animals. I made dinner, bathed both girls, and we all went to bed. One night down, the rest of our lives to go.

I never forgot that sense of freedom, even in the midst of my fear, when I chose gratitude. To this day, I still purpose to find what I can be thankful for within my circumstances, and then I camp out there.

The act of choosing gratitude shifts my focus from what I am missing to what I have been given. Gratitude frees me to enjoy life as it is today.

Practicing Forgiveness

Choosing forgiveness is easy to talk about, but very hard to do. It's been said many times that forgiveness is a choice, not a feeling. Choosing to forgive is a daily, positive decision that has cumulative effects. It is a process and the best gift you can give yourself. There is no better moisturizer or even facelift that can compare with the power of forgiveness. Anger weighs you down, causes frown lines, and more importantly, shackles your soul.

Some forgiveness, I've found, requires supernatural help, so I ask for it. While I am asking God for help, I am honest in my anger, even with God. I also speak positive words over my life and the life of my children. Surprise of surprises, forgiveness does grow.

For a time, I practiced saying my forgiveness out loud. There is a verse in Proverbs that says, "The tongue has the power of life and death, and those who love it will eat its fruit" (Proverbs 18:21). We have the power to speak things into our lives. The power of words is one of the great differentiators between humankind and the rest of life on earth. What we say matters. So why not speak peace, forgiveness, and hope over your life?

For me, that act of choosing forgiveness sounds like, "I choose forgiveness. Please, God, help me release my grievances toward _____, and heal my heart and mind."

I'm not saying this is an easy process, but it's better than the alternative—suffocating my soul with anger. Personally, I had some serious wrestling to do before forgiveness could happen. I eventually had to forgive myself for not seeing the clues of my husband's death, and to forgive my husband for his choices. In this process, I found so much compassion, so much love, so much understanding, so much gratitude for the gifts Jason brought into my life, our marriage, and the beautiful lives of my children. I loved him through the pain. I love him today. My family and I are healthier for this process. It took years, but it happened.

For the first three years after Jason died, the pain in my heart was excruciating. Though it lessened over time, my heart physically hurt. As I asked God to help me, I prayed this verse, begging for relief for my heart and soul: "In my anguish I cried to the LORD, and he answered by setting me free" (Psalm 118:5 NIV). I was looking for answers, certainty, comfort, and maybe closure, but God didn't provide explanations. I never got an answer as to *Why*. That is between God and Jason.

One day, after three years of praying this verse, God answered my prayer in a beautiful way. I had taken my daughters to Costa Rica as a way of doing something positive on Jason's third "Angel Anniversary," the date of his passing. We were visiting Los Lagos, a kid-friendly resort at the base of the Arenal Volcano. The extensive gardens were lush, with tropical landscaping highlighting natural waterfalls. There were mineral pools fed from underground hot springs, and a large waterslide that fed into a swimming pool. My girls squealed with delight as they took it all in.

The gardens were also the backdrop to a mini-zoo, featuring local wildlife, turtles, alligators, crocodiles, and lizards. There was a butterfly enclosure, with an abundance of butterflies, which fascinated my children by lighting on their fingers. I could hear the music of tropical birds and parrots singing as they flew from tree to tree. At every turn there was something beautiful to behold.

I felt content that my daughters were so happy and that I was, too, though I wished I could have seen this with Jason when we lived in Costa Rica. As I quietly meandered through the gardens, I happened to stop to wonder at yet another waterfall framed by the most inviting landscaping, and the thought occurred to me, "This is like a facet of heaven. If Jason is in a place like this, I do not begrudge him this beauty. I want him to enjoy it!" Then, imagining Jason standing in front of me at the base of a waterfall, I smiled as I thought, "My Love, I forgive you, and I forgive me for not seeing the signs. I love you with all my heart, and I want you to enjoy heaven to its fullest because this little taste is *amazing*. I am going to have a great life with our girls, and I'll catch you on the flip-side." With that, I blew him a kiss.

Then, the most surprising thing happened. It felt as if the shards of pain, like shattered glass in my heart that had been there for three years, were removed. I felt a lightness come over me and a joy fill my soul. It wasn't something I could have planned or manufactured on my own. It was a revelation. Forgiveness was the doorway to freedom and even joy.

In terms of time, this was a quick experience, maybe thirty seconds, but it set a new course for my life. I smiled and took a deep breath, and my girls came bounding toward me excitedly to lead me to look at a large turtle that was munching on mangoes. Walking forward, I stopped, took a picture of the waterfall, and laughing, I followed my daughters, free to join in their joy. Free!

God had kept His promise: "In my anguish I cried to the LORD, and he answered me by setting me free" (Psalm 118:5 NIV).

The Cell of Anger

Most people don't know that in my early thirties I spent some time in the slammer. About forty-five minutes. It was a lesson I will never forget.

I tend to best understand spiritual concepts out of physical experiences, like training for a race or gardening. The physical process helps me comprehend the internal steps needed to achieve a good result. Like when I think of spiritual discipline, I think of the discipline needed to exercise with a goal in mind, and those daily workouts help me understand the spiritual steps that are necessary to achieve success.

Obviously, God knows this about me and took the opportunity to teach me a powerful lesson about anger and forgiveness. It was in my first year of marriage to Jason, around 2001. At that time, we had a wonderful housemate, who helped us defray the costs of the house. Theresa was a fun and fabulous boarder, and we all had a great time together. She also had a front row seat to our first year of marriage, which for the most part was pretty amazing.

One night, though, I got quite annoyed with Jason, and I didn't want to let go of my anger. I didn't want to forgive him for whatever he had done. As I expressed to him why I was so frustrated, I could sense God gently telling my spirit, "Let it go. Let go of the anger. Forgive him. Anger can be a trap."

I have to confess that I sort of back-sassed God. "Not yet. Not right now. I'm too steamed. He needs to understand."

Although I felt I could not yet let it go, I *could* take a break and get some fresh air. It was around 9:00 p.m., and I wanted to take our dog, Natalie, for her evening bathroom break before going to bed.

Theresa was in the kitchen, so I asked her if she would join me outside. It would be nice to have gal-pal perspective, blow off a little steam with someone who knew and loved us both, and hopefully find some understanding.

As we talked outside in the cool of the evening, a police car drove past us. We lived in a good bedroom community just outside of Atlanta, so I figured the police were probably just doing routine patrols. As Natalie was locating the perfect area for her deposit, the patrol car rounded the corner again and stopped in front of my house. Two officers got out of the squad car and approached us.

Theresa and I stopped talking as one officer said, "Do either of you know Mishael Porembski?"

"Yes, officer," I replied, surprised. "I am Mishael Porembski. How can I help you?"

"Well, ma'am, unfortunately, you are under arrest. I have to take you in to the precinct," the officer replied.

To which I graciously exploded, "*What?*"

"Apparently, you have an unpaid traffic violation from two years ago that has just been sitting on our desk. The citation was for not having your insurance card with you during a minor accident."

I remembered. I had been at a traffic light looking for something in my purse. I thought I saw movement from the corner of my eye and figured traffic had started again. I reflexively took my foot off the brake, and soon bumped into the car in front of me. The person in front of me was very nice and didn't press charges. There was no damage to her back bumper. Nevertheless, an officer came to the scene, and I hadn't had my insurance card with me, so I received a citation. It had all been such a stressful blur. Somehow, I had remembered it as a warning, put the citation on the passenger seat to deal with later, and had forgotten to do so. Which means I forgot to go to the hearing for that citation. The police department hadn't forgotten my failure to appear in court.

This all came rushing back to me in one of those life-passing-before-your-eyes moments. I was guilty.

"Can I go inside to tell my husband?" I sheepishly asked the officer.

"Yes, but I'll have to go with you."

I suppose he wanted to shore up his bets that I wouldn't shimmy out our back door, make a break for it, and become a fugitive from the law. Jason was inside studying for a chiropractic test when we four entered the house.

"Honey," I started, "there is a squad car outside. This kind officer is here to arrest me."

"*What?*" Jason snapped his head up from his books.

"Yes, sir, I'm going to have to take your wife in to the precinct. She is under arrest. You can post bail there."

Jason stared in slack-jawed disbelief. As I walked out with the officer, I looked back. Jason and I hadn't concluded our argument. The tables were severely turned now.

"Honey, you *are* going to post bail, right?" I asked a little plaintively.

"Yes, Baby. Don't worry!" he answered, quickly closing up his books and looking for the car keys, and Theresa was scrambling to find her purse and join him in following the squad car.

I walked into the night air with the officer heading toward his vehicle. Before I got into the car, he handcuffed me with both my hands in front of me.

"Oh, dear God," I thought, "please, don't let this make the neighborhood newsletter."

I was certainly not in control of my destiny at that moment. How had things changed so quickly? I decided that I would be as kind and polite as possible. There was no way to fight this situation, so instead I must rise above it. If I was going to be a prisoner, then I would be a model prisoner. We arrived at the precinct, and I was fingerprinted. Then it was time for my mug shots. I decided that if I should ever become any kind of public figure, it would be prudent to take some good-looking mug shots. So, I posed as if I were at a Cover Girl photo shoot. I was then put in some sort of Plexiglas phone booth structure as they booked me. There was a phone in there for my one phone call. When I was told I could make my call, I called Jason's cell phone. He answered laughing, as he was in the lobby of the precinct and had just seen my mug shot.

"What are you doing back there?" he asked. "I've never seen such good mug shots."

"I'm having a fine time. Everyone is really nice to me, and there is no point making the situation worse with a bad attitude," I replied.

"Well, Theresa is going to post bail for you tonight, and we can pay her back tomorrow morning. You should be out shortly," Jason assured me.

"Thank you so much, Baby! I love you!" I gushed.

Releasing me took a lot longer than anticipated. The paperwork dragged on and on. I think maybe God wasn't done with His object lesson at that time. I was having a fine time chatting on the phone with Jason and then with a police officer, using their little push-button microphone system so I could talk to him through my Plexiglas walls.

After about forty-five minutes of soft incarceration, another officer opened my phone booth door and said, "I'm sorry it's taking a while, ma'am, but we need this space to process our next person, so we will have to put you into a holding cell until your bail posts."

Wait. What?

I took a deep breath. We were about to go deeper down the rabbit hole. I got up and followed the officer to a genuine jail cell. Everything felt like it was going in slow motion—the sound of my steps down the hall, the sound of the officer's keys unlocking the cell door, the sound of the lock clicking, with me on the inside. The cell was made of cement blocks painted beige, with a single, cold, metal bed-shelf protruding from the wall. No mattress.

I quietly walked to the metal bunk and sat down, pulling my knees up close to my chest. It was chilly in that room. I surveyed my surroundings. The door was shut and locked, with a small plate glass window looking into the bland, beige hallway. Time seemed to slow way down now. I waited. Five minutes passed. How long am I going to be in here? What shall I think about? There's no one to talk to. Well, I could talk to God.

Then the thoughts came, and I was no longer in a position to backtalk. *"My Child, when you let anger get the best of you, you put yourself in the position of being locked into a cell of your own making. That unforgiveness will wall you off from those you love and who would love you back. That is such a sad place to be. Such a solitary place. You must forgive in order to release yourself."*

You made your point, Lord, in spades. I took it all in. I sat uncomfortably on the metal bed. I could feel the cold seeping into my body. I started to feel the lack of control that I had in this situation. Isolated. Locked in. How long does it take to post bail? How long am I going to sit here? Dear God, will they put someone else in here? Then I had an idea. I could close my eyes and push back the image of where I was with some comforting songs.

So, I started to quietly sing a hymn I had learned growing up. Closing my eyes, I could imagine myself safely in church with my mother and brother and all my friends around me. I softly sang, "Oh, Lord my God, when I in awesome wonder, consider all the worlds Thy hands have made." I started to feel a bit better. So, I sang a little louder. "I see the stars, I hear the rolling thunder, Thy power throughout the universe displayed." I discovered that the acoustics in a cement block room were surprisingly good. I could make my voice echo off the walls.

So, I sang in my full voice, "Then sings my soul, My Savior God, to Thee, how great Thou art, how great Thou art," and by that time, I had almost forgotten where I was. I went into full concert mode. I didn't care who could hear me. I sang loud and proud. I finished that song and sang a few other hymns. I was just enjoying the feeling of singing to God, the amazing acoustics, and the sense that although I couldn't change my surroundings, I could change my response to them.

Then another surprising thing happened. My cell door opened.

An officer popped his head into my cell and gently asked, "Are you doing okay in here?"

"Well, it is a little lonely, so I just started singing," I quietly answered.

"How about if I leave the door open?" he responded.

"Yes, that would be nice," I replied, and so he did.

"What do you know?" I thought to myself. "Singing praise to God still opens jail doors!"

I was thinking of Paul's experience 2,000 years earlier in Philippi as he sat in a dank prison cell with Silas, and they sang songs of praise to God, which activated an angel to bust them out of prison.

Okay, I know my own jail stint was nothing compared to Paul's, but it was a good lesson for me. Do I think that singing will always inspire a police officer to leave a jail cell door open? No, but I do think that focusing on God, choosing to find the positive praise regardless of our circumstances, will eventually open the cell of anger that we construct and confine ourselves to in our own hearts.

I know that forgiveness doesn't happen in a day. It's a discipline, and a choice. Just like working out, sometimes it's painful. There is a great deal of sacrifice involved, too.

Theresa posted bail for me that evening. I left the jail around 11:30 that night. Jason and Theresa were waiting for me in the precinct lobby. We got a copy of my mug shots and laughed about the adventure. Jason and I had a long hug, and I said I was sorry for nursing my anger. I went to court eventually and presented my missing insurance card, paid a fine, and learned my lesson. I was glad all of that was behind me, but I have never forgotten that night, the cell I got myself into, and how thankful I was to be free again.

Sometimes, we don't know how to get out. The feelings of anger and unforgiveness can be brutal jailers, beating and bruising us. When that has happened to me, I say a simple prayer: "Dear God, please heal my heart and mind. Help me to release anger and choose forgiveness." Sometimes, I say that many times and then choose something positive to focus on, like my family, the nice weather outside, doing something for someone else, or the fact that I am alive.

I have prayed that simple prayer with my daughters for years since the death of my husband. I have prayed it when I needed to find forgiveness for Jason for not being here when my girls were asking for a father, for myself for not knowing his pain, for mistakes I made in our relationship, and for those I hurt and who unintentionally hurt us while we were all trying to find our footing in the aftermath of grief.

**When I am tempted to let my anger rage on
and allow my right to be angry take over,
I think of that cold, lonely jail cell that I am making
for my own soul with cement blocks of rage and unforgiveness.
Then I ask God to help me sing my way out
and choose a way of freedom.**

Practicing Reconciliation

"Seeking Peace gives more energy than being right. Ultimately even the most aggressive problems have spiritual and peaceful solutions."
– Michelle Fabulich Hodgson

I saw this quote in an Atlanta magazine, *Best Self*. Michelle Fabulich Hodgson was featured because she won the "Over 40 and Fabulous" contest. She looked great, but there was much more to her. Michelle founded a non-profit called Children Helping Children in honor of her son, Cole, who passed away in 2007. This unique organization mobilizes children and teens to help other sick children and to use their unique gifts in service projects for the community. In this article, she didn't go into the details of her grief journey, but she had some pretty cool clues, which are quite powerful, given that she practices this youthful perspective *after* the excruciating loss of her child.

"True youth comes from a youthful spirit. I still act like a kid—take risks, learn new things as much as possible and remember the joy of being alive. And, I can write on and on about multitasking, delegating, exercise, eating right and being organized, but the irony is that all of those things can fill up a day and create their own kind of chaos. There is only one true way for me to find complete balance, and that is connecting to the Source. If I do that, the rest of the day is in harmony.... Live every day fully in the moment. Pretend like it's your last day on the planet. We come from love, so be love and give love. Love is really all there is."–Michelle Fabulich Hodgson[48]

The aftermath of grief can be like a war zone. People are in pain and, as the saying goes, "hurting people hurt people." So, what do you do with the broken relationships that can happen after loss? Sometimes, creating reconciliation in relationships is like clearing rocky, dry land and turning it into a productive garden. It's tough business that takes time and consistent effort as you try to find a way to connect, make mistakes, try again, fail again, get deeply wounded, and then go back again. A great deal of pain and humility is involved, but land doesn't clear itself. Left on its own, vacant land produces high grass, thorns, and weeds where snakes make their homes.

God wouldn't let me walk away from certain people in the aftermath of grief. When I felt stronger, I had to return to them, and we both worked to heal our relationship after loss. In that process, I owned my offenses and the mistakes I had made toward others. This then inspired others to vocalize and own their actions, too.

My attempts at reconciliation certainly weren't perfect, and I sometimes had to take deep yoga-breaths and listen to another perspective. I was honest about my struggles, and so others were inspired to be honest, too. Then, in truth, we were able to forgive one another (and choose to forgive again and again privately), and that brokered a measure of peace. We have continued to build productively on that peace little by little. God blessed our efforts. I was amazed as I felt peace and genuine love start to grow. It started slowly and grew over the time we were together, but it was there.

This peace was backbreaking work. It required that I reach out again and again and that others reach back. Many times we each reached out, and maybe one of us wasn't ready, but each time someone reached out, something good happened, something grew, even if we couldn't see it.

Recently, I was able to hug and tell someone I had reconciled with, "I appreciate that you never left. We were both so hurt, and though we raged, you never truly left. That makes you family to me. You are truly my family."

Through talking about our hurts, we had cleared the big rocks, cut the high grass, dug up the stumps, and chased the snakes away. As we continued to be kind and forgiving, the ground was tilled, augmented, fertilized, and tilled again. Finally, the planting of peace was nourished in fertile ground. It was so beautiful to see my children play with those who had previously been distant, to see the smiles on everyone's faces, and to know that love was living where fear and misunderstanding had once ruled.

I am sure that there will always be work to do. There is always weeding to be done in a garden, but that's okay. That's the life of a gardener. Dealing with weeds is part of cultivating fruit, but our harvest of peace is sweet.

To those of you who need reconciliation, especially after loss, keep reaching out in a healthy way that also honors your boundaries. Remember, when people are grieving, it's like emotional drunk driving. We make so many bad decisions when we are inebriated with the pain of grief, and in that process there can be deep emotional casualties.

I pray you have the strength to keep reaching, keep clearing the rocky land of pride and offenses. It's hot, humbling, backbreaking, lonesome work, but the harvest of peace is worth it. The harvest will come. Don't give up! This is my hope and prayer for your journey. I say that humbly, because it is my continual prayer for myself in my own journey as well.

Prayer

Without prayer, I believe, we are like plants hidden from the sun. It's hard to grow without the power of photosynthesis. We need the energy from the sunlight to be healthy and to grow ourselves. Maybe prayer isn't about getting what I want, but about becoming who I am meant to be, for a purpose that is greater than only my comfort. Maybe prayer is about finding the path to genuine peace, even when I don't welcome or understand the circumstances. Peace is its own form of strength.

Prayer is simply starting the Divine Conversation. My prayers have been simple. I will share each prayer verbatim here:

Help. *This is a good one. I use this one a lot.*

Help me. *Just in case God didn't know who needed help.*

Help me, Jesus! *I say this repeatedly, out loud, as a parent. It also serves as a warning to my children that Mom is about to lose it.*

Help my family. *Save them from the mistakes of their mother and give my children wisdom to make good, life-giving choices.*

Give me wisdom. *Wisdom is a life-saver, and God promises in Proverbs and the book of James to give wisdom liberally to all who ask.*

Guide me. *Help me relax in the fact that You will guide me and my family.*

God, please heal our hearts and minds. *I have prayed this at night for years with my daughters. God has been very faithful to this prayer.*

Help me to be sensitive to You and those around us. *Help me to see the bigger picture. Help me to understand those around me, not just react to them. Help me to be sensitive to what You want me to learn today and how You may want me to help others.*

Please forgive me, help me to forgive myself and others *who knowingly and unknowingly hurt me or my family. Help me to have understanding and release actions that hurt and hinder my life, and give me the strength to release those around me and myself from perfectionism.*

Please give me Your strength to forgive. *Sometimes forgiveness isn't natural. God, please give me the strength to help me continually forgive.*

> ***Help me to be content.*** *Help me to be present and content in my present circumstances. Help me to see the joy in this moment and release my expectations.*
>
> ***Help me find gratitude.*** *Help me to be thankful for this time in my life and to recognize the blessings You have given me today even if I'm still steamed with You for what I have perceived that You have taken or withheld.*
>
> ***Help me to be sensitive to Your purposes and to be used by You.*** *Help me to see the bigger picture. Give me the strength to walk in faith and love. Help me find joy in Your purpose for me, which involves loving and serving others.*

If you would have told me, while I was married, that being a widow, writing a book on grief, and helping grieving families would have been part of my journey, I would have run screaming from the room. But now that I'm here, I have found that doing this work is actually very healing and joyful. It gives a purpose to my pain. In this space, I find relief, even joy for my soul.

These are the actual prayers I have prayed over the last eight years. I am not given to lengthy, wordy prayers. There were also some prayers with lots of expletives when Jason died and in the years following. You know what? God can take both kinds.

The eventual healing and good space my family is in now is a direct result of three things: prayer, support, and wise choices. That's our secret sauce.

There were also a few anchor verses that I kept saying in my mind and out loud:

"I shall not die, but live and declare the works of the Lord" (Psalm 118:17 NKJV). I said this one out loud when I was in deep grief. It gave me direction.

"I would have despaired unless I had believed I would see the goodness of the Lord in the land of the living. Wait for the Lord,

be strong and let your heart take courage. Wait, I say, on the Lord" **(Psalm 27:13-14).** This verse said to me that I would see the goodness of the Lord on this earth, in my lifetime. Just hold steady, don't do anything self-destructive, hold on, move forward, make wise choices, wait for good results, and have the courage to trust that God is still involved in your life.

"Trust in the Lord with all your heart, lean not to your own understanding, in all your ways acknowledge Him and He will direct your path" (Proverbs 3:5). This verse says to me to make trust a conscious choice. Don't let the circumstances dictate your destiny; reach out to God in prayer, make wise choices, and trust that God will direct your path.

"The eyes of the Lord run to and fro throughout the whole earth to show Himself strong on behalf of those whose hearts are loyal to Him" (2 Chronicles 16:9). This one I like for the Sci-Fi visual this makes me think of: eyes running all over the earth at the speed of light. I also like that this verse says that God will show Himself strong on behalf of those who stay loyal, which to me means staying connected in prayer, making wise decisions, and continuing the Divine Conversation.

Journey to the Sunrise

Discover how your faith will grow as you persevere through the journey.
Realize that we are all imperfect, and eventually someone you love
will really hurt you in one way or another.
Understand that with forgiveness comes a renewed life, and that
renewed life brings peace of mind, and seeking peace gives more
energy than being right.

Steps on the Path

- The act of choosing gratitude shifts your focus from what you
  are missing to what you have been given and frees you to enjoy
  life as it is today.
- When you are tempted to let your anger rage on and let your
  right to be angry take over, think of that cold, lonely jail cell
  that you are making for yourself with cement blocks of unforgiveness. Then ask God to help you sing your way out and
  choose a better way of freedom.
- Sometimes creating reconciliation in relationships is like
  clearing rocky, dry land and turning it into a productive garden.
  The work is worth it. Listen to others, talk about your hurts,
  continue to be kind and forgiving, and plant peace through
  positive actions in your relationships.
- Focus on positive praise regardless of your circumstances, and
  say a simple prayer: "Dear God, please heal my heart and mind,
  help me to release anger, and choose forgiveness."
- Choose to trust God by continuing the Divine Conversation;
  reach out to God in prayer, make wise choices, and trust that
  God will direct your path.

Chapter 16:
Reclaiming Ground

In my twenties, I created a documentary about my father, telling his story as a Polish-Catholic boy in the Nazi Bergan Belsen concentration camp. The title of that documentary was *Burning Questions*. Unbeknownst to me, that experience would become my primer on grief and grief recovery.

I grew up with a father who survived a concentration camp and, as a boy, saw his father ripped from his family by Nazi soldiers. As a child and young adult, I knew my father was grieving, but I didn't know how to help him. I only knew two people from his family, his mother and sister, who had immigrated to the U.S. after the war. Everyone else was still in Poland. When I suggested that my father go back with me to Poland so I could meet his family and make a documentary about it, you can imagine that his first response was an emphatic *No*. Eventually, he decided to go with me, and what I learned from his open-hearted journey helped me many years later when I lost my husband.

In no way am I comparing the two experiences, but the example my father gave me has always shaped the way I processed my grief. I was in my twenties when I shot that documentary. What did I know about grief?

I just knew that I always wanted to see the places that my father had been telling me about in his stories. So, I asked him to take me to those places and share his memories on-camera at their original locations. He graciously did, but I did not expect what happened. As he told me the stories in their original locations, sometimes he cried as the details all came rushing back to him. He told me that he could see everything vividly. It was painful, but it was also beautiful. It was calming and comforting for him to stop denying this part of himself. Each location and each story brought with it a gift of remembrance, and even freedom.

He turned to me after about a week of shooting on location in Warsaw, Poland, and said, "I had a dream last night, Daughter. I dreamed that I was driving, and the floorboards of my car were clear. I was driving over these terrible, angry, demon-looking creatures under my car on the road. As I drove over them, they turned to dust and blew away behind the car." He looked at me and smiled, "The demons are gone."

I never forgot that experience. There was something powerful for my father in returning to emotionally charged spaces and reclaiming them in the present day. That incredible exercise produced freedom for him.[49]

Going Home Again

Going "home" again will always be emotionally charged, whether a tragedy has rocked it or not. When I felt strong enough, I determined to return to the home Jason and I had shared when we were first married, in order to introduce my girls to it as a positive part of their family history.

About fifteen months after Jason died, I went back to the house where we had met and created a home together. It beckoned to me as a rich, powerful memory, and I needed to reclaim it. However, I was also afraid to go to the happiest place I had ever known and stand on the ground where we had laughed, planted a garden, and reveled in our love. Everything had been irrevocably changed. The other side of extreme love was the extreme pain of loss. I didn't know if I could stand going back. It was only twenty minutes from where we were now living, but it seemed a world away.

I could not let my fear constrict me, however, so I called Kristi, my former neighbor, and asked her if I could visit with her. It all came flooding back to me as I drove the old streets. I remembered riding in Jason's Beretta with the broken sunroof that flapped in the wind, our laughing and holding hands, and the feeling of deep comfort and security just being near him. The feelings of healthiness and freshness were all there just below the surface. I could feel them.

I took a turn and drove through Life University, where Jason got his chiropractic doctorate. I remembered the wooden gazebo where he would wait for me to pick him up, the walks through the wooded park there, the water wheel, the lazy lunches, the stolen kisses, the feeling of holiday as we would drive through campus to see the Lights of Life Christmas display, and his graduation. I could see it all like it was yesterday.

Then came the old neighborhood. It felt as warm and welcoming as it always had. We had known many of our neighbors. Jason used to say that living there was like living in a 1950s neighborhood where everyone was in community. As I pulled up next to my house, Kristi greeted me in her driveway.

The first thing I noticed was that the huge garden that Jason and I had spent five years planting was still there. It was overgrown and needed tending to, but it was still there. I could remember mowing the lawn, the rainy days when we would spread the compost, the laughter as Jason would sing a silly made-up song, "I fought the lawn and the lawn won."

There was a story behind almost every plant and tree. There were the trees that I bought on sale for $5 each, seven in all, and had stuffed into his Beretta—foliage sticking out of every window as I drove down the street to show Jason my conquest. Their trunks were thick with time now.

I walked the garden, remembering the beautiful times that we had spent. I smiled thinking of when we used to sit on our old outdoor bench in our bathrobes in the morning, him drinking coffee and me tea as we waved "Good morning" to our neighbors. We enjoyed the fruits of our labor in our garden—especially at springtime when it was in full bloom—and it was a joy just to sit there with him and watch the world go by. Strangers would stop their cars just to enjoy our flowers.

I could see Jason at the door calling me to share a homemade pizza with him as I was tending to the plants. In my mind's eye, I saw Natalie, our old dog, lying on the lawn with her front paws crossed, such the lady. I touched the stones that now lay askew around the base of the big pine tree that Jason had helped me bring to the house in my Ford hatchback one spring. I'm sure no one knew the secret story of these stones. As I placed my hand on them, I could see it all in my mind. Hear his voice again in my head. Feel his loving look.

It was the fragrance of home in my heart.

I thought to myself that since Jesus says that He goes to prepare a place for us in heaven, I would like it if He could make my spot that little cedar-sided contemporary townhouse in Smyrna, Georgia, with Jason waiting for me at the door holding his special pizza made with a smiling tomato-slice face and black olive hair. The angels would be playing Gypsy Kings, and we could sit by our fireplace and snuggle forever. That was as close to heaven as I had ever been.

We had some good fights there, too. After one lively discussion, I bought some toy guns that shot foam disks. We ran around the house shooting each other, laughing as we did it. I did not know the magnitude of the treasure I had until now.

I walked into Kristi's home, talking with her dad, and he gave me some great insight. Drawing from his own life, he said that as life changes, your needs change, and what you once thought was necessary becomes no longer necessary. It's like having a big house when you are raising a family, and then not needing it when the children are grown.

If you flow with that change instead of resisting it,
new opportunities and adventures open up.

I could relate, because while I had loved our home in that neighborhood, it no longer suited my needs. If I kept trying to live in that time, recreating it, I would only be frustrated and miss what had been given to me now.

Then it was time to go. I packed the kids into the minivan, hugged Kristi, and thanked her and her father for being there for us. As I drove to the corner, I remembered something. I stopped and went to the curb at the entrance to the subdivision and scanned the ground. There it was: our initials inside a heart still carved into the concrete. I rubbed my hands over the letters and recalled when I had scratched those initials into the fresh cement years before. I was glad it was still there.

It was hard to go back, but it was good too. I felt less constricted, and less afraid. There were still treasures there. Some things had changed, and others were still the same. Beautiful memories came flooding back and overwhelmed my senses.

Sorrow and joy slow-danced together.

I will never forget that time. Intentionally re-inhabiting our emotionally charged spaces has not been easy, but like my father, I wanted that freedom from fear. I wanted to see the pain turn to dust and blow away. When I feel a wave of grief—which happens still—I can return to those good memories and remind myself of the beauty that we have chosen and of the beauty that still lives in our family. That gratitude is a freedom for my soul.

Navigating Emotionally Charged Places

When Jason died, suddenly there were emotionally charged spaces everywhere. The mall, the church we attended, the playground, the grocery store, and even the gas station. One by one, I had to reclaim these spaces for myself. Sometimes I brought friends along, and other times I re-inhabited the spaces alone or with my girls. Some spaces you must occupy out of necessity, but others will take more time.

In more difficult emotional spaces, I intentionally layer a good memory over a past memory in the same space. This act creates positive momentum forward and eventually gives me freedom in that area of my life.

One of these intentional re-layerings was on a trip to Costa Rica with my daughters. It was how we spent the third "Angel Anniversary" of his passing. I went back to the little townhouse where Jason and I lived when we opened his chiropractic clinic in San Jose and I gave birth (in a hospital) to my firstborn daughter, Arie. Arie really wanted to see the house from when she was a baby. In my rented car, I took us there.

Things had changed. First, the townhouse had been painted from a light yellow to a burnt orange and was now being used as a place of business: a lighting showroom. In the rooms that were once our bedroom, office, nursery, living room, and kitchen were scores of lighting fixtures with price tags covering the walls and ceilings.

I asked the woman working there if we could look around. She kindly agreed. As I went up the narrow staircase to our second floor, I was transported to the time when we lived there. I could almost hear Jason calling up from the kitchen to say good morning and what would I like for breakfast.

At the top of the stairs, I closed my eyes. If I stood still enough, I could imagine Arie as a baby in her crib and Jason walking over to hold her. I remembered the calm with which I woke up in our cool bedroom, sunlight coming in through the arched windows.

I could see so many memories in my mind's eye, but I kept getting jarred into the present, continually interrupted by Arie and Sophia.

My girls, then two and five years old, were running from room to room, turning every lighting fixture off and on. At least four ceiling fans were twirling and no fewer than twenty light fixtures were glowing.

**I was trying to concentrate on the past,
and they were having a ball in the present.**

I wanted to get annoyed. Let me have my moment to reminisce, but I stopped myself. I realized, *This was the moment*. This was what was real now. The magic that I was trying to recapture was still there; it had only transformed into the laughter of my children in the present. It was then that I realized that I could never really recapture the magic of the past. There is only the present moment.

I discovered that the magic of life—the magic of feeling content or enjoying that perfect day or the exhale you feel when you love so deeply and someone loves you back, that joy of living—it only happens in the present moment. It was happening then in the laughter of my children as they gleefully tried to turn on *every* light fixture in that showroom that had once been our little home.

There it was. A new memory was made right alongside the ones I already cherished. A new experience was layered in the same place as a favorite memory. I like that they co-exist. I don't want to forget the past, because those memories are a part of who we are, but I also want to make new memories in those spaces so that they don't become taboo. I don't want these emotional spaces to seem so sacred that we never enter that space again.

Be warned: going back to a place of significance can bring with it intense feelings, so be prepared. Bring a friend, or possibly your kids. Or invite a friend and their kids to come along. (Consult a professional counselor if you need to). Generally, kids live in the moment and that is a gift they give us if you let them. Be ready that your sacred space may *not* be sacred to them and that's okay. The memory is special and that can never be changed, but be open to flowing with the present moment and to seeing what gifts still await you now.

I'm glad I went back to that house in Costa Rica with my girls.
That journey taught me that those significant places or memories
in our lives can be launch points for new moments of joy.
We just need to bring a fresh perspective and an open mind.

Let me add that I could not have thought this way in the early months of my grief journey. This perspective came with time and prayer. So, forgive me if this sounds easy, because I know it's not. But being constricted from your own life is worse.

When I try to hold someone in my life, try to make sure that they stay, it is exhausting. I think I tried to do that for a long time with Jason. Even after he died, I didn't want him to go. I craved his presence and I tried to invoke it (not with mediums, mind you), to search it out by going back to our favorite haunts. I even traveled to Costa Rica to recapture the space where some of my most treasured memories with him occurred. The journey was good for me to do, but what I found was not what I intended to find.

I became thankful for the life I had with Jason, for the children I have now, for the friends and family who walked alongside me, for a beautiful day, and for wonderful memories.

It's easy to let the past overwhelm the present
and to let past hurts cloud a perfectly sunny day.
When that happens, make a conscious decision
to pull yourself back into the Here and Now.

I practice pulling myself into the present moment by focusing on something that is immediately near me, like my daughters' smiles or the blue sky. That present-moment focus helps me allow thoughts of the past to flow by, and I can relax into the immediate. It's also good to slow down for a day or so after visiting an emotionally charged space to let your spirit rest. The next day after visiting our old home in Costa Rica, I was tired. Processing all those thoughts and emotions takes effort. So, I gave in to my desire to get quiet. In the morning, I snuggled into bed with my girls and we watched a movie together. I felt at rest that there was another space I had reclaimed, layering positive memories in the present while savoring the treasured moments of the past.

Journey to the Sunrise

Discover those moments when sorrow and joy slow dance together. **Realize** that when you feel overwhelmed, you can return to those good memories and remind yourself of the beauty that still lives in your family. **Understand** that if you flow with change instead of resisting it, new opportunities and adventures open up.

Steps on the Path

- Pause, take a deep breath, and enter into an emotional battleground with the courage to create joy.
- It's easy to let the past overwhelm the present and to let past hurts cloud a perfectly sunny day. When that happens, it takes a conscious decision to pull yourself back into the Here and Now.
- As life changes, your needs change, and what you once thought was necessary becomes no longer necessary.
- Find your own way to re-inhabit a difficult emotional time with a positive experience.
- Focus on what you have been given now. Recreating the past will only be frustrating and might even cause you to miss what God has for you today.

Speak Life: Train Your Spirit(Please Say Out Loud)

I have continued to press into the heart of grief when I felt most dry. I have chosen gratitude, forgiveness, prayer, kindness, and generosity of soul in the most parched of circumstances. Even when the grasses around me were flaming hot with the heat of loss, I have purposed to press on, seeking God in prayer, worship, and Bible reading, as an act of will. By the grace of God, I will not run from the desert, but instead will make positive choices in the midst of my tragedy, practicing spiritual discipline, which will yield a mighty harvest in due time. I will follow the ancient paths back to God, trusting and believing that the mighty floodwaters of the Spirit will come, the refreshment from the hand of God.

Step 6:

Cross Your Finish Line

Do you not know that in a race all the runners run, but only one gets the prize?
Run in such a way as to get the prize. Everyone who competes in the games
goes into strict training. They do it to get a crown that will not last,
but we do it to get a crown that will last forever. (1 Corinthians 9:24-25)

Run Your Race

"Come on, Mom, you can do it!" Arie called to me as we swam a quarter mile together in open water. We were at the Calloway Gardens Triathlon. Arie and I were just finishing the initial swimming portion of the race, and I would be the last one out of the water. I had been recovering from a frozen shoulder injury most of 2015, so I was lurching along with a lopsided freestyle—a long right stroke and a short left stroke. It was a wonder I was not swimming in circles. Lifeguard boats were trailing me to ensure I was in no danger of drowning, which, in five feet of water, was not a major threat. Arie, at ten, was swimming slowly and easily by my side as I struggled through the last few yards.

We made it out of the water together. With our exit, we officially concluded this portion of the race for everyone. People on the sidelines clapped and shouted encouragement as my oldest daughter and I jogged to the transition area, and we quickly exchanged our swim caps and goggles for bike helmets and sneakers.

Hopping onto our bikes, we took off for the scenic views of the lush gardens at Calloway. Arie continued to encourage me, but now she escalated it to a challenge.

She cried, "Let's power ten, Mom," and then she zoomed past me like a rocket.

My jaw dropped. This was new. Naturally, I had to kick it into high gear. I love my child, but I couldn't yet be lapped by a ten-year old, even if she was my own. Arie knew my nature and taunted me. I caught up to her and passed her, just to show I still had it. She laughed, and we both raced each other for a little while. She was giving me a run for my money, and I was proud of her.

After a while, we relaxed a bit to enjoy the view from our bikes. Together, we sailed passed well-manicured gardens and meadows. Arie commented on her favorite ponds and lakes, pointing out birds and turtles, and I tried to etch into my mind forever the dappled sunlight and my daughter's blond hair, flashing in the sunshine, flying in the wind before me. Together, we were free. I was in awe that we were able to share this moment. I could not have believed this was possible when our hearts shattered at Jason's passing those years ago, and now I was so thankful to experience this race with her. It was amazing and beyond anything I could have asked for or imagined.

When we finished the bike portion and transitioned to the run portion of the triathlon, we continued to stick together. Arie and I were about to enter one of my favorite parts of the race. This final portion is why I race with my children and why I encourage people to cross finish lines as a healthy form of grief recovery, no matter how long or short the race is.

There is a beautiful life lesson to be had here, and it works best when you are submerged in the race experience.

As Arie and I ambled along, we were passed by a teenage boy. He was all knees and elbows, long and lanky, in that process of getting used to his growing body. His family was following alongside the racecourse in a golf cart. They cheered him on, saying, "Go get 'em! You can do it!" as he ran by. Laughing, they drove past us to keep pace with him.

"Do you see that, Arie?" I asked. "Do you see how closely his family members are following him and cheering him on? They love him. They are fully aware of him, and they want him to race well."

It was beautiful to see such devotion, even when the cheers were directed at someone else. We felt encouraged by the overflowing affection.

"It's like Daddy," I told her. "This is the picture of those who have gone before us and are cheering us in our race of life. I believe they are not far, they are aware, they want our best, they love us, and they'll be waiting to hug us at the finish line."

> *Therefore, since we are surrounded by such a great cloud of witnesses, let us throw off everything that hinders and the sin that so easily entangles, and let us run with perseverance the race marked out for us.* (Hebrews 12:1)

We were about a quarter mile from finishing, and we could hear the party music and the dull roar of cheers as people crossed the finish line and their names were called out on the loudspeaker. This was the object lesson of how to frame our lives after loss. We were in it, living it and racing it. Arie and I talked about how entering heaven and racing in life are so closely joined.

First, there was a welcoming party waiting for us. Our Peruvian family had come to share the weekend with us. Before the race, we had enjoyed a wonderful time relaxing together, sharing meals, and conversing while my daughters and their little cousins played together. Then, after a great weekend together, my family and younger daughter, Sophia, were gathered at the finish line to celebrate our crossing over.

We rounded the corner from the tree-lined shade of the racecourse, into the final stretch toward the finish line marker standing tall in the sunshine. Energized, my daughter and I sprinted together to the finish. The music was pulsing as we approached. The festive mood was palpable. There was a party waiting on the other side! As we entered the finish chute, our names were called over the loudspeaker. My heart swelled as we crossed the finish line together and were greeted by our family members rushing in to hug and cheer us. I always choke back tears at the end, because I know that this is just practice for the real thing.

One day, when this life-race is done, I will cross over and be welcomed with great celebration to a party of cheering family and friends who have gone before us. Each time I cross a finish line, I imagine Jason cheering, arms outstretched to hug me when we are finally reunited.

This is one of the reasons I started racing. I'm practicing for the real thing. So much good has happened in our lives as a result. When I am weary, I know God refreshes us through others who are cheering us on our journey. I imagine our family, led by Jason driving a crazy heavenly golf cart, laughing and cheering us along our life course. Life itself is an endurance race that can change directions, just as a triathlon changes course in the swim/bike/run portions, and our prize is the legacy of encouragement and inspiration our life story leaves behind for others.

There is another reason I love participating in a race, whether it is a 5K, 10K, or sprint triathlon. It's the empowering realization, "If I can do this, I can do anything!" That's what I said to myself when I crossed my first finish line.

Each race is its own challenge, and I had that same thought crossing the finish line this time. In this race, I had to struggle to perform with an injured shoulder, but there was something good in pushing myself again. I would have never traded making those memories during this race with Arie.

Finish lines inspire new goals and a new sense of potential in life.

Chapter 17:

Becoming a Victor, Not a Victim

C rafting your new normal after loss takes practice in creating a
new life pattern and then repeating that pattern. One of the most
effective patterns for me after becoming a widow was the discipline of
training for a race. The distance didn't matter. What mattered was the
process. It goes something like this: set up a goal with a specific deadline that includes a date in time. Break down achieving that goal into
monthly, weekly, and daily tasks. Get support as you move toward that
goal. Finally, cross your finish line.

It's hard to think about what the next phase of your life will look
like when you don't feel well. Training for a race event will help you
to feel better, clear your mind, and train you for accomplishing your
future goals. This process is a practice, a discipline, a repeatable pattern.
It does not depend upon your emotions.

One day, I hope you will say, like I did, "If I can do this, I can do
anything!" If you can discipline yourself to achieve these goals within a
supportive community and then accomplish your goals, you can set your
sights higher and higher! First, a race, then, maybe it's back to school
for an advanced degree or moving to a new location or changing careers.
When you feel stronger and have established a pattern for moving forward, life opens up into your Great Adventure!

Stories of Triumph

Here are a few stories of triumphal moments from Team Lady 180
widows and my daughters, Arie and Sophia. (At the time of this writing,
our single mom members haven't completed a triathlon yet, but they
soon will).

Kimberly Guinn: widow for one year, with triplet daughters

Before my husband, Frank, was killed, I had done exactly one Sprint Triathlon. It was in Clearwater, Florida, and I swore that day that I would never ever do another one. It was hard. I was not comfortable on the road. I was done, and I had no issue letting anyone know it. But if I have learned one thing in life, it's to never ever say the word "never."

After that, I continued to run and to support Frank through his runs. Then, in a moment, all that changed. I was no longer supporting him. I was completely without him. I was in the deepest and darkest place in my life. I was quick to reach out for help. I connected with other widows and read every book about widowhood I could find. One piece of advice I would receive over and over again was not to make major changes in the first year. However, I am not a person to follow advice. The biggest change I made in my life came about when I uttered the words, "I'm going to finish his IRONMAN."

I am not a racer. I am not competitive. I don't even like to run. I am scared to death of the bike at this point because my husband was killed while riding his bike, but I was determined. Little did I know that this phrase would be the catalyst from which I began to heal from this tragic loss.

When I began to train, I knew I was in over my head. So when Frank's Triathlon coach offered to coach me, I jumped at the chance. He set up a plan for me to follow. I am a drama teacher, so the summer months were easy. However, when school began, I had to completely rethink my training schedule. I quickly realized that it had to be a part of my life. My principal now doesn't bat an eye to see me strolling into school with my bike beside me. I would set it up on the stage and train during lunch, planning sessions, and even theatre rehearsal. Eventually, even my students accepted my crazy new training program.

From this, I learned to take time for myself. Training with the finish line as my focus forced me to get out of my comfort zone. I had a year to be ready to do something huge, and I didn't have time to wallow in my grief. I had movement, and I quickly learned that movement was healing. During my training, I talked to Frank. I laughed at him. I cursed him. I told him all the things I needed to say to him. When the grief was overpowering, I would run until my lungs would almost explode, I would scream and cry, and then I would push through and keep going. It kept me moving, and it kept me sane.

Finally came my moment of crossing the finish line. I had pushed through a very hard race. I was doing a 70.3 half IRONMAN, which was more than I ever thought I could do. It was hot, and the wind was killer. At one point, I was passed by the one and only Sister Madonna. She is a nun in her 80s who races both full and half Ironman races. It was humbling. Even more humbling was to finish an hour after my brother-in-law, who only a year before was run over in the same wreck that killed my husband. All of those feelings and fears and doubts were gone the second I saw the finish line. It was surrounded by my family and friends. They welcomed me into their arms. My eight-year-old triplet girls crossed the line with me.

The DJ calling the race asked me how I felt crossing the line, and laughing while crying, I replied, "It feels so good!"

In that moment, I took back the city that Frank and I loved. I reclaimed the place where he had been killed.

I felt that I had done something I could never have done before.
I felt true happiness in that moment.
It was something I had not felt since my husband had died.

The impact of my training on my children has been interesting. At first, I was worried that my training would take too much time from my children. I worried how it would affect them, but then something happened. They became interested in my training. They started asking to run or bike with me. They were so very proud when I crossed the finish line. They all wrote stories about the weekend, and the overall theme was that they were proud of their momma. A few weeks after the race, Makenna (one of my triplet daughters) and I were swimming at the gym. She swam up to me and asked if she could do the IRONMAN, too. I laughed and told her she had to be eighteen to do the IRONMAN, but we could start with something smaller. Since then, she has been training, and this fall, she will complete her first sprint triathlon, at eight years old.

LaTonya Pringle: widow three years, with one daughter

The day I participated in my first triathlon was one of the greatest days of my life. You may be asking yourself, "Why?" I mean, who would really want to subject their bodies to such exhausting activity? Who wants to swim a quarter of a mile, ride a bike for nine miles, and then finish with a two-mile run? Well, of course, I would—and so would a lot of others. However, for me, the Calloway Gardens Triathlon was much more than a triathlon. Participating in this race was the day I reclaimed my life.

You see, just over two years earlier, my husband and best friend passed away suddenly. In that moment, I stopped trusting. I stopped trusting myself, because I hadn't recognized that my husband's health was in jeopardy. I stopped trusting my body, because my seemingly healthy husband's heart had just stopped beating, forever. Even more disheartening was that, for a time, I stopped trusting God. I mean, why would He allow me to experience life as a young widow and single mom? Even more hurtful, why does my daughter now have to grow up without her daddy? Her dad was not only a great husband but a great father also.

What I knew for sure was that my life would no longer follow the "status quo." No one ever imagines or dreams that she will get married, buy her first house, and become a widow by the age of thirty-three. I figured, since everything is different—since my life has been suddenly flipped upside down—I should go ahead and continue to do things differently. I wanted to think of something challenging I would absolutely never do, not in a million years. I needed to find someone and something that would help widows like me reclaim their lives, deal with the pain of grief, and honor my loved one through living an absolutely amazing life. That group, for me, is Team Lady 180. We hold each other accountable, but we also laugh and cry, cheer each other on, and celebrate our children's birthdays together.

Most importantly, we understand the journey. We understand that what others see as a small step is really a giant leap of faith. Not only are we a Team, we are a family training together, and ultimately triumphing together. So, the day I participated in the triathlon was the day I began to trust again.

I began to believe that no matter how difficult, challenging, or unfair the circumstances may be, somehow, some way, all things work together for my good.

For me, the start of the triathlon was difficult. It seemed as if I wasn't going to be able to participate. First, I lost a piece that snaps my front tire to my bike. It was nowhere to be found. I spoke with the bike specialist available on site for the triathlon, and he didn't have the piece I needed. I thought I would have to drop out, but my girls on Team Lady 180 were there, and they went to work asking strangers if they had an extra bike for me to use during the race.

They found a wonderful lady who allowed me to ride her bike. I completed the swim part, which was not as difficult as I had anticipated. I got on the bike and was riding along, when the chain popped. *Shoot!* I remember thinking. *Okay, don't give up. Try to fix it, and just maybe someone will stop and help.* Not only did someone stop and help me, she said she wouldn't leave me. She stayed with me the rest of bike ride, even stopping to fix the chain each time it popped. I must mention that Team Lady 180 had also made classes available that taught us to be prepared for the unexpected, such as chains popping or flat tires, during the triathlon.

For me, the triathlon was a metaphor for life. It may not be easy. Yes, there will be challenges along the way, but there will also be a Team of friends, family, and even kind strangers who are more than happy to lend a helping hand and put their goals on hold to help you achieve yours. When I got to the finish line, my Team Lady 180 gal pals were triumphantly awaiting to celebrate this accomplishment with me. This experience was much more for me than just a triathlon. It changed my life.

I think the best part of Team Lady 180 is that it continues beyond the triathlon. Lessons of love, support, encouragement, and understanding are continually paid forward as new widows come in and each member enters a new phase of growth in her own time. Team Lady 180 teaches women dealing with grief to acknowledge that grief in a healthy way. It is a sisterhood no one ever wants to join, but one that is there when you need it. It is teaching women to support each other as a Team, to train together, to mentor one another, and then to triumph as we reclaim our lives.

Arie: Ten Years old

First, the swim is personally hard for me, but I still worked on it. It was hard knowing people were doing better than me. My mind would try to make me lose hope and tell me I was not going to make it, but I learned to push all that aside and power through. On my bike, it was a different mojo. I felt like I was soaring. When I would pass people, the feeling was amazing. Now, the run was where sometimes my mom had to push me through a little. I would be so tired that every step felt like I was dragging ten elephants. Then, going up that last hill, I could see it, the finish line! Somehow, the tiredness went away. A wild rush came over me. Mom and I sprinted through the finish line.

Crossing a finish line is like doing a hard math problem, like multiplication. If I work at it and solve one problem, I think to myself, "I can do the next one, and then the next one after that." It's the same with crossing a finish line at a triathlon. If I can accomplish that, I can do the next hard thing, and then the next, until I am unstoppable.

Crossing the finish line is magical. You just can't explain it!

Sophia: Eight years old, upon crossing her first triathlon finish line

First of all, finishing a race is really hard. When I see my family cheering for me, I feel happy and think, "Let's go!"

I think of my dad in heaven cheering me on, too. I think it helps other families who lost a loved one because their family and friends can be at the race with them and they can know that their loved ones in heaven are cheering for them, too, like their family that is here.

Journey to the Sunrise

Discover the wonder of your loving family and friends cheering you on.
Realize that finish lines inspire new goals and a new sense of potential in life.
Understand that life's changes will bring depth and unexpected beauty into your life, and you can begin to enjoy living in that space.

Steps on the Path

- Crafting your new normal after loss takes practice in creating a new life pattern and then repeating that pattern.
- Break down achieving that goal into monthly, weekly, and daily tasks.
- Get support as you move toward that goal, and finally, cross your finish line.
- It's hard to think about what the next phase of your life will look like when you don't feel well.
- Training for a race event will help you to feel better, clear your mind, and train you to accomplish your future goals.
- This process is a practice, a discipline, a repeatable pattern. It does not depend upon your emotions.
- One day, I hope you will say, like I did, "If I can do this, I can do anything!"
- When you feel stronger and have established a pattern for moving forward, life opens up into your Great Adventure!

Chapter 18:
Grief Growth

I never really believed people who said they enjoyed working out. People at the gym are generally breathing heavily, slick with sweat, red-faced, and clench-jawed. They don't look like they're having fun. I always assumed that people who said they enjoyed working out *really* meant they enjoyed *having* worked out. The feeling of having passed through that difficult time is great. I can see—once I've caught my breath—that my discomfort had a purpose, and I feel stronger.

When we've gotten to the other side of grief—not that it ends, but that we can finally say, *I can do this*—our triumph is something like that post-workout feeling. Only it's multi-dimensional. The trial has tested our minds, bodies, spirits, and relationships, and we have learned to use each of these areas of our lives more purposefully.

Our Triumph also involves what we do with our new superpowers. We can view the tragedy as a finite event that has recolored our entire lives. Ever notice that all superhero stories involve some kind of tragedy happening to the main character? The tragedy somehow produced a kind of super-growth. Maybe this theme isn't so off the mark in real life.

As we emerge from the grief with a better understanding of ourselves, our limits and our strengths, we begin looking forward from the crisis. All of the momentum of our positive decisions, our victories over what had seemed overwhelming, can then flood backwards over the months or years of grief and pain. Then we can find the beauty that has forged us into better tools and more sympathetic, intentional people. That in itself is a super-power.

Scientists are just beginning to study the phenomenon of post-traumatic growth at places such as Yale University and University of North Carolina. Apparently, severe trauma does not need to have only tragic effects. The definition of post-traumatic growth by the post-traumatic research group at UNC-Charlotte defines this phenomenon as "positive change experienced as a result of the struggle with a major life crisis or a traumatic event. Although we coined the term post-traumatic growth, the idea that human beings can be changed by their encounters with life challenges, sometimes in radically positive ways, is not new."[50]

In his book *Upside: The New Science of Post-Traumatic Growth,* Jim Rendon cites a study by Assistant Professor Tzipi Weiss, "who studied growth across dozens of cultures, examined seventy-two breast cancer survivors. Some of those cancer survivors had contact with another survivor who reported growth [after trauma]. Weiss found that just having contact with someone who had grown was one of the biggest factors in predicting post-traumatic growth. In addition, those women who knew someone who had grown after trauma reported higher levels of positive change than did other survivors."[51]

When grief is approached in a healthy way, it can result in personal growth and "fundamental, sometimes dramatic" change.[52] Psychologist David Feldman, Ph.D., says, "Trauma survivors who experience PTG acknowledge their sadness, suffering, anger, and grief, and are realistic about what happened to them. But in the midst of their pain, they're able to ask: Given where I am in my life, how can I build the best future possible?" Feldman, who wrote *Supersurvivors: The Surprising Link between Suffering and Success*, argues that when people work through the grief process, they can "convert the worst thing that happened to them into the best."[53]

Grief changes you. Over time, some of those changes can be spectacular, given the right choices.

Though my life is still a work in progress, those life changes brought on by grief have created depth and unexpected beauty for me and my family.

Our Beautiful Stained-Glass Heart

In my experience, the path is rarely clear, and the reasons behind our trials are rarely obvious. I believe that uncertainty is itself a part of the plan. Proverbs 25:2 says, "It is the glory of God to conceal things, but the glory of kings is to search things out." For me, this means that the journey is an adventurous scavenger hunt, and God prompts us with clues.

One of those prompts occurred when I was at the hairdresser. Part of my Beauty Creed is that getting a haircut is like buying a dress that you will wear every day. So, I tend to buy extremely nice ones. Also, that big hair will balance out my ample assets. I go to a trendy salon in Atlanta, and I never tell how much I spend there.

At first glance, I didn't recognize my stylist, Naomi. She had changed her hair from a brown bob to a bleached blond pixie cut. She wore a kelly-green mini dress with plaid platform pumps. She looked very artistic.

The haircut was perfect timing for me. A woman's relationship with her stylist is sacred ground. You tell her things that you may never say to anyone else. As always, Naomi and I chatted while her fingers nimbly worked on my split ends.

We talked about my recent road trip. She told me that she had taken one, too. She agreed that cutting loose on the road always brings a renewed sense of self.

I told her of the Costa Rican cloth hammocks that I had hung in what was once my dining room, just for whimsy. She was delighted. We laughed at how befuddled I made the Home Depot salesmen when I was shopping for the right hooks to hang the hammocks. I shared how wonderful it was to relax in that room with the neighborhood kids, and how I was considering a nice shade of metallic purple for my new "Costa Rican Oasis."

Then we talked about men, past and present. We shared thoughts and stories, and in the process, she said something beautiful.

She said, *"My heart has been broken so many times that now it's like a mosaic that creates a beautiful picture. The broken pieces are different hues of red and reflect the light now in different ways. I prefer the beauty of a broken heart to that of pristine innocence. It's like a stained glass window."*

Naomi didn't shrink with fear from heartache. Instead, she was strengthened by it. I believe that God speaks in unusual ways, infusing hope through others. For a split second, I thought I might have seen a glimmer of His knowing smile housed in a bleached pixie cut and platform heels.

A Lesson from Job

In the biblical book of Job, we see the process of grief and loss illustrated in a dramatic, even hyperbolic way. As the account goes, Job was a God-fearing, prosperous man, but he lost his children, home, and possessions in a short span of time. Then, Job was afflicted with painful boils, which were so disfiguring that his friends didn't even recognize him. God never explained Himself and never tipped Job off to the fact that he was at the center of a cosmic drama between the Almighty and Satan. God did, however, offer Himself and His presence to Job. Though Job was deeply hurt and had serious questions, he was determined to stay in relationship with God.

However, that's not the end of the story. Job had his own triumph. The Bible tells us that once Job emerged from his trial, the second half of his life was sweeter than the first. He wasn't gifted with a duplicate life; his new life was different, and sweeter.

> *The Lord blessed the latter part of Job's life more than the former part. He had fourteen thousand sheep, six thousand camels, a thousand yoke of oxen and a thousand donkeys. And he also had seven sons and three daughters. The first daughter he named Jemimah, the second Keziah and the third Keren-Happuch. Nowhere in all the land were there found women as beautiful as Job's daughters, and their father granted them an inheritance along with their brothers.* (Job 42:12-15 NIV)

Maybe the thought of getting more oxen and sheep hits a flat note in today's world, but there's more to it. The point is that Job held on even when he didn't understand God's agenda. Job chose to trust God, affirm life, and continue to grow after unthinkable trauma and loss. In that ancient time when women weren't given an inheritance, Job actually grew ahead of his time. He became a trailblazer and took a step toward gender equality by giving his daughters an inheritance along with their brothers.

Moreover, Job's journey is still relevant today, because his grief journey wasn't only about him. It was also about us. Through Job, God gives us an example of real hope in the midst of trauma. We can now see that what seemed then to be some sort of cosmic sport between God and the Enemy actually created a blueprint for healthy grieving for millennia to come. The fact that my Jewish friend, Michael, came and sat silently with me on the day I learned of my husband's death, in the epicenter of my grief, was a direct product of Job's grief thousands of years ago.

**Through his trauma, Job grew into a deeper faith
and left behind a legacy of writing that still influences
the grief journey of millions of people even today, right now.**

Do all stories end like Job's? No, this kind of ending was hard won. It doesn't just happen. There was a commitment on Job's part to stay the course with God even when God didn't offer an explanation for Job's losses.

If we are honest, sometimes it doesn't end in a way that looks pretty. Take John the Baptist, for example, who was the natural cousin of Jesus. The book of Luke tells the story of John sitting in a dank prison, incarcerated for voicing his beliefs, waiting to be beheaded while Jesus was out and about preaching. John wants to know, before he literally loses his head, if he's on the right track. He needs affirmation that his *cousin*, Jesus, is indeed the Messiah, God incarnate, because this stuff just got real. John sends messengers to Jesus to ask for confirmation, and here is his Cousin's reply:

> *So he replied to the messengers, "Go back and report to John what you have seen and heard: The blind receive sight, the lame walk, those who have leprosy are cured, the deaf hear, the dead are raised, and the good news is preached to the poor. Blessed is the man who does not fall away on account of me."* (Luke 7:22-23)

At no time does Jesus say, "While I'm doing all these miracles, I'll swing by and get you out of jail." Or even, "You're not getting out of jail; it'll get worse before it gets better, but here's *why*." I think it's more like, "I *am* at work. There will be a blessing, but it will come with great sacrifice. Yours included. Can you *trust* Me in this process?"

That's fairly tough to digest.
When we don't get a Divine explanation of why bad, unbelievably tragic things happen, can we still choose to trust and move forward in the life-race toward the prize?

I wouldn't want to sound like one of those well-meaning friends at the funeral who talk about closed doors and open windows, or the strengthening benefits of things that fail to kill us. I can eventually enjoy lemonade, but that doesn't mean I don't think of chocolate milk-shakes sometimes. It is right to grieve with those who are grieving in the Ground Zero of loss, but eventually, there's the next step. I believe this next step is a Bible verse that has, admittedly, annoyed me for years:

> *Consider it pure joy, my brothers and sisters, when-*
> *ever you face trials of many kinds, because you know*
> *that the testing of your faith produces perseverance. Let*
> *perseverance finish its work so that you may be mature*
> *and complete, not lacking anything. If any of you lacks*
> *wisdom, you should ask God, who gives generously to*
> *all without finding fault, and it will be given to you.*
> (James 1:2-5)

Who's going to voluntarily sign up for that? Who wants to invite trauma into their lives and then think that it's a reason for joy? I don't elect to have trials in my life, and I haven't thought they were a reason to be joyful when I was deeply grieving.

It was only years after the loss of my husband
that I began to understand the wisdom James is sharing with us.
I believe he is talking about the transformative power of grief.

From my perspective as a widowed mom, I believe this passage is trying to explain that, in time, you will consider it unbelievable joy when you face trials and persevere through them. Your faith cannot grow without being challenged. If you persevere through the journey, you will be transformed, fully stepping into who you are created to be. If you need wisdom for this journey, you need only to ask, and God will generously give you wisdom so that you may complete this journey with success.

When Jason first died, I wanted to outrun the grief that burned me from the inside out. The grief was debilitating, and I desperately looked for a way to dull my constant pain. Over time, however, the sense of grief changed, and transformed me with it.

The grief made me more sensitive to others and took our family on a journey that changed our lives—is still changing our lives. Without our grief, we would not have met wildly inspirational people like Scott Rigsby, whom my children still call "Super Legs." We would not have engaged in triathlons as a family. We would not have met Lori Apon, "Queen Widowed Mom." We would not have known our Team of soulful, adventurous, hilarious, empowered widows and single moms. We would not have written this book or known God in this deeply dependent way.

That's one reason why I enjoy running races, and why I enjoy *having* worked out. On the other side of that finish line, we can better hear the cheers of the people who have been helping us along, we can better see the distance we have come, even if the entire race felt like just an accumulation of one agonizing step after another.

When you have been very thirsty, that pure, fresh water tastes amazingly *sweet*.

Journey to the Sunrise

Discover the moment when you start to believe that no matter how difficult, challenging, or unfair the circumstances may be, somehow, some way, all things work together for good as we pursue a relationship with God.

Realize that if you need wisdom for this journey, you need only ask God, who will generously give you what you need to complete this journey with success.

Understand that part of the transformative power of grief is an overhaul of your priorities.

Steps on the Path

- When we don't get a Divine explanation of why bad things happen to us, can we still choose to trust and move forward in the life-race toward the prize?
- Read the book of Job and see how through his trauma, Job grew into a deeper faith and left behind a legacy of writing that still influences the grief journey of millions of people today.
- Record the amazing insights God gives you from reading this story from the Bible. Then prepare to start your own amazing adventure.

Chapter 19:

Starting Your Great Adventure

Etched on a stone in my garden, next to my Japanese maple tree and encircled by irises from the garden I started with Jason, is a daily reminder:

"Do something every day that makes you happy."

Does that mean that you throw caution to the wind and only do things that make you happy all the time? You can, but then who's going to do the laundry or pay the bills? Believe me, that path leads to a dark, water-less home, with wilting vegetables, a defrosting refrigerator, and nothing but pajama pants to wear. I'm speaking as one who knows.

There's a balance between sparking joy in our lives and being responsible. I'm not telling you to ditch your responsibilities. I am suggesting that you intentionally explore what sparks your joy and interest in life. There's a simple way to do this by creating "The List."

The List

If you are ready to start an amazing adventure, make a list of all the things you once loved to do, but have stopped doing. Then pick your top three choices.

Next, make a list of all the things you always wanted to try and have never done, and then pick your top three choices from that list.

Now, pick *one* item from either or both lists and Plan to Do it! It sounds so simple, but it yields amazing results.

I have employed the power of "The List" many times, and each time I try an item from my list, I find a new ticket to adventure for my family. We meet new people, try new things, and discover fun surprises.

I'll tell you my two top favorites. I picked flamenco dancing from the list of things I used to do to make me happy. I used to be in a flamenco dance troupe in my twenties. Also, from the list of things I always wanted to try, I picked pottery. I chose to do two items at once, and I was smiling from ear to ear through the process. I met amazing women at my flamenco dance class, a few of whom were widows, too. I loved hearing one of the dancers, a sassy sexagenarian with a flower in her hair, stomp her black dance shoe and say, "¡Bailemos!" which is Spanish for "Let's Dance!" I loved her spirit and her seasoned feminine strength even in the face of her own widowhood. She inspired me every time I went to class. I also learned a great deal about my spiritual life from my pottery classes. There was so much to be gleaned from the process of creating something from clay, smoothing the rough edges, and learning to produce a high-fire, multidimensional glaze.

Now it's your turn to start your list and even ask a friend to join you as you try some fun adventures.

There is a difference between happiness and joy.
Happiness is dependent on your circumstances.
Joy is an intentional approach to life, even a spiritual discipline,
that is a consistent result of your spiritual connection to God.

I believe you need moments of both joy and happiness. My point here is to spark your interest in life and nourish your sense of adventure as a form of grief recovery. I want you to explore life and discover that there are still amazing adventures to be had. Creating "The List" is a great place to start. Why? Because there's something really sexy about a person who is positive.

You can shop all you want, buy the hottest clothes, even nip and tuck your body, but the *sexiest* thing you can do is so simple. Enjoy Your Life! I realize this is a special challenge after loss, so I'd recommend baby steps.

Over time, learning to enjoy your life creates a vibrant calm within you, which attracts happy, healthy people to yourself. In an article entitled "Laws of Attraction: How Do We Select a Life Partner?" in

Psychology Today, Noam Shpancer, Ph.D., highlights some of the most desired traits that attract people to us: "Research on the personality factors that attract us to others (and others to us) has identified two personality factors that are considered across the board desirable: competence and warmth. Competent people, that is to say intelligent and socially skilled, are considered more attractive. Kind people with a warm personality are also more attractive. Warm and wise is a winning pair in the mate selection tournament."[54]

Nourishing joy and creating happiness are intentional and healthy for your life, and this activity has long-reaching, positive effects. There is a discipline to doing "something every day that makes you happy." Although we probably can't take a vacation every day, we can plan large and small adventures. For example, when my extensive amounts of laundry became an intolerable burden, we make a film festival out of completing the laundry together. There are bigger things, too, like planning a fun vacation, taking a hike or bike ride, or camping with your kids (be wise, and get expert advice on that one).

To spark some ideas, here are a few things from my list.
- Helping someone else or volunteering for a group you believe in
- Taking a flamenco dancing class
- Training for a triathlon
- Making pottery
- Painting
- Taking a road trip
- Exploring another country or culture
- Learning a new language and meeting up with a local cultural group that speaks it fluently
- Playing in the park
- Watching a Screen on the Green movie in the park during the summer time
- Shopping at Goodwill
- Going to a yard sale or auction
- Visiting a farm
- Listening to Brazilian drumming music
- Listening to Cuban jazz music
- Painting a room a new color
- Catching up with an old friend or family member.
- Horseback riding

- Taking a day trip
- Learning photography
- Taking a new class in something interesting, like cooking or archery
- Reading a good book
- Salsa dancing
- Taking swing dancing classes
- Doing Zumba classes at my gym
- Attending a *Little House on the Prairie Festival* in the summer
- Learning a new skill
- Hanging hammocks in my house
- Wearing red
- Seeing a theater performance
- Seeing my favorite dance troupe, Alvin Ailey
- Going to a baseball game with friends

Now it's your turn. Try making your own list. My hope is that you'll meet new people and experience new discoveries that will take you on some fabulous adventures. Maybe you'll even write about it afterwards, because this is part of *your story*, which is part of your lasting legacy.

The Grief Adventure

Costa Rican landmarks dot the timeline of my life, and I suppose it will always be that way. Somehow, I find the road back to myself there. It is the deep place where I become still again.

The country of Costa Rica had also come to represent an alternative life for me. It was where I went in my imagination: life was slower, we played instruments instead of watching television, there was a live-in maid who did all the laundry and cooking, and I shopped for my food at a farmer's market where someone played Latin music on a xylophone as I selected exotic fruits.

I first visited Costa Rica in my early twenties on a mission trip, and I fell in love with the place. I returned when I was married, and Jason and I enjoyed a second honeymoon. In 2004, we actually lived there long enough for me to give birth to Arie. We had opened a chiropractic clinic for Jason a month after she was born.

One of my most savored memories is when Jason and I were visiting our friends, Steve and Chris, who told us about Montezuma, a wonderful little out-of-the-way beach that we should visit. We took a bus ride to Puntarenas, then a ferry ride, and then another bus ride that included chickens onboard, until we finally made it to Montezuma Beach. Once I stepped off the bus, I knew it had all been worth it. Montezuma was this idyllic little beach town with one main street and sun-washed, multi-colored buildings. We pulled our rolling luggage down a dirt road to a little hotel called La Cascada ("The Cascade"), a name that made perfect sense, because the hotel was near a low waterfall.

The highlight of my trip with Jason was when we went horseback riding up a mountain and then down to an even more remote beach, which looked like something straight out of the movie *Blue Lagoon*. A high precipice dropped right into the ocean, and a waterfall tumbled over its edge into a natural pool that had formed from lava rock jutting up from the ocean. It was a pool fed by a freshwater waterfall that was on the edge of the ocean. It was so beautiful that it didn't look real.

It was stunning to see — and even better to get into. We got off of our horses, climbed the rocks, and eased ourselves into the cool water. The sunlight glinted off the waterfall that poured into our pool, while the ocean waves crashed on the rocks behind us. I was in love with my husband. We laughed so much that day, later returning to the hotel and enjoying a siesta together, and then enjoying a succulent dinner at the beach restaurant, Playa de los Artistas. That time will forever be etched into my memory. Before we left, we purchased two cloth hammocks as a memento of that time. They were the ones I hung, years later, in my dining room, converting it into a peaceful, tropical space.

I have always idealized that trip to Montezuma, and the town had become a sealed, sacred memory. I had not been back since that first time with Jason.

Eventually, I made my way back to Costa Rica to help Steve and his wife celebrate Steve's fiftieth birthday in 2014. I was hungry for an adventure, and a trip to the remote town of Santa Teresa to be with a group of friends sounded like the perfect opportunity. I didn't even ask where we were going or what we were doing. I just booked my ticket. There was no itinerary. I simply trusted the rest.

Once in Santa Teresa, I relaxed and enjoyed the resort's secluded beach. One morning, I got up early to walk along the shore. It was on those long lazy walks that God seemed to come alongside me, and I could just enjoy His company. No big agenda, just shells and the sound of the ocean breathing. I was reminded how comprehensive and creative God is. Though I can never fully understand Him, I can rest in knowing that He loves me. When I clear my schedule to be with Him, some really beautiful things happen.

I walked along the ocean's edge in the early morning hours. The beach butted up to the jungle while mountain ridges dropped sharply into the ocean, and massive rock formations, ten stories high, jutted up from the ocean waves. The sand was crusted with rocks and millions of broken shells. I had left my shoes behind at the beach house.

Little did I know that where I was staying was only a ten-minute car ride to Montezuma Beach. I had not realized that Santa Teresa would be that close. In the distance along the shoreline, I thought I saw a familiar land formation with the waterfall in the distance that dropped into the ocean, like the special pool in Montezuma I had visited with Jason years before. So, I started walking toward it. It was almost like walking in a dream. Could I really be that close to such a core memory?

As I kept going, I realized that the cracked rocks and broken shells that were mixed into the sand hurt my bare feet. Compelled, though, I gingerly walked for a couple of hours toward that memory. Eventually, the rocks and shards of broken shells were too painful, so I turned back. Maybe if I had walked another forty-five minutes I could have reached it, but what would I have found? I don't know. I considered trying again the next morning—this time with shoes.

When I turned to walk back to the beach house, I wondered what I would have done had I reached my destination. Maybe I would have sat there alone, remembered our laughter and wonder at the waterfall, like I've done before while visiting other places that were significant to us as a couple. Those experiences have not been especially satisfying for me.

It occurred to me as I was walking back that Jason wasn't mine to keep. God had shared him with me, but he was never mine.

As I stepped along the rocky patches of the shoreline, with the waterfall at a far distance behind me, I realized that walking and finding shells with God was incredibly peaceful. God and I have vacationed together before. I have always taken solitary adventures. Now that I am a widow, God seems to lavish me with moments that tell me I am loved. He romances me. This was one of those times. I couldn't have predicted it.

Relaxing, I welcomed a pack of friendly dogs that walked alongside me for a while, watched a surfer crest a wave, and smelled the salt air. I was content to simply enjoy the present moment.

Dive In

"Will that be eight people for the zip-line and ATV party package to Montezuma?" the concierge asked from a small wooden cabana at our beach house resort on that same trip.

My heart was beating fast. I was ready for a new adventure. We would zip-line and ride on all-terrain vehicles with a pack of fun friends into the heart of my memories with Jason at Montezuma Beach.

I had never zip-lined before, much less in the jungle. As we rode in the pickup truck to our launch-point, I became quieter, my fear of heights really kicking in. Eventually, I gained confidence as I worked through the zip-lining course.

It was exhilarating to fly through the jungle. My friends laughed with me, and we cheered every time one of us reached our platform. Eventually, I discovered that if I focused on all that could go wrong, like plummeting to my death or my harness breaking, then I would become paralyzed with fear. If I trusted the cable and enjoyed the exotic birds and vegetation, it became a marvelous experience. At one point, following a friend's example, I even zipped upside down!

After the zip-line, we rode on ATV vehicles all the way to Montezuma, along dirt roads that were punctuated by rolling farms, slowing down for the herd of cows blocking our way. I was having so much fun on the ride that entering Montezuma snuck up on me. Suddenly, there it was: our hotel, La Cascada, just to the right of a gently flowing waterfall.

Across the street, we stopped for a meal at Playa de los Artistas, the same beautiful restaurant with seating made of tree stumps directly on the beach. I hadn't known we would eat there until the guide stopped and announced the plans.

We all sat at a long table under the shade of a palm-frond-covered pavilion. The food was still wildly delicious. We had the seafood platter with scallops, shrimp, and lobster. My mouth still waters as I write this, because the tastes were so amazing.

After lunch, as everyone was talking, I excused myself from the table and walked out to the beach. I found a shell to take home with me as a reminder that I was actually in this place that held such sweet memories with Jason. I was able to remember our time together, the way he used to hold my hand or make me laugh, and I was also thankful for a table full of new friends to enjoy this present time with. Both moments could co-exist.

With lunch over, it was time to take a hike. Our guide led us over large rocks that crisscrossed and dipped into the cool, rushing current of the wide stream that fed the waterfalls near La Cascada. With each step, I got closer to one of my most magical memories. Years ago, Jason and I had also hiked to a waterfall next to the hotel. What would I find when I got there?

I could hear the rush and roar of the waterfall before we arrived. The way into the jungle had at times become narrow and required me to step carefully, but now the path opened into a clearing with wide stones surrounding a natural pool fed by a waterfall pouring down from a jungle cliff, two to three stories high. The fresh water seemed to dance on its way down, beckoning me to play.

The memories came flooding back. Meanwhile, friends from our group were shedding their backpacks, some to rest on the warm rocks with their feet in the cold water. Others stripped to their bathing suits and dove in to swim their way to the waterfall.

I stood on the edge and took it all in, seeing both my time with Jason and my time in the present moment simultaneously, with the waterfall connecting both of those moments.

I was wearing the same Athleta swimsuit, decorated with colorful, curled scrolls, that I had worn on my first triathlon with my widowed Teammates of Team Lady 180.

I stood at the edge of the pool and remembered how Jason and I once swam to the spot on the rocks just below the waterfall. I could imagine seeing him there, and with that image in my head, I dove into the natural pool. The shivery water sent a tingle over my body as I plunged in and then surfaced. As I looked around, I was surrounded by a cathedral of trees reaching for a blue sky. I swam to the rocky cliff wall and heard a "Whoop!" as someone jumped from behind the waterfall out into the pool below.

I was at the rocks where Jason and I had been years ago. Even though I knew the rocky wall behind the waterfall would be slippery, I decided to climb it to experience the back of the waterfall. It felt right to do something fresh and different in this space. When I reached the leaping point, I stopped. It wasn't like I had imagined, being behind a waterfall. The force of the water was a constant roar, powerful and refreshing. The water didn't just come down; it bounced off the stone wall behind me and shot out horizontally as well.

I stood there, my bare feet gripping the rock, my body leaning against the stone wall behind me, and my heart beating fast. I put my hands up and closed my eyes; the water was dancing all around me. I thought, this is what's God's love must be like—overwhelming, powerful, roaring, refreshing, exotic, and healing.

I took a deep breath and pushed off, leaping to the water below. When I surfaced, I felt enveloped in love. The love of God that had brought me this far, the love of my late husband who brought me to Montezuma all those years ago, and the love of friends who enjoyed this moment with me now.

There was love going back. There was love in the remembering, and love in the journey.

Journey to the Sunrise

Discover the love that lives in the remembering and in the journey.
Realize how important it is to do something every day that makes you happy.
Understand that there is a difference between happiness and joy. Happiness is dependent on your circumstances. Joy is an intentional approach to life, a spiritual discipline that is a result of your spiritual connection to God.

Steps on the Path

It is time for you to start your amazing adventure.
- Make a list of all the things you once loved to do, but have stopped doing. Then pick your top three choices.
- Next, make a list of all the things you always wanted to try and have never done and then pick your top three choices from this list.
- Now, pick *one* item from either or both lists and Plan to Do it! It sounds so simple, but it yields amazing results.

My hope is that you'll meet new people and make some new discoveries that will take you on some fabulous adventures. Maybe you'll even write about it afterwards because this is part of *your story*, which is part of your lasting legacy.

Can you plan a trip, long or short, to empower one of your core memories?

Speak Life: Cross Your Finish Line
(Please Say Out Loud)

I have arrived at the Okavango at just the right time. I celebrate my Victory and the Victory of my Teammates! We have come a long way! We drink deeply of the fresh water, now spilling into the tremendous basin, shaped like a giant hand, reminding us of God's provision. The floodwaters are rising, and the basin steadily fills. We rest and refresh ourselves, because this is just the beginning. The light of dawn is peeking over the horizon. It is the start of a New Day. I have come far, but my journey isn't over yet.

Step 7:

Live Your Legacy

"Surviving is important. Thriving is elegant." ~ Maya Angelou

Cleaning the Bricks

While we were traveling around Warsaw making my documentary, *Burning Questions*, about my father's childhood trials in the Nazi concentration camp at Bergen Belsen, my dad told me a story I will never forget. At the end of the war, the city of Warsaw had been demolished. Eighty-five percent of the buildings had been destroyed. Anyone who had been away at war or in concentration camps returned to an unrecognizable city, marked by piles of rubble, broken glass, and dust. Those who had not been away had their own memories of watching the destruction occur.

My father asked his eighty-six-year-old Aunt Stefania why the people of Warsaw didn't just start fresh after the war and build a better city in a new location.

Aunt Stefania was a fiery, passionate woman packed into a petite and powerful five-foot frame.

Her eyes sparked, and she said, "Oh no, we had to rebuild the city right here, just as it was, to show that they had not beaten us."

She went on to tell us that the people of Warsaw worked in their spare moments and every weekend, putting their city back together stone by stone over the course of fifteen years. Those who had no construction skills spent their time cleaning the bricks—chiseling off the hardened mortar so that the bricks could be reused. For fifteen years, they cleaned the bricks of their broken buildings and used them to rebuild their businesses and homes, just as they had been before, with graceful architecture and intricate, historical details.

My father told me, "You can only do that if you have love, love for your city."

As I see it, the people of Warsaw began to craft their revival soon after the war. By rebuilding their structures with the same bricks, they were determining to "re-layer" their city. The rubble of war would not be the end of their story. Those bricks would go on to embed themselves in new memories. The work of the citizens would weave Warsaw's history into a seamless whole.

To honor the hope of recovery, the citizens of Warsaw were making a living monument that they still live in and enjoy today. It was important that they used those same bricks. Sometimes, in the rebuilt structures, you can see scars on the stones, a few amputated toes on the historic statues. Those scars are part of the legacy of violence that razed the buildings, but since those stones and statues make up part of the present-day businesses, they also speak of survival, recovery, and triumph.

Immediately after Jason's death, I felt my marriage was a hollowed-out shell, and my family was a wasteland of grief and hopelessness. I realize now that I was only living through a moment in time, a part of the process. When Jason and I promised to make our marriage a lasting legacy, we were making an eternal promise, one that didn't end with his death. Cleaning the bricks means using all the gifts our marriage has produced—even the scarred and messy parts—to create a beautiful and lasting teaching tool to help other grieving families. In so doing, our living monument to hope fills our hearts with purpose and joy.

If we take the broken bricks of our lives, clean them, and use them to rebuild our own monument to hope, we can build something that will help others, as we also honor our past.

I'm not suggesting, like the people of Warsaw, that you rebuild your life structure after loss exactly as it was before. That's not what I've done with my life. Certainly, new, modern life in Warsaw, Poland, inhabits the rebuilt buildings of the past. I am suggesting that there is healing in repurposing the pain of your past to help others. Take the experiences you've had, clean them until they become the lessons that you have gleaned, and use them to empower those in your life. That is your monument to hope and a significant step in your recovery.

Chapter 20:

Crafting your Legacy

Sometimes, cleaning the bricks from the rubble of our lives seems to be more than a laborious, fifteen-year process. There are some spaces that seem like they can't be re-layered. They are the scenes of great trauma, or they are too intensely personal, or they represent something that can never be recovered. There are wrenching moments of finality on this journey, such as when I interred Jason's ashes two years after his death, or when I decided to remove my wedding ring.

I also got rid of our minivan because I could not sit in the driver's seat without recalling that moment after I found his note telling me that he wasn't coming back for three days. He had left without warning.

For some people, *setting off in a whole new direction seems the best therapy*. There's a healthy way to head in a different direction: we should try new things—things we might never have done with our lost loved ones, as a way of internalizing the lesson that we can never be the same, that we have been changed. We cannot return to the way things were, and sometimes it feels like we no longer even *have* a comfort zone. So, we figure this would be a great time to step out of that zone.

The problem is, unless we find a way to clean them up and put them to use, we will keep on stumbling over the bricks left over from our previous broken dreams.

Wasps in the Cracks

I didn't have to look far for an object lesson for that truth. God had one parked right in my driveway for almost three years. When I got rid of my minivan, I gave it to my father. Right after our loss, my dad would travel to Atlanta every four weeks to spend a week or so and help me do the "tough stuff." He lived in Florida, a fourteen-hour drive from me, and he needed a reliable car for the journey. Besides, I wanted a fresh start, so I bought a brand-new 2007 Honda minivan for myself and my girls.

Then my father had a stroke in 2012. It changed his ability to walk and live independently, but never dulled his mind. During his recovery, he did a stint in a skilled nursing home for a few months of rehab to learn to walk with the aid of a walker. In time, it became obvious that his life had changed and he should move in with my daughters and me.

When I flew to Florida to pick up my father from the nursing home, I drove him to our home in that same old minivan, now packed with all the things we could fit from his life in Florida. We parked that older minivan in my driveway in the hopes that Papa, as we call him, would eventually recover and be able to drive again. Though he constantly feels dizzy from vertigo, my father quietly uses every inch of his life, which once included world travel with national news correspondents and US presidents, but now is kept closer to home. He instructs my daughters and dispenses hard-won wisdom. He inspires and encourages me in building the active grief support group, Team Lady 180, which I had searched for so desperately in my early grief journey.

After two and a half years with no marked health improvement, we decided to sell his minivan. He suggested to me that I keep the minivan and drive it myself, but I rejected the idea. I didn't want to be reminded of the pain of loss. Besides, I suggested we sell it to help pay to make this book happen. He agreed.

Unused and parked in my driveway for all that time, the 1995 minivan had a sun-worn paint job, and the tint on the windows was cracked, peeling, and purple. I had no desire to drive it. Every time I looked at it, I could still see myself sitting in the driver's seat, calling Jason on my cell phone, pleading on his voicemail for him to come home, while Arie cried in the backseat asking where Daddy was. I didn't care if that minivan went to the scrap heap. I certainly wasn't going to drive it, but I could sell it.

In the process of getting the van ready to sell, God taught me a thing or two about cleaning the mess, reclaiming a sealed space, restoring the damage, and then refueling your dreams.

First of all, whatever you have sealed off doesn't stay that way. Cracking open that minivan was not like cracking open a hermetic seal on some ancient Egyptian tomb. It wasn't even like opening an old photo album to revisit static memories captured on a snapshot. The same rule applies when trying to restore a relationship that I had stepped away from because I was in too much pain. There was no emotional cryogenic freezing in the meantime. My first lesson when I tried to re-enter the monstrous minivan was that, even when we've temporarily turned away from a memory or relationship, life still breeds in the cracks and crevices.

When I first unlocked the old minivan, opening the driver's door, I jumped back in surprise. Actually, I jumped back and ran screaming into my house. A family of wasps had made a large nest in the door jamb—and under the front hood of the car as well. The sealed minivan, it turned out, provided an ideal space for wasps to multiply.

To reclaim the space, I had to open the van to the sunshine, reveal the wasp nests, get my helpful neighbor to spray them (activate your support resources at hand), knock the nests down, and stomp them.

Those wasps can represent the stinging conversations you may have to have in the process of reconciliation, or the discomfort of revisiting places packed with overpowering memories. Spray those past hurts with forgiveness. Kill the offenses through compassion and understanding before they continue to multiply and then swarm (unless the offense endangers you physically or in an abusive way; then, consult with a professional counselor). Protect yourself as best you can from the pain when you seek to re-layer memories. Bring supportive friends or plan definite activities that will structure your visit, but wade in there and face them.

Once the wasps were removed, it was time to clean up the van. I took the time to clear the clutter and throw away old garbage. The inside smelled bad, so I deep-cleaned it. The analogy here is probably pretty straightforward, especially when dealing with difficult relationships. I had to remind myself of the people of Warsaw cleaning bricks. It was a tedious, sort of violent process, chipping away the chunks of mortar to uncover the straight, usable brick. Even the least skilled volunteers could do this chore. It just takes dedication.

Next, I needed a new battery. Taking out the old, worn-out battery and replacing it with a new one reminded me of how God tells us to come to Him to renew our spiritual strength in His love. Ezekiel 36:26 says, "I will give you a new heart and put a new spirit in you; I will remove from you your heart of stone and give you a heart of flesh." Romans 12:2 takes it a step further, "Don't copy the behavior and customs of this world, but let God transform you into a new person by changing the way you think. Then you will learn to know God's will for you, which is good and pleasing and perfect." With a new battery, the car started to run, and I took it for a spin around the block.

Next, the vehicle needed to get some intensive repairs so the mechanical parts could function. I think it was especially important for me to note that some of my minivan's rehabilitation work could not be done by me. I had to take it to a professional to get any major overhauls done. Just like we have areas in our lives that have to be repaired, spending time in prayer and meditation with the "Master Mechanic" and with a professional counselor gets our hearts to run with healthy precision.

Then, I gave it a new identity and a new outlook. Once the minivan was running, it was time for new tags, a new paint job, and new window tinting. Finally, that 1995 minivan was pretty, gassed up, and ready to sell. She looked like a little classic car.

I smiled, thinking, "Look at me, restoring and releasing the past like a pro."

However, God wasn't finished with His lessons for me. I listed the 1995 minivan and my own 2007 minivan at the same time, to see which one would sell faster and help pay for producing this book. My 2007 minivan sold within twenty-four hours, and I realized it was logical to sell my newer minivan and gain more funds so that this book could exist. However, that meant I was now *back* in the old car, re-inhabiting the space where I could recall so vividly those moments of loss.

Well played, God.
He put me in the center of the Divine Switch-a-Roo-Ski.

When I thought about it, looking past that one memory of intense loss, this minivan also represented my father's determination to drive fourteen hours each way from Florida to Atlanta, so that he could support my young family in our grief. There were actually some great memories with Jason and Arie in this minivan, and I even drove my newborn, Sophia, home from the hospital in this vehicle. I could still imagine her, pink, sweet, and snug in her baby car seat.

I didn't have to let the memories of loss and trauma define my life. Those memories were a part of my experience, but not all of it. My daughters, though they missed the built-in DVD player of the 2007 minivan, could now help me create new, laughing memories in what had once been my old vehicle.

Cleaning up, reclaiming, restoring, and refueling the 1995 minivan allowed me to release my more expensive 2007 minivan and get the funds to move forward with publishing this book.

Ultimately, my van of vexation became a tool to move my life forward, an important element in crafting my legacy. Physically, it is still contributing to my everyday life with my daughters and father. It is also helping to enable the next step in my journey, transforming my tragedy into triumph, and paying forward the blessings my trials have brought.

Unsealing parts of our pain is messy. Sometimes, in our absence, wasps have started to breed in the dark cracks, like lies that threaten to sting us once we open the sealed places to the sunshine. When you are ready, and with support, consider taking the necessary steps to breathe new life into those sealed places. Restoration and reconciliation will take time, but once the hard work is done, your effort just might be the vehicle that helps you move forward and even fuel your new purpose.

I still drive my old 1995 minivan. My daughters like the warm cloth seats, and I like the fact that I can load it with bikes, even scratch it with my bike rack, and I don't mind. More importantly, it now reminds me of the love of my father, good times with Jason, the laughter of my children, and moving forward in purpose.

The Legacy of Your Written Words

One of the ways to "clean the bricks" of dreams that have been bombed is to tell your story. In crafting my own lasting legacy, I have found one tool that has been absolutely vital—writing. Tell your story, even if you are just telling it for the sake of your children. Write down the stories as they come to you, both celebratory and soulful. There doesn't have to be an order to it. For years, I just wrote thoughts and feelings down as a way of processing my grief. As I continued on this journey, those stories eventually took the shape of this book.

Your stories become part of your family's oral traditions and help to build a kind of narrative identity for your family. The week my husband died, my father reminded me of my grandmother's survival in the concentration camp, and then demanded that I, too, survive the loss of my husband. I knew this story well. When he challenged me with it in my early moments of panic, I knew this was part of my family narrative. Part of our legacy as Porembskis was to persevere through extreme difficulty, and to follow in Babcia's footsteps. I would later return to my maiden name as a constant reminder of my father's and grandmother's strength and determination.

Creating your lasting legacy can start with simply documenting your thoughts. In this way, the pattern and process become easier to discern. This book is partly a compilation of my journey as a widow over the last eight years, along with helpful health strategies. The stories from the early days after Jason's death are very different from the stories that I tell now.

I remember once interviewing a woman as part of a video for Arts in Medicine, an innovative program to use the arts to help people living with injury and disease, at Shands Hospital in Gainesville, Florida. This woman talked of her illness and how painting helped her heal.

She said something I will never forget: "I painted through my pain, and eventually I painted myself well."

Her paintings changed through the course of her journey. As she focused her mind and energies on what she wanted in her life, she painted *that* life. In time, her perspective transformed, and freedom came.[55]

At the beginning of my grief journey, I balked at grief groups that suggested that I journal my experience. Why would I want to journal such pain? Why record such anguish? The answer was that I needed to express it. Writing or painting or any sort of healthy artistic expression gives your mind the means to process what has happened. You will change over time, and this expression can be a very real part of your healing.

Our stories have the power to inspire others, and helping others is another powerful source of joy and healing for our hearts and minds. When our pain has a purpose, we can focus on how telling our story may help someone else, and that effort can lead to joy in the present moment.

Writing out my discoveries on this grief journey has been an excellent way to "write myself well." Over time, I can see the trajectory of God's faithfulness, even in the most painful circumstances. This book has been a most difficult thing for me to write, but it has also brought incredible healing by giving purpose to my grief journey and crafting it into a teaching tool that I hope helps and inspires others on their grief journey. Expressing my adventure through writing has been its own contribution to transforming our family's trials into triumph.

Whether your paint your story, write your story, or find some other way to share your story, there is an eventual, surprising release and joy in giving purpose to the pain.

Your pain is part of the living legacy of your family.
The choices you make with your pain can craft your family
narrative far beyond your days here on earth.

What do you choose as your Lasting Legacy? Making wise choices today and again tomorrow and the next day puts you on the path of a purposeful life. If you make mistakes, join the club. We all do, and that's okay. Just make the next best decision after that.

Journey to the Sunrise

Discover the steps it will take to rehabilitate neglected memories and relationships.

Realize that you will keep on stumbling over the bricks left over from your previous life unless you find a way to clean them up and put them to use.

Understand that if you take the broken bricks of your life, clean them, and use them to rebuild your own monument to hope, you can build something that could help others, as you also choose to honor your past.

Steps on the Path

- One of the ways to "clean the bricks" of dreams that have been bombed is to tell your story. In crafting your own lasting legacy, you will find telling your story is vital to transforming your trials into triumph. Even if you are just telling it for the sake of your children, write down, paint or otherwise express the stories as they come to you, both celebratory and soulful. There doesn't have to be an order to it.

- Your stories become part of your family's oral traditions and help to build a kind of narrative identity for your family. Whether you paint your story, write your story, or find some other way to share your story, there is an eventual, surprising release and joy in giving purpose to the pain.

Chapter 21:

Paying It Forward

O ne thing I noticed while on this grief journey is that when I helped others, my own load seemed lifted. Even when I just went to a support group and could share with another widow some nugget of hope, I walked away feeling happier, lighter.

"Improve Your Health by Helping Others" on the University of Texas MD Anderson Cancer Center website says,

> Sometimes, one of the best ways to promote your own health or to cope with a health problem is to forget yourself and concentrate on helping others...People who exercise often talk about feeling 'high' during or after a workout – a happy feeling of warmth, a sense of calmness, and a release of stress. These same feelings can also be felt by those who help others. This 'helper's high' is believed to be caused by the release of endorphins, the body's natural pain reducing chemicals. In addition to relieving pain, endorphins also produce good feelings.[56]

After knowing great grief, I found that what used to make me happy didn't work for me anymore. I was surprised that helping other widows and single moms now gave me joy. So, I simply followed my newfound source of bliss. I have to admit, I am not a naturally altruistic person, but that simple act of helping others made my heart bubble with joy, and I jumped in because I desperately needed a delightful heart.

Part of the transformative power of grief is an overhaul of your priorities. Loss radically shifts your perspective, and you reprioritize what is important and what is trivial in life. That shift of priorities has the real potential of adding depth and joy to your life.

Eventually, that transformation in my heart led to other changes in my life, such as starting the non-profit 180 Your Grief, Inc., under which our Team Lady 180 group functions currently to help support widows and their kiddos, as well as single moms and their kids. These groups provide fun, supportive Teams for widowed and single moms and their families to train for races as a form of grief recovery.

One of the "Gifts of Grief" is that it makes you sensitive to the needs of others, and if you start to ride that wave by responding to the needs of others, it can take you to amazing places and fill your heart with joy. This is the transformative power of grief.

Grief has the potential to shatter our dreams of safety, sensitize our hearts, and widen our perspective, so we can genuinely understand and help others. The amazing trade-off is that when we do so, our hearts are filled with incredible joy.

Michelle Menifee: widow one year
When I learned the love of my life, Edward "Eduardo" Menifee, had cancer, I was crippled with grief, heart-broken, depressed, and lost for words. *What will I do? How will I ever make it? How could this happen? What about longevity? What about our future plans?*

We had more places to visit, more lives to touch, more love to share, more lessons to teach. We were a team! It was difficult to imagine life without my "Eduardo."

Family members and friends were concerned. I was encouraged to seek traditional counseling. Encouraged to move forward. Encouraged to face the realities of life. I kindly declined.

One day, while searching online, I discovered "Team Lady 180," a non-traditional meet-up for widows. The statement, "Outdoor fun & health/wellness support for widows" struck my attention. Since linking up with Team Lady 180, I've opened myself up to the newness of life.

New friends. New beginnings. New acceptance. As I learned more about the organization and participated with the planned activities, I found myself increasing in strength, growing in grace, learning about new resources, socializing with others, and feeling better about life.

Truth be told, this is the sorority none of us made plans to join. Mishael's energy, drive, and love for others serves as an outlet for inner peace, a network of like-minded individuals, a bridge of hope, and a source of motivation, reminding sisters to press forward. I'm most grateful to God and Mishael for guiding me through one of the most difficult seasons of my life.

Today, I'm at peace with continuing the non-profit programs founded by my husband some forty plus years ago. Helping others is our living legacy. Initially, it was difficult returning to the prisons and community centers. One evening after conducting a class at Metro Transitional Center for Women, I dreaded leaving the center, knowing that I would no longer receive those calls from my husband asking, "How did it go?"

As I opened my car door, one of the residents approached me and said, "Ma'am, thank you for coming. Thank you for believing in us. I never met your husband, but his spirit was here tonight. You're supposed to be here. You filled us with so much hope. Your words made us feel important. Please come back."

I nodded my head and said, "I'll definitely be back."

As I sat in the car, the thought entered my mind: *God used the Angel Resident to speak to me in person*. This indeed encouraged me to press onward. From that day forward, I pledged that I would surround myself with the positive support needed: my family and friends, Team Lady 180, and others, to build upon the strong foundation established by my love, Edward Menifee.

I now live life with his spirit dwelling within me. I understand the true meaning of "soul mate." To the worship centers, I go. To the prisons, I go. To the community centers, I go. No, I'm never alone. Thank you, God and Team Lady 180, for the turnaround.

The Pay-It-Forward Widow

In those first weeks and months after Jason died, an unusual phenomenon took place. I call it the "Pay-It-Forward Widow." Widowed women of various ages came to my home to encourage me. I really appreciated their presence, and each one gave me a gift of insight that I still carry with me today.

The first was Mimi, the widowed mother of one of my dear girlfriends, Amy. Mimi was at my house the day I found out Jason had died, and she offered me these words of wisdom: "Don't run. Don't do anything or make any decisions from fear. Move forward from faith." This wise widow was right. I needed to pause before making big decisions while I was grieving. I needed to hold steady and let the pain of grief eventually lift so that I could recover, rebuild, and discover what inspired me after grief had done its transformative work.

I didn't need to run, I needed my own community. I needed other widows who had been on this journey longer than I had to encourage me. I needed to be inspired by women who understood my pain. I needed to see other widowed moms and solo moms living well, being strong. I needed it for my own survival and for the healthy survival of my children.

Once I had gained a healthier perspective, I knew it was time for me to accept the mantle of Pay-It-Forward Widow myself. Since I knew what it was like to hide behind a chair and cry, feeling alone and outcast with a Scarlet "W" on my chest, I became quick to reach out to other widows. I knew which platitudes were useless to say, and I knew what the wreckage would look like. So, I could wade in and help those who were grieving in practical ways. When I was able to give comfort to a new widow, it was like I was somehow reaching back in time and comforting myself in my own raw anguish.

Leveraging Your Pain into Your Purpose

Leveraging your loss to help others makes you into a very specialized leader, one who understands and empowers a specific area of pain. When I became a widow, I sought out other widows, specifically widows who were dealing with suicide, and were living healthy, inspired lives. I needed their positive example like I needed oxygen in my lungs. They gave me real hope. These women leveraged their loss as a laser-focused form of inspirational leadership that directly impacted my family.

When I started to visit other widows to offer support, something amazing happened in me. I can only describe it as a bubbling up of joy in my spirit. It was the most unexpected thing. As I shared my story to help others, I found a new source of delight. My spirit was being refreshed.

Making positive choices in the face of the death of my husband actually changed the purpose and the source of joy in our lives. Did

I set out to do that? No, it was a discovery, and it happened over the course of several years. Now, our discovery can help make your journey more efficient.

Helping others makes your load lighter and will even spark joy in your life.

As you continue to help others, your life may actually change for the better. Your kind of grief gives you an opportunity to become a specialized tool to help others in their loss. What if you take these same steps, Empower Your Ground Zero, Forge Your Team, Train Your Mind, Body, Spirit, Cross Your Finish Line, Live Your Legacy, and Unveil Your Triumph, and apply them to the loss of a marriage, loss of a loved one, life trauma, or even the loss of a job? I believe you would empower your journey to leverage your pain into a purposeful teaching tool.

While I would never have chosen this life, after eight years of being a widowed mom, I can say that the grief changed our family and actually made us more than we would have ever been without it. We are more compassionate to the loss of others, more understanding when people are drunk with the pain of loss, and more willing to seek out what is really important in life. We are experiencing more joy simply from helping others.

Grief completely changed the trajectory of our lives. I would have never chosen this life, but now that I am in it, it has changed me in important ways, and I don't know if I could have been changed any other way.

The Gift

A beautiful and brilliant friend asked me not long ago, "I think a lot about my aunt who passed away recently. I used to send her care packages with little presents, like the licorice she liked and books I thought she'd enjoy. I never realized how often I think about her from day to day. What am I supposed to do with all these impulses?"

Those desires are still there for a reason. Unless you find a way to turn these tiny reminders outward, they will become pinprick invitations to grief—not healthy grief, but self-indulgent sadness. Instead, use those stray thoughts and impulses towards the happiness they were originally meant to produce. They are your invitations to widen your circle. I suggested to my friend that she still put together care packages, but now send them to her son, another family member, an older neighbor, or a friend in need. You don't have to stop your loving acts. Let them grow.

Something similar happened to us with Jason's birthday, our wedding anniversary, and his Angel Anniversary (the day he went to heaven). For Jason's birthday, my girls and I started giving a surprise gift to a friend who had the same birthday. It was fun to put the present together and to know we had surprised someone. A few years later, I decided to start giving a gift to someone in-need on that day, and it was even more fun. Then in 2014, my girls kicked it up a notch and suggested we give presents to widowed families in-need. It was a modest enough project for Jason's birthday—collecting gift cards to give to families that we knew were struggling at Christmastime and the holidays.

Moms in my neighborhood thought it would be a sweet little project for my daughters and some neighborhood kids to do. Our neighborhood got involved and had a large yard sale. We decided to take the $600 we made at the yard sale and convert it into gift cards to give to widowed families with children. The kids from the neighborhood got together and made a short video to promote our idea. GiftCardsGivingHope. org was born. We posted the video on YouTube, and within days it was on the local NBC station. In the four weeks before the holidays, we collected $10,000 in gift cards and gift certificates for widowed families in-need!

This was an amazing way to inject joy into our lives during Christmas. As our neighborhood community and businesses donated gift cards and gift certificates, my kids and I were positively gleeful as we distributed them to widowed families for their holidays. I was surprised to again experience the childhood joy of Christmas when I saw how happy these families were to be able to buy food and presents during the holidays. Then, the ladies at Modern Widows Club caught the vision, and using the videos our neighborhood kids had made, were able to raise funds for their widowed families in-need also. This past holiday season, we did the same activity, now including our new single mom Team as well.

How can you take one step to celebrate your loved one in a ritual or activity? Can you do something to help someone else in the process? Can you give a surprise gift to someone, maybe even someone you don't know, during the holidays or on a birthday in honor of your loved one? Can you celebrate a special day that you shared with them by inviting others to share a new fun moment with you? These moments are invitations to grow, to expand your circle, and you never know the spark that will set off a firework in your life to help others.

Speak Strength over One Another

In 2014, I was on a girls' weekend near Boston, Massachusetts. A few of my high school friends and I flew to Boston to be with one of my high school besties, Michele Slobin. She is a graphic designer who created the cover for this book and our leadership guide. I brought my daughters as part of our summer vacation. What happened there was pure magic.

Once we settled in and started talking, it was like each woman was able to see the strengths of our seventeen-year-old selves and remind one another of our innocence and dreams in our present forty-six-year-old selves. We were wiser, savvier, and we had all been to the rodeo a few times. Now, as women, we could remind one another of who we were at our core. We could re-envision dreams we had dreamt when we were younger, honor the journey we had been on, support one another in our struggles, listen to our new dreams, and inspire one another to press onward.

Once, while we were driving together to explore Boston, Michele said to our Team of ladies, "I need you girls to tell me something good about myself."

What a beautifully vulnerable and powerful request. We all took turns telling Michele what she meant to each of us, what we loved about her as a girl in high school, and now as a woman, and the strengths that we saw in her then and now. Then the group focused on each woman in the car. Taking turns to build one another up.

Then those women focused their light on both of my daughters, then ages seven and ten, telling Arie and Sophia the strength, beauty, and talent that they saw in them and the promise that their strength held for them. I could see my children's faces shine. I could see each woman's soul being fed. We all went onward that night as more empowered women.

That is also my hope and prayer for the Teams that this book may inspire. Maybe you haven't known one another since you were thirteen years old. That's okay. The point is to build an authentic, inspirational community that helps all of the members achieve their goals.

Yes, exercise. Yes, train your whole selves, but most of all,
listen, learn, dream, and support one another.
That is the secret sauce.
That's how you help others, and, in doing so,
bring triumph and transformation to your lives.

Grief Never ends...but it changes. It's a passage,
not a place to stay. Grief is not a sign of weakness, nor
a lack of faith. It is the price of love.–**Author Unknown**

Journey to the Sunrise

Discover the moment you choose to honor the beauty of your past and enjoy the present as well. What does that look like?

Realize that you can leverage your loss to help others. Can you volunteer for a local charity? Can you help a neighbor or friend?

Understand that grief will completely change the trajectory of your life. Instead of focusing on the question of "Why did this happen?" ask yourself, "What will I do with the life I have now?"

Steps on the Path

- When I helped others, my own load seemed lifted. Even when I just went to a support group and could share with another widow some nugget of hope, I walked away feeling happier, lighter.
- Grief has the potential to shatter your dreams of safety, sensitize your hearts, and widen your perspective, so you can genuinely understand and help others. The amazing trade-off is that when you do so, your heart will be filled with incredible joy.
- Pray about becoming who you are meant to be.
- Your eventual vibrant healing is a direct result of three things: prayer, support, and wise choices.
- How can you leverage your loss to help others and speak hope to those on your Team?

Chapter 22:

Play On

In the twilight between sleep and wakefulness, I heard the most beautiful acoustical guitar music the morning of April 2, 2007. I would later learn that Jason had already died before dawn. I remember lingering in that morning twilight for as long as I could because the music was so relaxing, so natural, and such a lovely, refreshing way to wake up. I was sleeping with Arie and she awoke in a great mood, too. The house was filled with joy. It felt like Jason was there.

We used to have a quirky family game. Arie would run around the kitchen counter and we would try to peg her with an inflatable beach ball. Jason was a sure shot, and it was hilarious. It felt so much like he was there that morning that Arie and I played that game together, and we laughed and laughed.

I had forgotten that memory until much later, when, in my eighth year of his Angel Anniversary, after several days of intense feelings, I awoke refreshed and at peace. Sometimes, I get tangled in the memories of the details and the recognition of the jagged hole his absence has left, and I forget that even in that terrible time, there was also beauty.

My friend, Steve, in Costa Rica once said something to me that forever helped reframe my perspective on loss. He and his wife, Chris, were our neighbors when we lived in Costa Rica. They knew us well before and after Arie was born. When I went back to Costa Rica on the third anniversary of Jason's passing, Steve and I sat down one morning to talk.

Shaded by palm trees and magenta bougainvillea flowers, with our feet dangling in his neighborhood pool, Steve turned to me and said something like, "Mishael, I'm not so sure that death is as bad as we think it is. There are a few things in life that look really intense, but something beautiful is also happening. If you look at birth, it's messy and painful. It looks like the mother is almost dying, but actually a baby is being born. Same with making love. If you were to look at it for the first time as an objective observer, it can look intense and even painful, but we know something beautiful is also happening, maybe even a baby is being made. I think that possibly it's the same with death. It looks awful, it feels awful, but I believe that there must be something beautiful happening there, too. A birth back into heaven."

I've also come to believe that even the grief, though the most intense pain I've ever known, is doing something beautiful in us, too. It is transforming us into a deeper, kinder, more sensitive and useful tool to help others in their loss, even though the price we pay for that transformation is inexplicably high.

The intensity of grief can make a person either bitter or better. The feeling is so painful that I have come to call it a "fire of the soul." Sometimes it's a raging inferno, burning us from the inside out. My first reaction is to run hard from it, but I've discovered that it may be working to burn away whatever is blocking the release of the light that is meant to shine through us.

I've mused for years over what Steve said. His words helped unchain my pain that day. Maybe that's what the guitar music was about that morning on April 2. Something terrible had happened, but something beautiful, too. Jason was already in a beautiful space, and maybe God was giving us a moment of peace and joy before the details and overwhelming feelings of loss came crashing in. The resulting excruciating journey of recovery for my children and myself could not be avoided. So I say again, even though my family has worked hard to heal well, for the health of yourself and your family, always choose life, even in the most crushing of circumstances.

In 1873, Horatio Spafford learned that four of his daughters had died in a shipwreck in the middle of the Atlantic. His heart was cracked so wide open by grief that he went on to write the song, "It Is Well with My Soul," which still comforts hearts today, almost a hundred and fifty years later. He and his family later created a foundation, the Spafford Children's Center, which today continues to help 30,000 children annually.

**That's the transformative power of grief.
It shatters our safe lives and opens our perspective to a higher purpose. This makes me ask the question over and over again, Out of this destruction, what is being created?**

Without knowing the history behind the creation of this classic hymn, only that I loved it growing up, Jason and I had the song "It Is Well with My Soul" played at our wedding. That was the guitar music I heard on that April morning.

Also at our wedding, my high school friend, Joe, read from 1 Corinthians 13. The last verse was, "These three things last, Faith, Hope and Love. But the greatest of these is Love." This is the stuff of eternity. The love gently serenades our soul. The love overcomes the details, overcomes the pain, and waits to joyfully greet us when we cross our own finish line of this life's journey and step with victory into eternity.

I'm not saying this to discount the pain of loss or to condone self-destructive choices. Only to report that there was beautiful guitar music in the twilight of that morning on April 2, 2007. I choose the beauty, over and over again, because that's where he is now.

Let the music play on.

Journey to the Sunrise

Discover that grief isn't something to be raced through once you're in it, because grief has the potential to be powerfully transformative. **Realize** that, if you let it, grief can be the path to your purpose. **Understand** that you are not defined by what happens to you. You are defined by your choices within your circumstances.

Steps on the Path

- When we are making positive choices in the face of difficulty, it seems that those choices then choose us back in some kind of universal dance with our soul.
- The transformative power of grief is that it shatters our safe lives and opens our perspective to a higher purpose.
- Out of this destruction, what is being created in your life?

Speak Life: Live Your Legacy
(Please Say Out Loud)

The Okavango Basin has filled to overflowing and I am being refreshed. Now the fresh waters spill their borders and begin to fill the dry, ancient riverbeds. The water is streaming into the desert, rising with volume, heading to pools and watering holes to revive life all around it. Like those refreshing waters, my heart overflows with streams of kindness that surge forward to help and refresh others in their loss. I will look for these opportunities of service, as they will become a spring of life within me. This is part of my Living Legacy. The sun is rising, and the landscape of my life is transforming right before my eyes.

Step 8:

Unveil Your Triumph

What the caterpillar calls the end of the world the master calls a butterfly.
- Richard Bach

For your husband is your Maker, Whose name is the Lord of hosts; and your
Redeemer is the Holy One of Israel, Who is called the God of all the earth.
(Isaiah 54:5 NASB)

Flood of Love

Every year for the last four years, my daughters and I have taken a one-hundred-and-seventy-year trip back in time. This year was the 178th anniversary of the Marietta Camp Meeting. It stems from a practice that started when the founding families of Marietta, Georgia, would gather together for a week of spiritual revival meetings after their summer harvest. Eventually, it became an annual tradition, so they built wooden cabins around a large wooden pole-barn structure and made it permanent.

I stumbled onto this tradition quite by accident, when I saw a road-side advertisement for their Vacation Bible School one year. My girls attended this VBS in an antique one-room schoolhouse. While they were in class, I took the opportunity to attend their morning revival meeting for adults. It had become my time to purposefully be still for a week in the summer, and take time to pray about what the school year will hold before the bustle of the academic year began.

I had attended the revival meetings for two days and was sitting on a wooden bench during the service when a woman approached me.

323

"Is this seat taken?" she asked.

"Oh, no. Please, join me," I whispered.

I smiled as she sat down next to me. The morning revival meetings were mostly attended by a conservative, senior audience—median age around seventy—because most of the younger people were at work. Moreover, those attending were members of the families "camping" for the week. So, I stuck out a little in my colorful skirts and cowboy boots. Folks were used to this, though, and always made me feel welcome.

"My name is Mishael. What's yours?" I asked the young woman now sitting next to me.

"Patrice. Nice to meet you," she replied in a hoarse whisper.

We shared a hymnal and sang songs together that were over a hundred years old. She was a tawny, highly fit African American woman with pink streaks in her long hair. Her long, well-manicured nails had some kind of intricate pattern painted on them, and her hipster outfit looked like it came from the trendy, mid-town area of Lil' Five Points. I was curious to learn more about Patrice.

After the organ played and the service ended, I turned to Patrice and asked, "So, how did you find out about the camp meeting?"

I did not expect her response. She was an effervescent woman, full of joy and laughter.

Speaking with a Southern drawl, she answered, "Well, I was in the grocery store and I felt the Spirit telling me to talk to this man about Jesus. So I introduced myself and asked him if he knew Jesus. He did, and he asked me if I knew about this camp meeting and said I should go. I thought that was where the Spirit wanted me to go, so I got in my car and came here. When I started to walk down the aisle and saw the crowd, I said in my heart, 'Oh noooo, Lord, You want me to come here?' I wanted to turn back to my car and go. But I didn't. You know why? Because when God asks us to do something, it's timely. If we don't do it when the Spirit leads us, we might miss what He has for us, *because it's timely*. One action depends on another, and if we respond ten hours later, that opportunity might not be there anymore."

Talking to Patrice was like looking at the sun, she was so joyful and bright. I sat stunned, smiling, taking it all in. I was reminded of "Bud," the man I met at the mall who told me about "speaking to the bones" of our lives, like Ezekiel did. His timely words of hope were given to me because he obeyed God and left his mechanic's shop to go to the mall, not knowing whom he would meet, but ready to be used by God all those years ago. It was happening again.

"Patrice, I think your word is for me," I finally said.

"Well, Hallelujah! That's great! I'm so glad. Don't be afraid to move when the Spirit leads," she encouraged me.

We talked for a while longer and then went our separate ways.

I had thought that Patrice was just chatting with me, but at this point I recognized the message she was delivering:

Don't be afraid to move when the Spirit leads.
Because when God asks us to do something, it's timely.

Soon after I talked to Patrice—before I could plunge back into the minutia of my work—God intercepted me with the reason. When I got home, I noticed that a neighbor had called me. When I called her back, she said, "Mishael, my husband and I feel strongly that we are to sponsor you on a spiritual retreat. It will be for three days. You would have to be ready to go in forty-eight hours."

I promise, I am not making this up. I couldn't believe it.

I replied, "That is so kind of you to offer, but I cannot accept such a big gift. I have to be responsible and work on my book (*this book*) and clean my house. I don't have time to get all the food together for my father and kids so that I can leave in two days. I really appreciate your offer, though. That is most kind." After saying goodbye, we hung up.

My neighbor called me back. "Mishael, my husband and I really feel you need to go on this retreat. We will provide food for your girls and father. I will watch your daughters the whole time you are gone."

This was totally out of the blue. My kind neighbors had never suggested anything like this before in the seven years that I've lived near them. Besides, it was the last week of summer, and my neighbor was a teacher. She was willing to give up her last weekend of summer before her work started in order to send me on this retreat. I was being asked by persistently generous neighbors to abandon my pressing responsibilities, ignore my deadlines, and take a holy adventure.

I asked my girls what they thought. Arie, ever the supportive Teammate, quickly hijacked my cell phone and texted my neighbor that I would go. It was settled.

I had no idea what to expect, and my neighbors asked me to trust them.

"Let the retreat be a surprise," they encouraged me.

So I did. It was a women's retreat in the North Georgia Mountains. I didn't know anyone.

That weekend was a time that God romanced my soul in so many details that I cannot write them all out here. I was told that every retreat has a different theme. This weekend, the theme was "Traveling with God," and the woman who was leading it was married to a Jewish man, so the whole weekend honored the Jewish-ness of Jesus, or Yeshua, which is the name His original disciples would have called him.

The weekend wasn't about achieving or doing or being good enough. It was simply about God romancing our souls. It was about understanding grace and God's unconditional love for us. It was about being wholly accepted, wanted, and cherished by a Heavenly Father and Heavenly Husband.

At one point, in one of the chapel services, rose petals were spread all over the floor. It was early morning, and the small one-room chapel was lit only by a multitude of candles. We sang with no instruments, and the music felt like a colorful fire to me. I could feel the love of God seeping into my soul. I closed my eyes and remembered the rose petals that had lined the aisle as I walked to my husband on our wedding day. I remembered the scattered rose petals that held raindrops at his second memorial service. Now there were rose petals here, as I felt deeply refreshed by God. *Timely indeed.*

Later on that weekend, we were given nails that had once been used to secure railroad ties. They were to be reminders of the nails that were driven in Jesus' hands and feet, the sacrifice of love that was made so that we could forever be connected with God. That railroad nail was identical to the nails that I still have from the blacksmith at Stone Mountain Park. I thought, *His past sacrifice enables the present transformation.* That is how God had made "all things new" through the fire of grief, the life and joy that is now possible because of the sacrifice made then on the cross.

At the end of the weekend, we were given a copy of a Ketubah, which is a Jewish wedding contract. It is considered an integral part of a traditional Jewish marriage, and, among other things, outlines the rights and responsibilities of the groom in relation to the bride. This contract was meant to remind us that Jesus wants to be our Heavenly Husband. I felt my eyes well with tears. So many details resonated with me. The rose petals, the railroad nail, and the Ketubah were all signs that were personal to my journey to show me that God knew me, understood, and was reaching out to me as I simply made time for Him and simply asked Him to come close to me.

If God knows me and cares for me, then I don't have to be constantly vigilant against unknown danger. I can relax knowing that because He loves me, as I make wise choices and seek Him, He will direct my life. It might not look like the life I had planned, but the peace of being connected with God far outweighs the comfort of having predictable plans.

At the end of the retreat, each of us was asked to give a brief talk to a room full of people about what the retreat meant to us. As I stood at the podium, I noticed that the neighbors who had sponsored me on this retreat were sitting in the audience.

"There is a desert in the Okavango basin, in South Africa," I began, "and every year, the elephants, led by a wise matriarch, start on a journey into the heart of the desert, looking for water. The Grandmother elephant knows the ancient paths through the parched land. As they travel, the climate gets hotter. What little grasses that are left smolder in the desert sun. Yet they press on, deeper into the heart of the desert toward the Okavango basin, because they know the floodwaters are coming. Buffalo and zebra herds follow the elephant families, instinctually knowing that the elephants will lead them to life-giving water.

"Miraculously, the parched elephants arrive as the floodwaters overflow the basin, which overflow into streams, which travel to fill pools, until eventually the pools and streams overflow, and four thousand square miles are flooded with life-giving water. In a matter of days, the desert transforms into lush grassland, teeming with life. The elephants splash together, playing in the pools that were once a barren wasteland. The gazelles leap with joy, the zebras chase one another, kicking up water as they run.

"This time at this retreat, knowing how much God loves me, letting that love flood my heart—this was the fountainhead of the flood that has refreshed my soul and transformed the landscape of my life."

This wondrous retreat occurred just as I was finishing writing this book. I have before recommended journaling, or "painting yourself

327

well," or building a garden, or stitching a pillow, as a way of working through the grief journey. I know when I look at the Kitten Pillow that my grandmother made for me that arthritis plagued her with every stitch. I promised in the Introduction that I would unearth my messy stories, no matter how painful, because the naked truth was necessary. As I continued writing these stories, I resurrected ancient anxieties, which made me again feel vulnerable, alone, exposed, almost unscabbed. I sometimes felt my widowhood weighing heavily upon me, less a badge of courage than a brand of solitude and damage.

Around these feelings I had hope, however, because I knew how to ask for help and how to turn towards health. God heard me, as He always does, and answered at this retreat with refreshment for my spirit. He told my story back to me, taking possession of my most important images—the railroad spike, the rose petals, the Spirit-driven stranger—and bathing them with His love, and returning them to me as a wedding gift.

> *The LORD will guide you always; he will satisfy*
> *your needs in a sun-scorched land and will strengthen*
> *your frame. You will be like a well-watered garden, like*
> *a spring whose waters never fail.* (Isaiah 58:11).

Our adventure doesn't end here. This is only the beginning, the beginning of a new day in a refreshed land, a land teeming with life.

Chapter 23:
Woman of Valor

An excellent wife, who can find? For her worth is far above jewels.
(Proverbs 31:10 NASB)

The description of the perfect woman in Proverbs 31 used to frustrate me. The Proverbs woman was the perfect wife. I wondered, "How can I ever measure up to this married superwoman? Does my marital status determine my worth?" But then I began to look at her more closely. In various translations of the Bible, the Proverbs woman is referred to as a "perfect wife," an "excellent wife," a "truly good wife," a "capable wife," and a "competent wife"—and the apparent demotions in praise for her wifely abilities among the versions are somewhat dispiriting all by themselves. But other versions speak only of an "excellent woman," a "virtuous woman." In the Orthodox Jewish Bible, this perfect female is called *aishet chayil*, a "woman of valor."[57]

What does valor mean? "Great courage in the face of danger, especially in battle. The medals are awarded for acts of valor. Synonyms are: bravery, courage, pluck, nerve, daring, fearlessness, audacity, boldness, dauntlessness, stout-heartedness, heroism, backbone, spirit, (informal) guts, true grit, spunk, moxie"; "Strength of mind or spirit that enables a person to encounter danger with firmness: personal bravery."[58]

Who is a "woman of valor"? She need not be a wife. In fact, according to Chaviva Gordon-Bennett, a Judaism expert, the one woman in the Bible who is specifically called *aishet chayil*—the one woman who fulfills all the many qualities that make for the perfect, excellent, virtuous, competent woman—was a widow.[59] According to Gordon-Bennett, "One reference to a woman of valor appears in the Book of Ruth, which tells the story of the convert Ruth and her journey with her mother-in-law Naomi and marriage to Boaz. When Boaz refers to Ruth as an *aishet chayil*, it makes her the only woman in all the books of the Bible to be referred to as such."

Even more, Ruth earns the title of "woman of valor" because she insists on supporting her mother-in-law, Naomi. Without Ruth, Naomi's story is tragic. Naomi has been called a female version of Job because of the trials she undergoes: she moves with her husband and sons away from their famine-stricken home. Then, her husband dies, leaving her a widow, and dependent on her two sons. Her sons marry, but then they also die. Naomi now has no means to support herself, and no protectors—she is too old to have more sons, and too old for a new husband (she says this). So she sends her daughters-in-law back to their own families, because they at least are young enough to remarry. But Ruth refuses to abandon her mother-in-law. She vows to stay with Naomi, saying, "whither thou goest, I will go; and where thou lodgest, I will lodge: thy people shall be my people, and thy God my God: 17 Where thou diest, will I die, and there will I be buried" (Ruth 1:16-17 KJV). Ruth's biblical vow to be part of Naomi's Team has endured through the ages as a beautiful love pledge, often used in wedding ceremonies today.

Ruth, the woman of valor, is a widow without a job or a place to live, supporting her mother-in-law, another widow in need. Eventually, Ruth marries Boaz and gives birth to Obed, bringing honor to Naomi also. Obed later becomes the grandfather of King David, and great-grandfather to the eminently wise King Solomon.

Ruth is an example for all those determined to journey through grief with faith and perseverance, and, in so doing, transform their tragedy into triumph.

Gordon-Bennett tells us that Ruth is the original Proverbs 31 woman. In fact, the book of Proverbs is believed to have been written by Ruth's great, great grandson, King Solomon. I think it's inspiring to view Ruth as that proverbial "empowered" woman. We know that she knew grief, poverty, and loss, but she persevered, refused to stop following God, and lent her strength to another suffering widow. We also know that the strength she showed from the beginning and the wisdom she imparted to her progeny must have been drawn, in part, from her early sufferings.

This makes the widow Ruth the original Woman of Valor. As such, she is considered the Greatest, Wisest Matriarchal Leader on the journey through the desert of grief into the flood lands of transformation and triumph.

Here is a traditional Jewish translation of Proverbs 31:10-31
Eshet Chayil–A Woman of Valor
A woman of valor who can find? She is far more precious than jewels. The heart of her husband trusts in her, and he will have no lack of gain.
She does him good, and not harm, all the days of her life.
She seeks wool and flax, and works with willing hands.
She is like the ships of the merchant; she brings her food from afar.
She rises while it is yet night and provides food for her household and portions for her maidens. She considers a field and buys it; with the fruit of her hands she plants a vineyard.
She dresses herself with strength and makes her arms strong.
She perceives that her merchandise is profitable. Her lamp does not go out at night.
She puts her hands to the distaff, and her hands hold the spindle.
She opens her hand to the poor and reaches out her hands to the needy.
She is not afraid of snow for her household, for all her household are clothed in scarlet. She makes bed coverings for herself; her clothing is fine linen and purple.
Her husband is known in the gates when he sits among the elders of the land.
She makes linen garments and sells them; she delivers sashes to the merchant. Strength and dignity are her clothing, and she laughs at the time to come.
She opens her mouth with wisdom, and the teaching of kindness is on her tongue.
She looks well to the ways of her household and does not eat the bread of idleness.

*Her children rise up and call her blessed; her husband also, and
he praises her:*
"Many women have done excellently, but you surpass them all."
*Charm is deceitful, and beauty is vain, but a woman who fears the
LORD is to be praised. Give her of the fruit of her hands, and let
her works praise her in the gates.*[60]

You Are a Woman of Valor

It is a long journey, even an adventure, to the fountainhead of the
flood lands. I hope that as you have taken wise steps on your journey,
you feel your soul refreshed and transformed. Then, the streams have
indeed invaded the desert, changing the arid plains into a lush paradise.

This *180 Your Life* journey is meant to be transformative, in mind,
body, and spirit. Part of your "Unveiling" is realizing who you are now.

You are not just a survivor, but a warrior, a Woman of Valor

Your pain gives you the power and the opportunity to reshape your
life with a clearer purpose. It has been said that grief unveils your true
self. I hope that through this journey, your heart has changed and is
better able to handle life's challenges. When you have done the hard
work, committed to the quest, braved the fires of pain, pushed through
the drought of the soul, you emerge empowered, strengthened, and
wiser. You are becoming a leader and a warrior of the spirit, trained to
defend, mentor, and protect those who are still hurting.

This is my prayer of valor for you as you forge ahead into the next
chapters of your life. May you be clothed with dignity and strength, and
laugh without fear of the future. May you work industriously, opening
your hands to the poor and putting your time and efforts to promote
honor and kindness over the fleeting activity of charm and vanity. May
grief so transform you that your true self is revealed, your very best
self. May this legacy of strength cause your children to rise up and
call you blessed.

May you move forward on this journey, crafting the next chapters
of your life, grounded in peace and valor. May you use your strength,
forged in the fire of grief, to help those on your path, standing shoulder
to shoulder with your Team, moving forward as an army of hope.

Journey to the Sunrise

Discover what being a woman of valor means to you.
Realize that you are not just a survivor, but a warrior.
Understand that you can move forward on this journey, crafting the next chapters of your life, grounded in peace and valor.

Steps on the Path

It has been said that grief unveils your true self. I hope that through this journey your heart has changed and is better able to handle life's challenges. You have done the hard work, committed to the quest, braved the fires of pain, pushed through the drought of the soul, and have emerged empowered, strengthened, and wiser. You are now a leader and a warrior of the spirit, trained to defend, mentor, and protect those who are still hurting.

Speak Life: Unveil Your Triumph Woman of Valor
(Please Say Out Loud)

My heart has changed and is better able to handle life's challenges. I am committed to the quest of a renewed life. I will leverage my loss to help lead others, knowing I am a warrior of the spirit, trained to defend, mentor, and protect those who are still hurting. I will be clothed with dignity and strength. I will laugh without fear of the future. I will work industriously, opening my hands to the poor, and promote honor and kindness over the fleeting activity of charm and vanity. May this legacy of strength cause those I love, mentor, and influence to rise up and call me blessed .

Certificate of Completion

_____

this _____ day of _____ in the year _____

has completed the
180 Your Life Journey to Renewal
and is hereby confirmed to be a

Woman of Valor

A Woman of Valor who can find? For her price is far above rubies.

~Proverbs 31:10

Chapter 24:
The Dawn Rising Within You

Is this not the fast which I choose,
To loosen the bonds of wickedness,
To undo the bands of the yoke,
And to let the oppressed go free
And break every yoke?
7 "Is it not to divide your bread with the hungry
And bring the homeless poor into the house;
When you see the naked, to cover him;
And not to hide yourself from your own flesh?
8 "Then your light will break out like the dawn,
And your recovery will speedily spring forth;
And your righteousness will go before you;
The glory of the Lord will be your rear guard.
9 "Then you will call, and the Lord will answer;
You will cry, and He will say, 'Here I am.'
If you remove the yoke from your midst,
The pointing of the finger and speaking wickedness,
10 And if you give yourself to the hungry
And satisfy the desire of the afflicted,
Then your light will rise in darkness
And your gloom will become like midday.
11 "And the Lord will continually guide you,
And satisfy your desire in scorched places,
And give strength to your bones;
And you will be like a watered garden,

And like a spring of water whose waters do not fail.
12 "Those from among you will rebuild the ancient ruins;
You will raise up the age-old foundations;
And you will be called the repairer of the breach,
The restorer of the streets in which to dwell.
(Isaiah 58:6-12 NASB)

I can only express it in these terms: not only do you arrive at the dawn of a new day, the rising of the sun also happens within you, shining ever brighter in your life as you become your best version of the person God created you to be. You are beloved and fit into a Master Plan.

My prayer for you is that, through your own journey, you have transformed from within, no longer wandering in the night of the soul, but rather radiating like the rising sun. My prayer is that, in time, hope shines *through* you, by your life's example, as an ever-brightening dawn of a new day. Let your goal be a life that has been transformed by grief, from pain to purpose, from tragedy to triumph.

My prayer for you is that at the appointed time, the streams of renewal will fill their borders, the pools and watering holes bulge to overflowing, and yet the floodwaters of renewal will continue to pour in. My hope is that you are refreshed and renewed, and that your new growth yields the jeweled fruits of love, patience, perseverance, forgiveness, joy, kindness, generosity, and peace. May these super-fruits nourish and empower your spirit as you have reclaimed your life, cleared your ground, pressed into grief and faith, spoken to your bones, nourished your body, and started the Divine Conversation. I pray that this process has helped you find the source of Life-Giving Water.

Reader, you have braved the cold night of the soul, forged your Team, unwrapped the python of constriction, and strengthened and disciplined your body. Though parched, you pressed into the desert, determined to cross your finish line, purposed to rebuild and refresh others, and now you emerge triumphant.

The hot fires of grief have *transformed* you into a warrior,
nay, a *Band of Warriors*.

I know that this journey doesn't end here, but my prayer is that you move forward in supportive community. Keep working the steps, mentoring newcomers, and moving forward together. There is an African Proverb often quoted by Jeff Shinabarger, the founder of Plywood People, a non-profit in Atlanta leading a community of start-ups doing good:

"We go faster alone but farther together."

My prayer is that you are empowered on this journey and, at your own pace, help one another to face what lies ahead. Cheer and inspire one another. My heart is proud of your journey, proud to see you stand strong, warrior sisters, ready for your adventure.

Each person heals at her own pace. I did not feel fully recovered in a year's time after my major loss. That's okay. I discovered these steps and committed to working them. I still do. Grief, like the overflowing Okavango, is cyclical. There will be times of refreshment and times that feel dry. Now, I know what to do. I have a plan and a community. Whatever ground of peace I have claimed has been fought for, but there are treasures to be found in the effort, for the process of searching for hope has changed me. Although it was incredibly uncomfortable at the time, I now find it more interesting than immediate relief would have been. I have discovered that grief isn't something to be raced through once you are in it, because grief has the potential to be powerfully transformative. If you let it, grief can be the path to your purpose.

I've said before that I am especially moved by object lessons. I believe we should celebrate our victories, and this is a celebration of the sunrise, the Unveiling of Your Triumph. I have presented this process as a year-long journey—even though it took me far longer to reach the place of peace and refreshment—and I structured the book in terms of twenty-four chapters, two per month, in accordance with the Mourner's Kaddish, which spans the year following the death of a loved one, and culminates in an Unveiling ceremony for the loved one's headstone. The twelfth month marks the end of ritual mourning, which is also a year of ritual praise, and the Unveiling becomes a celebration. I encourage you also to mark your triumph with an actual ceremony. If you have embarked on this journey with a friend or in a group, you might share a meal together, and afterwards start the ceremony. You can fashion your own elements, or refer to my suggestions in the Leadership Guide at 180YourLife.com. I also provide "Woman of Valor" Certificates and other resources available as a free download to honor you and the members of your Team.

I have learned that we are not defined by what happens to us. Instead, we are defined by our choices within our circumstances. When we are making positive choices in the face of difficulty, those choices then choose us back in some kind of universal dance with our soul.

My own dawning feels very different as I approach year nine than it did even in years five, six, seven, and eight. The point isn't an arrival; it's continual renewal. I think that happens best in community. Our lives aren't comprised of only one day, but of a series of sunrises and sunsets, all strung together in the timeline of our lives.

Our New Normal

What does the dawn of a new day look like? It's finding beauty in your new normal and in the life you have been given today. It's peace in your heart. On the eve of my fourteenth wedding anniversary, my daughters and I were having a slumber party in my bedroom. I remember, years ago, anticipating my wedding day the night before with excitement. I was to marry my best friend, Jason. It happened to snow the next day. It was a bright, crisp winter's day that could only be made more perfect by gently falling snow. It was the stuff of magical, soft-edged memories.

So was this day. My daughters and I had just finished eating popcorn, snuggling in my bed, while watching an animated movie together. I marveled now at Sophia's belly laugh when it filled the room, or when she danced with such conviction and flair. Or how Arie's long hair framed her face like golden fire in the sunshine when she sailed high on the playground swings.

We call December 17 our "Family Anniversary." It's the day our family started, and that is indeed something to celebrate. When Jason and I married, we committed to let God use our marriage for His purposes. We saw marriage as a calling, a loving vocation. Our marriage mission statement was simply, "To Love Unconditionally, Laugh Often, and Leave a Lasting Legacy."

That mission helped focus our day-to-day decisions, and it still guides me. Looking back, I have to say that life as a widowed mom is not what I expected. Still, knowing the gifts I have now, I am so thankful that Jason and I started our family.

Lying in my bed that night, with peacefully sleeping children beside me, I was grateful for a sense of joy. I can attest that life can be so bitterly harsh and still so beautiful. Although I would not have chosen single parenthood, since I was here, I could appreciate that I got a front row seat to watch how truly amazing, giving, and loving friends and family could be. I could see my daughters blossom, raised in a beautiful community of generous friends who had become our supportive family.

I got to taste the faithfulness of God, even though I certainly railed at Him for no short amount of time. Quietly, and sometimes not so quietly, I wondered if God was practical and powerful enough to remove the pain. That pain did not quickly subside.

A friend once said to me, "Like a baseball player, you always swing for the fences."

The pain was so intense, so unrelenting for a while, that I swung hard in the opposite direction, coloring with bold strokes. I resolved not to participate in those dark days, when memory and loss and grief blocked out all possibilities of joy. Instead, I anticipated those times, especially anniversaries relating to loss, and planned for an "Opposite Day." I was determined to love life again and to teach my daughters to celebrate life regardless of circumstances. That habit stuck, and now it's the mode of our family. Life is something to be enjoyed, savored, and "adventurized." My determination to find hope and adventure looked pretty colorful at times.

Today, I don't have to try hard to make a great day out of a landmine of memories. It's already beautiful. I'm relaxed in my home, quietly at peace, and simply content with my children, who are the great living gift of my marriage. I will always be grateful to Jason for the time we had together, the love we shared, and the beautiful gifts of our daughters.

I will always remember our wedding day, whose simple decor was love and laughter. I remember Jason bending at the waist, overcome with tears as I walked down the aisle on my father's arm. By the time I met him at the preacher's feet, there wasn't a dry eye in the house because the room was so filled with love. I am grateful for the time I had then and the time and people I am gifted with now. The heart is big enough to love both. Both are vibrantly beautiful.

Life wasn't perfect then, and it isn't today. We weren't the perfect couple. We aren't the perfect family. Life is messy, but it's still incredibly beautiful. It's still deeply loving. It's still a grand adventure. For this and so much more, I celebrate our Family's Anniversary.

We will have a good day today, not because I'm swinging hard for the fences to find joy, but because I'm peacefully savoring the gifts I have already been given.

I feel such gratitude for the support of friends and family that helped us get to this wonderfully normal, lovely space. It is my quiet triumph and a deliciously happy moment. Look for those moments in your life. They are the gifts of your new normal starting to bud and flower in your garden of grief.

Bringing the Flowers Forward

Gardening took hold of me when I fell in love with Jason. To harness this intense attraction before I had even told him I liked him, I started to dig large holes in my yard. It was a great way to get my energy out. Having these holes in the yard begged for plants, and that's when my gardening phase was born. After we began dating and eventually married, my gardening bug didn't go away. Together, Jason and I created a beautiful landscape that was like a well-manicured mini-park.

My daughters and I eventually moved to a different neighborhood after Jason passed, where we began another garden filled with our favorite flowers and fruit trees. We could wander among the vegetation we had planted and inhale the sweet scent of a purple plum, warm with sunshine, or sample the sweet-tart bite of a ripe blackberry. Then, one Christmas season not long ago, I called the current owner of our old townhouse where Jason and I had created our first garden together. We had planted a great many irises, and I asked the current owner if he minded letting me dig up a few to bring into my current garden, which my daughters and I were cultivating. He graciously offered to let me dig up *all* my irises and *all* the flowers Jason and I had planted. As a generous bachelor, he was glad to simplify the garden Jason and I had left behind.

It took several days, but I mined for those irises and unearthed about 500 of them and planted them in our current yard. I learned a wonderful lesson from that exercise. Our life can be like a garden, and we can let the beauty of the past *coexist* in healthy ways with the beauty of the present.

Another lesson of gardening, which I relearn every year, is that vast amounts of work do not necessarily yield immediate results. The wonderful growth may only manifest much later, sometimes in surprising ways. The lives of those seeds and tubers under the ground are undergoing their own change, and like all things alive, what they make of their surroundings—soil, water, fertilizer, sunlight, neighboring plants, and animals—can be beautiful and unexpected.

Grief, and our growth through grief, can do the same. Every year on the day that Jason died, April 2, my family and I celebrate his "Angel Anniversary." We celebrate Jason's life and mark the changes that our lives have undergone throughout the previous year. On the first anniversary, we joyfully released balloons over children laughing at a playground. On the second, we gathered friends and family for the second memorial service with all of Jason's favorite foods and music. On the third, my girls and I took a trip to Costa Rica and re-layered memories of an earlier time, of when Jason and I had vacationed and even lived there with my oldest daughter. For the fourth, my girls were old enough to appreciate Disney World, so we sampled the Happiest Place on Earth.

On the fifth anniversary, we weren't able to plan an elaborate celebration because I was still recovering from walking pneumonia. I enjoyed a full night's sleep, and I awoke on his Angel Anniversary feeling refreshed. As I walked outside to inhale the fresh air, to watch the new life of spring budding and the dogwood petals gliding to the ground, I found my gift from God to remind me of Jason.

An iris was blooming, gently bobbing in the spring breeze. The first of the five hundred irises we had brought forward from our old house, honoring our earlier life. It was waving at me, sassy in the spring sunshine. I could sense the joy in its timely appearance, as if the iris were laughing and twirling at its own beauty, enjoying the secret it was sharing with God and me.

I thought of the joy felt by the desert when the floodwaters finally come, when God makes streams in the wasteland: "The desert and the parched land will be glad; the wilderness will rejoice and blossom. Like the crocus it will burst into bloom; it will rejoice greatly and shout for joy" (Isaiah 35:1-2).

I could imagine that lone iris almost prancing with delight in its triumphal beauty, like my bedazzled poodle from years before. I could almost hear the laughter of my Heavenly Husband in the rustling of the leaves.

The Year of the Bloom
I woke up today feeling rested and refreshed.
I had a glorious nine and a half hours of sleep,
which in itself is a miracle.

The saying that "sleep is the new sex"
Is no joke.

The sun is shining.
Dogwood petals are gently falling off of the trees.
It looks magical.

Spring is in the air,
and I feel at peace.

Today marks the fifth year that our lives changed forever.
Early morning, April 2, 2007, my husband
stepped off of this earth
and into heaven.

I wondered then how I would
ever survive that day,
Let alone my life.

Back then, looking ahead five years
seemed like an eternity.
But here we are.
It's not the life I would have chosen, but it's still a good life,
One that Jason helped me build.

I still see his mark in so many ways.
I see him in the compassion of Arie
and in the quick wit of Sophia.

344

In the sweet cards that Arie gives me nearly every day,
And when Sophia plays his music and dances on a desk.
Good Memories, Good Children, Good Family, Good Friends.
He's a part of it. A part of making it and sustaining it.
And I am thankful for it all!

I happen to believe that
Love never dies.

And there have been occasions when a wonderful gift confirms
that belief.
It's fun to look for the gift on a special date.

This year was no different.
There are several gifts,
And I will tell you of one.
I couldn't plan anything big because I'm recovering
from walking pneumonia.
So this morning, I walked outside into the sunshine
and soaked in the day.
And there was my gift.

An iris blooming.
Gently bobbing in the spring breeze.
It wasn't just any iris.
It was from the very first garden that Jason and I had
planted together.
Over a year ago the owner of my old home and my old huge garden
let me come back
and dig up all my irises.
What a kind gift that was.
The fifty iris tubers we had planted over
fifteen years ago had multiplied.
And now there were over five hundred.

I dug them up like buried treasure
and brought them to my new garden at our current home.
Knowing that inside every gnarled tuber

was the living potential for one of the
Most audacious flowers.
Taking the best of the past and letting it live with the present.

And there it was,
First bloom of my irises.
On April 2.
Beautiful and Big.
Sexy and Sumptuous.
Sparkling Petals Unfurled.
Delectable Purple Color.
The First of Five Hundred.

THE YEAR OF THE BLOOM

Those who sow in tears will reap with songs of
joy and they will come home with arms full of harvest.
(Psalm 126:5-6)

Closing Thoughts from Mishael

T hank you from the bottom of my heart for trusting me enough to be dedicated to the process of this sacred journey. You hold in your hands my own monument to hope. This book is built with the broken bricks of my shattered dreams. Now, I hope that it may become a building block in your own monument of hope as you give purpose to your pain. Each of us becomes a living part of this collective movement, forged in the fires of grief, whose intent is to share hope and inspiration with others. Your growth and success give purpose, even joy, to my pain, and I hope that in some small way, God has used my story to inspire your journey. Thank you for taking these steps, though our journey isn't over. I hope that you continue to work these steps in supportive community, helping and mentoring others whom you find on your path.

I pray that through this process, you have found guideposts along the way that lead to a new day and the refreshment of your mind, body, and spirit. To confront loss, live with grief, have your soul wrenched and wrung out by tragedy, and then to embrace the discipline of healthy choices, stay in community while you feel spiritually dry, and engage in the Divine conversation. These are the decisions that empower grief to yield great treasure in your life. This treasure can transform your life into a place of green renewal, worth far more than mere wealth. Moreover, I pray, by the grace of God, that these choices breathe out renewed life, creating a band of empowered, hope-filled warriors, able to help and inspire those who are new to the transformational journey of grief.

Thank you for taking this journey with me. I hope that you don't stop here but continue onward. I still work these steps in my life every year. Each year brings new discoveries, new adventures, and new refreshment. Move forward as a warrior, forged in the fires of grief, trained to protect and guide in hope those who are new to this wondrous process.

May you move forward on this journey, crafting the next chapters of your life, grounded in peace, triumph, and God's unchanging love. May you laugh and always walk toward the sunrise. May you go with God.

My scripture prayer for you comes from Isaiah 45:8 (NET Bible)

O sky, rain down from above!
Let the clouds send down showers of deliverance!
Let the earth absorb it so salvation may grow,
and deliverance may sprout up along with it.
I, the Lord, create it.
Be the Light,

Mishael

Afterword

Most of my good family adventures start with a bargain or a wild idea. This one started with both. I purchased annual premium passes to Stone Mountain Park, and with those passes came free tickets to its sister park, Dollywood, in Pigeon Forge, TN. Pigeon Forge is right next door to Gatlinburg, TN, where Jason and I had spent our honeymoon. I hadn't returned there in fifteen years. So, on the spur of the moment, on the last day the Dollywood tickets would expire and while in the final editing phase of this book, I reached out to Lydia, a friend now living in Tennessee, to ask if I could crash on her couch with my daughters to save some money. She asked if I would like to stay in one of her recently acquired eleven rental cabins.

"You have cabins?" I asked. She happened to have had a cancellation for the next two nights. My girls and I left the same day for Pigeon Forge. I had no plan except to use our free Dollywood tickets.

I had not reclaimed my honeymoon space, and now my daughters and I were on an unexpected road trip traveling there together. It rained the entire time, but that didn't matter to us. I reminded myself that my sacred spaces might not be sacred to my children, and to enjoy their desire to discover and have fun. We went to the Tennessee Aquarium, just as I had on my honeymoon, and the girls ran from exhibit to exhibit.

I hope you are seeing this, Baby, I quietly thought in my mind, *because our girls are amazing. Thank you for marrying me, thank you for our children, and I love you.* I met a young woman as we both dangled our hands in the stingray-petting pool, and she told me that she was on her honeymoon. I smiled nostalgically as she shared a loving look with her new husband, and I wished them blessings on their marriage.

The next day, it poured, and my girls and I suited up for Dollywood. Jason and I had also been there years ago, and it was like opening a Christmas present to see how the amusement park had both changed and stayed the same. Arie was now eleven years old and Sophia was eight. This was the first time both of them were old enough to ride the larger roller coasters.

Then it happened. *The moment*. I can never predict it or force it. It just comes. We rode a few roller coasters, starting with the smaller ones, to prepare Sophia for the scarier ones. Arie and I were thrilled that Sophia was now game to ride the big coasters every time. It was so fun to ride the rails together. By far our favorite was this huge, old-fashioned wooden coaster called Thunderhead. The girls wanted to ride in the front car. Arie rode in the very front, with Sophia and me directly behind her. The coaster started slow enough, and then catapulted our car into an unpredictable wild ride. We took the turns so fast that each of us lifted out of our seats and were only held by the restraints. I held Sophia's soft little hand and was amazed that she didn't scream. I found myself laughing. Arie screamed with delight, and I reveled in it all, laughing into the turns. I knew that we would be all right because we were attached to the rails, and now we three thrilled at the ride. The force of the coaster blew back our rain ponchos as we climbed to frightening heights, then plunged to the depths and whooped into the unexpected twists, and ended with that released-compressed air sound you hear when a train has just stopped. Our hair was wet and wild, as we sat silent for a second and then erupted, "That was the best!" We unbuckled and then raved about our adventure all the way to the picture counter, where we bought a photo of us as a memento of our ride.

I remembered that moment years ago when Jason first taught me to laugh into the turns, as I silent-screamed in the front car of our roller coaster ride. Now, with our children, that tradition lives on. It took a great deal of effort, prayer, and patience to get to a place like that again, our New Normal, our Grand Adventure.

By the grace of God and the love of my family and friends, it is a beautiful, spectacular life.

I pray that you may also journey to the place where you can laugh into your turns, love the ride, honor those who have gone before you, and revel in the love and life you have today.

Friends and Family Photo Album

My father and grandmother, **Jan Porembski** (Papa), and **Julia Porebska** (Babcia) after WWII in a British refugee camp in Germany. The Kitten Pillow my Bapcia (grandmother) embroidered for me even though she had severe rheumatoid arthritis. My father as an NBC Network News staff cameraman. My Polish Great **Aunt Stefania** (my father's aunt) with me in Poland. She is the one who told my father and me the account, firsthand, of how Warsaw was built by cleaning and repurposing the bricks of the bombed buildings. My mom, **Thea Porembski**, and me several months before she passed away in 2007.

Our wedding day in Atlanta, Dec. 17, 2000. Arie as a baby in 2004. Family photos taken in March 2007 a few weeks before Jason passed away.

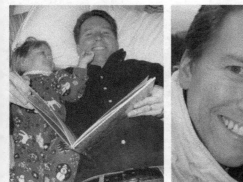

Love, Grief, and the Great Adventure: My second honeymoon with Jason in Montezuma Beach, Costa Rica, 2003. Sitting on the rocks after hiking to a waterfall near La Cascada hotel. The remote waterfall that Jason and I rode horses to on the beach in Montezuma. Me, returning to Montezuma eleven years later, via zip line.

Jason & Mishael's second honeymoon at Montezuma Beach in Costa Rica.

Watch the video of my journey back to Montezuma Beach, layering new memories in an emotionally charged space.

180YourLife.com

Growing Up: Sophia as a newborn with me at the hospital, 2007. Baby Sophia & Arie at Sophia's first Easter, 2008. My pajama pants phase, which lasted an undisclosed amount of time. A few years later with my daughters, thankfully not wearing pajamas publicly. Arie and Sophia, journalists in training. Taking an outdoor adventure together to honor Jason's angel anniversary. I try to do things with my girls on significant holidays that teach them about activities their father liked to do. Taking a "Grief Adventure" is our way of having fun and honoring him on a special memorial day.

Our Nanny: Caroline, when Arie was three and Sophia was a few months old. Caroline with Arie wearing a hat. Caroline with Baby Sophia. Caroline was very self-sufficient: she could farm, make clothes, and prepare farm-to-table food. She is pictured with Arie after working in our garden. Caroline's original GoNannies.com photo in 2007, which is how she connected with our family. At that time, she identified herself as a "Plain Person," a lifestyle that combines the ingenuity and simplicity of the Amish life but is comfortable in a modern setting with technology. Caroline visiting our family in Atlanta more than eight years later, in 2016.

Traveling to Costa Rica in 2009 with my daughters, ages five and two. **Re-layering a memory:** Horseback riding on the beach with my girls just as I had with Jason years before. **The Waterfall** where I found peace about Jason's passing at the Los Lagos Resort. Afterwards, feeling joyful at Los Lagos. **Our Old Home** in Costa Rica in 2004, around the time Arie was born. Then, in 2009, my girls and I visited the same house, which had become a lighting fixture store.

Family Training is Fun: Mishael's prairie skirt phase. This photo made me realize it was time to make a change. Training single-mom-style, using a child recumbent bike attachment. Arie & Sophia triathlon racing together. Me at my first Olympic triathlon. Arie, age seven, at her first tri race, the Iron Kids Triathlon. Sophia training, thanks to a scholarship with Atlanta Tri Stars, an Atlanta-based triathlon group for children in association with Atlanta Triathlon Club.

Fun Moments: Engagement: Jason proposed at this waterfall in Georgia, in April of 2000. Married six years, I'm three months pregnant with Sophia in late 2006. **The night I lost Sophia** in the laundry. Can you find her ear? Arie and Sophia collecting gift cards for widowed families in-need for the holidays **(GiftCardsGivingHope.org). Flamenco dancing,** doing one of the things that sparks joy for me from my "List" of favorite things. **Creating a Family Adventure:** Taking my girls on a trip after reading all the *Little House on the Prairie* books. Camping on the original Ingall's claim in De Smet, South Dakota, in pioneer attire, at the Laura Ingall's Wilder 40th Annual Festival.

Flamenco photo courtesy of Gina Palermo. PromotionOnline.biz

Inspirational Widows: One of the original 8 Team Lady 180 members, **LaTonya Pringle**, widowed 3 years, completing her first triathlon. LaTonya is now studying to become a grief counselor. **Lori Apon** (aka "Queen Widowed Mom") with her eight children, photo taken 8 weeks after her husband died from suicide. Next photo, years later with her eight grown children. Lori started a widows' ministry, WidowLife, through her nonprofit, Perspective Ministries. **Michelle Menifee** with her late husband, Edward Menifee. Michelle continues Edward's work with prison inmates after his death. (BasicsProgram.org) **Kimberly Murray Guinn** (left), her brother-in-law, Andrew Powell, and sister, Sandra Murray Powell, at the finish of their half IRONMAN. Kimberly completed the half IRONMAN triathlon one year after her husband's tragic death. She raced in the city where her husband was killed by a distracted motorist while he was cycling in preparation for his half IRONMAN. Kimberly and her triplet daughters.

This book was created by many amazing friends & neighbors rolling up their sleeves & working together. Here are some of them: **Jyn Hall & husband Steve Keck** (Jyn is our expert video producer and first hospital-diaper-changer of baby Sophia). **Dawn Davidson**, graphic illustrator for images in this book, together with her family and Mishael's family. Mishael and neighbor/editor **Dr. Bridget Heneghan**. Mishael with her high school "bestie" and 180 series book cover designer, **Michele Slobin**. Neighbor, nonprofit board member, and business analyst expert, **Christina Loud**. Former neighbor and certified personal trainer, **Coach Tara McLain** (in the jacket) and the wonderful, powerful, unstoppable women of Team Lady 180.

Team Lady 180 photo courtesy of photographer Gina Palermo. PromotionOnline.biz

Appendix 1

C asserole Killer: A Practical Guide to Empowering the First Few Weeks and Months of Your Grief Journey or the Grief Journey of Someone You Know

If There's Anything I Can Do

Get used to it. That's what everyone is going to say, and then they will deposit a very kind casserole. The truth is that food is great, but your fridge ends up bulging with carbs.

People generally don't know what to do when a family is grieving. So, here's your cheat sheet. I've compiled lists of things that generally need to happen in the first days, first week, first few weeks, and first months.

The real deal is that you have a limited amount of time to harness all that community goodwill and direct it in a systematic, productive manner. Generally speaking, the attention to your grief has a shelf life in your community of about seven to ten days. Years ago, families used to wear black for a year as a sign of grief, and it would remind the community to support a grieving family.

Today, we have the internet. Take these lists and let them be a kickstarter to inspire what you and your loved ones will need after loss. Truthfully, if you are the person experiencing loss, try to get someone else to take charge of all this. People don't want to sit around and be sad. Give them jobs. They will feel productive, and it will make life easier for a grieving family in the long run.

To empower this grief process, you have to get people to commit to a schedule, like on SignupGenius.com. Make a list of their talents and see where they can plug in for the future. "Tax accountant...great! Thanks for the casserole. Can we make an appointment to see you in two months as a grief gift for X? That would be a really big help." You get the idea. Who's going to say no? Your grieving family will get some much-needed help from your community.

People want to help; they just don't know how. The grief scene is messy. You need someone, like a family member or best buddy, to have clarity and control while a grieving family is in the shock of loss.

It's all going to clear in about ten days, and like anesthesia, all that commotion in the home will die down and the remaining family will feel the loss in a million unexpected forms. That's when the consistent contact is needed most. That's when you will appreciate the steady stream of people coming to help. I suggest it's needed for a solid six months.

I've said that grief is transformative, but not just for those who have directly lost a loved one or are experiencing other forms of grief. Grief is like the "all skate" session at the roller rink. For those who support the grieving, grief can be transformative, too. It will make you stronger, more empathetic, and less afraid of the messiness of life.

So, grab a clipboard and a computer and let's get this party started. Remember, keep your sense of humor; it's going to be a long road. I give you permission to kindly be in other people's faces, to be forward and ask for help. Go forth, coordinate, and steer this grief ship in a positive direction.

The Grief Cheat Sheet

First Week Top Ten List

1. Stabilize your blood sugar.
Make sure you have good, nutritious food to eat.

Green smoothies, green juices, green powder supplements, salads, healthy snacks, and balanced meals. These foods help normalize blood sugar and prevent the high and low blood sugar spikes that can contribute to chemical depression. Try not to eat only simple carbs. Focus on complex carbs and good proteins.

I take GABA and 5HTP supplements, which have been known to calm the brain, help induce sleep, and activate the pleasure centers of the brain without the side effects of alcohol or simple sugars. Of course, check first with your health practitioner before changing your diet or taking supplements.

Minimize alcohol consumption. You will feel worse and more prone to depression afterwards.

2. Have sleep aids on hand.

Magnesium powder and liquid calcium/magnesium supplements found at health food stores, and over-the-counter natural sleep aids may help in getting some sleep, initially. Sleep is usually the first thing to go when tragedy strikes. Consult your doctor first before taking any sleep aids. Visit 180YourLife.com for a listing of my favorite supplements.

3. Exercise.

Take a walk with a grieving person. Even if it's just for 10 minutes. Eventually you might work up to 5 miles, but in the first week, 10 to 20 minutes is a minimum per day. The vitamin D from the sunshine is calming to the nervous system. If it's possible, get the body moving, because it will combat extreme stress and help induce sleep.

4. Get the memorial service ready.

Compile favorite musical pieces, designate persons for eulogy speeches, compile a photo montage, have someone videotape the memorial service (lots of amazing things are said about the person who has passed that children may want to view later), post the obituary in the newspaper, and coordinate with the funeral home. Decide to bury or cremate if advance plans were not already made.

5. Coordinate meals.

Designate someone to coordinate meals. Have friends plan healthy meals rather than bring random food. Otherwise, the family may have too many comfort foods and not enough nutrition for the weeks ahead. Consider ordering pre-prepared meals from places like Dinner A'Fare. That is a great grief gift.

6. Create a list of all the bills.

Designate a trusted family member or friend to organize the bills so they get paid. Make an appointment with a financial planner. If there is not enough money to cover the family bills, people can make a tax-deductible donation to a church or synagogue or another nonprofit, designating that those funds go to the family. Check to see if there is a processing fee from the non-profit, but the majority of the funds should make it to the family, and your donation will be tax deductible.

7. Coordinate with the coroner to order 20 copies of the death certificate. You will need these to handle the estate later.

8. Coordinate childcare and serving meals to the kids. Sometimes the kids and their meals get forgotten in all the bustle of grief.

9. Designate someone to prep clothes for the memorial service (launder and iron clothes for the kids and family).

10. Kids still need to play. If there are young children, have someone take them out to the park. Kids still need to play even where there is grief. It will be a good way for them to do something normal.

Note: If you have life insurance, have someone close to you contact your life insurance representative and notify them of the family loss.

Weeks 2-6 Top Ten List

1. Make a list of all friends who want to help and their areas of expertise. Then give them jobs in their area of knowledge and invite them to participate on an online schedule.

2. Volunteer website. Harness their willingness to help. People want to do something positive with their grief. Let them.

3. Meet with a financial planner. Make your own will, and, if you are not a solo parent, designate legal guardians for your children. Be pro-active. You are may the only pony in the show for your kids, and you need to have emergency plans in place. God forbid, something should happen to you; you don't want your kids to become wards of the state if there is no legal guardian named for your children in a new will.

4. Find grief support for the surviving spouse and children. Google "Spousal grief support" and "Grief support for children who have lost a parent" along with the locations nearest you. Make an appointment and start going as soon as possible. Consider individual and private family counseling as well.

5. Thank You Notes. Have someone make a list of all the items given to the grieving family and write thank you notes. I don't think this should be done by the grieving spouse unless he or she really wants this task. Have someone make the list, get the addresses, and write the notes, leaving the signature area blank for the surviving spouse to sign.

6. Coordinate teams for childcare, weekend events, and visits to the house. After the bustle of the memorial service, the house gets horrifically quiet, and the reality of the loss settles in with the surviving family. This is the time when the family needs friends the most, and most people have returned to their lives. Offer to take the kids for a fun afternoon or even for the weekend to give the surviving spouse a break. Also, offer to have someone sleep over during that time so the surviving spouse isn't alone in a very quiet house.

7. Create teams or hire out for lawn care, **home care, laundry, food, and exercise.** Loan teenagers, in groups of two or three, preferably with adult supervision, once or twice a week as a mother's helper and/or sitter, or send a maid service to the house to do a deep clean. Exercise your discretion to make sure teens go into a safe environment.

8. Start dealing with the estate. Contact all financial accounts. Use Death Certificates to close credit cards, student loans, anything that is in the sole name of your spouse. Close email, Facebook, and other online accounts. Once you get the Death Certificate, submit that right away to the life insurance office.

9. Contact the social security office, bring the death certificate, birth certificates for the family, and the marriage certificate, plus proof of residence to start your social security benefits. Check SocialSecurity.gov for a full list of what is needed for you to receive benefits after the loss of a spouse.

10. Create a schedule for the family. Re-establish order in the home with a routine and, for a time, have friends and family join in that routine.

Months 3- 6 Top 10 List

1. Consider taking a vacation with a friend. Change the scenery. Go see something beautiful.
2. Take a healthy cooking class with a grieving friend.
3. Hire a trainer or commit to an exercise plan with friends.
4. Create a new family budget with a financial planner.
5. Register for a future event like a 5K, 10K, or sprint triathlon. Train as a group of friends around the grieving person and give yourselves 4-5 months to train.

6. Organize your home. Go room by room and get rid of things that are not necessary. Make every room in your home beautiful. Consider painting some rooms a new color or selling furniture off and redecorating a room.

7. If you are ready, set a date with a friend to deal with the deceased person's clothes and personal items. Save special pieces and give other clothes away, or send them to family members

8. Think about simplifying your life. Are there relationships that are weighing you down? It's okay to calmly and kindly communicate that you need a break from them. Nourish yourself in mind, body, and spirit and circle back, if necessary, when you feel stronger.

9. Create more efficient family processes. Think about creating a chore/reward system for your children. Learn about efficient single parenting strategies. Get ideas from single parent/grief support groups. I actually watched a great deal of the show *Super Nanny* on Netflix. I got some great strategies on how to positively motivate my children from that show. Also, I watched a great deal of *Dog Whisperer*. I know kids aren't dogs, but Caesar makes some great points about projecting fear and stress into your environment. Just good food for thought.

10. Do something productive with your grief. Don't veg out in front of the TV. Okay, I give you permission to veg for a few weeks. But the sooner you get moving, the sooner you will feel better. Start a small garden. Paint a picture, write in a journal, and meet with people who understand your grief. I'm telling you, don't do this alone. You can lose years that way.

11. Organize your financial papers, personal information, and family passwords into a searchable database. You need to find family information quickly and accurately. Use a folder system.

12. If you have photos all over your house of you and your loved one, consider changing out some pictures with new photographs. I personally needed a break from seeing lots of photos of Jason, so I took many down, except in my kids' rooms. When I was ready, I put some back up, along with new photos of our family as we created new memories.

Grief Gifts

Hire a nanny for a week

Have multiple families lend a teenager once a week, so that twice a week, there is a mother's helper for a 2-4 months.

Hire lawn care service or coordinate for 4 months

Purchase 2 weeks of healthy meals for the family using a catering service. Check 180YourLife.com for our favorite links.

Pay for a session with a financial planner

Give a series of massages for the surviving spouse. (This gives the calming gift of human touch, which the spouse is really missing)

Offer a coupon book of free sitting services

Arrange for private family counseling sessions

Give a gift card for a pair of walking/running sneakers from a running store that will give a professional fit.

Pay for healthy cooking classes

Books to buy:

Check out my website 180YourLife.com for my list of favorite books to empower your grief journey.

Kitchen Items to buy:

High Power Blender

High Power Juicer

Top Ten Mistakes of Widowhood & Loss

1. Don't blame yourself.
2. Don't move or run away from your life.
3. Don't sit and watch TV all day.
4. Don't drown your sorrows in sugar, alcohol, or simple carbs.
5. Don't date or sleep with the first guy who shows interest in you, unless he is your husband.
6. Don't think your life is over.
7. Don't do the grief journey alone.
8. Don't rush the process.
9. Don't keep frenemies.
10. Don't try to fit your life into someone else's.

Top Ten Tips for Getting through Widowhood & Loss

1. Let people help you.
2. Know that this will take time.
3. Take care of yourself first.
4. Set a goal for yourself and go after it.
5. Go on a fun adventure.
6. Make The List (3 things that used to make you happy and 3 things that you've always wanted to try and pick on to DO).
7. Ask your kids what they would like to do and do it with them.
8. Do something silly.
9. Try something new.
10. Enjoy simple pleasures.

Top 10 Tips for Getting Through Grief

1. Don't go it alone. Find a community of widows, or people who understand your loss, who are your age to hang out with. Also search for a youth-oriented grief community for your kids to start processing their loss.
2. Get outside for at least a 10-minute walk every day.
3. Remember: Grief is confusing and mentally exhausting. It's like brain fog.
   Recruit your friends to help while you are feeling tired. Accept help. Write out lists for everyday tasks.
4. Create a list of friends and their specific skills. Then ask them for help that is in their skill set. Friends and family want to help, but they don't know how in a grief crisis. You have to act as a master coordinator and give direction to helpful offers.
5. Create a schedule for volunteers that covers childcare, laundry, yard work, meals, and home organization. You will need this for at least two months.
6. Keep a schedule for the family. Even if you don't feel like it.
7. Plan something fun once a week. Feeling follows action. At first it will be a form of discipline to get outside and do something fun, but eventually you will enjoy it. Ideas include a walk in the park, going to a movie, making a meal with friends.
8. Nourish your body during grief. Don't get lost in comfort foods, which will feel good at first, but later will leave you feeling more exhausted and depressed. Focus on green veggies, green

juices, and green smoothies. The chlorophyll, enzymes, and vitamins from raw fruits and veggies actually refresh your blood cells and help calm your nervous system.

9. Take a five-minute vacation from grieving. Look around you and appreciate what you do have. Family, friends, a roof over your head, sunshine, food on the table? Focus for five minutes on the blessings. You need "Gratitude Commercials" to take a break from grieving.

10. Laughter and loving your life honor your loved one who has passed. Do something creative to express your grief. Writing, drawing, dancing, music, pottery, flamenco dancing…anything that expresses your feelings in a productive way. You will feel relief by unloading your burden in an expressive way.

Top 10 Grief Mistakes

1. Thinking that this will last forever.
2. Thinking that you will never laugh, love, live a happy life again.
3. Isolating yourself and your family. Seek counseling.
4. Thinking that the best part of your life is in the past. There is beauty in the future.
5. Thinking that healing will just happen. You have to be proactive; claim your healing through wise decisions.
6. Dulling the pain with substance abuse, excessive screen time, or overeating.
7. Trying to make yourself believe platitudes without taking action.
8. Thinking you can handle this all on your own. Grief is like an emotional amputation. You have to re-learn your life. Seek and accept help during this process from a supportive community.
9. Living your deceased spouse's or loved one's life through your current life. You will do that for a time. Just be open to what you want for your life. That is a valid and important question. Dream a little.
10. Making big decisions quickly…like moving or changing a job. Grief is transformative. Your new life will emerge in time. Stay where you are if you can for a few years. It will hurt terribly for a while, but you will also give yourself time to figure out what you want and need in the upcoming chapters of your new life.

Go-To Grief Busters

First, don't try to fight sugar cravings with just will power. You'll probably lose over the long term. That's why it's so important to understand how different foods affect you chemically. Sugar makes you feel great and then, hours later, causes a crash. Simply put, it spikes and then drops your blood sugar, and it has chemically addictive properties. Purpose to eat 5-6 healthy small meals throughout the day to stabilize your blood sugar levels and make sure to drink 8-10 glasses of water.

Second, get outside. Take a walk in the sunshine. The sunshine helps boost vitamin D in your body, which naturally calms your nervous system, benefitting your digestive system, which may later help with sleep. Think about it: don't you have a great sleep after a day at the beach? That's vitamin D working. Consult your doctor to see what's best for you.

Third, make some fresh green juices or green smoothies, and drink them on an empty stomach. Preferably in the morning before breakfast. In the afternoon works too, for that late-day-lag feeling. The live magnesium, natural vitamins, and minerals in these drinks help to calm and nourish the body.

Fourth, take a shower and make yourself look good, even if you feel bad. Hey, why not kick it up a notch? Book a salon appointment for a nice cut and color. While you are at it, get your makeup done. When you look and feel clean and fresh, people respond in a positive way to you, and that helps stop the negative spiral of grief.

Fifth, recruit a friend to exercise with and schedule dates to meet. When I'm grieving, it feels like I'm slogging through cold molasses. The simplest things feel overwhelming. So ask for help. Don't stay stuck. Exercise will get your endorphins going. It will lower your stress. You will feel more relaxed afterwards; your digestion will probably benefit, as will your sleep. Exercise makes your body work more efficiently. Just start with a simple walk around the block and work up from there. I promise, you will start to feel better.

Sixth, tidy up. A clean house feels like a hopeful space. So crank some good tunes and scrub away! If I'm feeling overwhelmed and it's in my budget, I treat myself to the help of a maid for several hours. If that's not affordable, then offer to tag-team house cleaning with a friend. You help them one day, and they help you another. It's so much more fun to do things together.

Seventh, do laundry and put clothes away. Organize your space. If you don't have clothes you love, take a friend and drop by a Goodwill store in a nice neighborhood to give an inexpensive boost to your wardrobe. You can experiment with new looks, and it won't break the bank.

Eighth, laugh. I give you permission to kick back and watch a comedy (just don't watch them endlessly) or go hang out with friends and family who make you laugh. Proverbs 17:22 says, "A joyful heart is good medicine, but a broken spirit drains one's strength." That's actually true.

Ninth, after a good laugh, do something that makes you happy. Take a bike ride, work in the garden, look up something fun to do in your area with friends and family. Intentionally craft your time, don't just let the day roll on without purpose or let it get filled with responsibilities. Give yourself a break. You'll come back to your responsibilities with a fresh perspective.

Tenth, don't go it alone. Activate grief recourses in your area. I know it sucks. Keep taking one more step, making one more good decision. Eventually, the wise decisions will start folding in on themselves, snowballing into your Great Adventure.

> Every one of us is called upon, probably many times, to start a new life. A frightening diagnosis, a marriage, a move, loss of a job... And onward full tilt we go, pitched and wrecked and absurdly resolute, driven in spite of everything to make good on a new shore. To be hopeful, to embrace one possibility after another—that is surely the basic instinct...Crying out: High tide! Time to move out into the glorious debris. Time to take this life for what it is.

> —Barbara Kingsolver from *High Tide in Tucson*

Support Groups

For more resources and to link with others practicing the *180 Your Life* program, visit 180YourLife.com.

Suicidepreventionlifeline.org–Suicidal thoughts are common in those who are grieving. Don't suffer alone. Find a support system. Reach out. Don't isolate. Suicide.supportgroups.com

DailyStrength.org/c/Widows-Widowers/support-group–An online resource that includes numerous communities. This is a link for widows/widowers.

Training Links: We will be continually working to get discount codes for various races. Visit our website to see if we have a discount for a race in your area.

AtlantaTriClub.com

Team Lady 180 trains with this team. They are very supportive and knowledgeable.

TrainingPeaks.com

A great site for finding or purchasing a training plan.

Sign Up for Races! This is a great starting point for finding races in your area.

IronGirl.com

This is such a fun female-empowerment race! I love the vibe, and it's a significant training goal.

GirlsontheRun.org

My kids naturally want to do what I'm doing. So they want to train and race like mom. What a great way to teach our kids to take positive steps through loss and life. Girls on the Run is a great organization that couples positive life lessons with training girls in the sport of running.

IronKids.com

My oldest daughter completed her first tri at the Iron Kids Triathlon at 7 years old. It was a great experience, and she felt so accomplished to do something that I did too. Check for races in your area. Also check for kids' tri clubs in your area.

Active.com

This is a great resource for finding races at discounted entry fees in your area.

TheColorRun.com

Hands down, this is just a fun race to do. You start clean and end with different colored powder sprayed on you at various stations. At the end, I looked like some Disney Aboriginal Tribeswoman. I loved it, and so did my kids.

Appendix 2

Taste of Triumph

Breakfasts:
Sweet potato and oatmeal pancakes: blend together 2 – 3 egg whites, 1 cup cooked oats, and ½ cup sweet potato. Throw in a few walnuts for texture. Use blended batter like a pancake batter: spray pan with olive oil spray, pour batter onto hot pan, let cook on one side until batter bubbles or mixture seems "set." Turn over and cook on other side until the mixture is the texture of pancake.

Hearty oatmeal – add mixture of some or all of walnuts, chia seeds, flaxseeds, and Brazil nuts to cooked oats. Sprinkle with nutmeg, cinnamon and/or allspice as preferred.

Smoothie (see some recipes below)

Lunches:
Ezekiel English muffin with turkey, spinach, tomatoes, and avocado. Side salad to supplement sandwich with olive oil and vinegar for dressing. Include nuts and seeds on salad as crunchy topping.

Baked salmon with roasted broccoli and sweet potato.

Smoothie (see some recipes below)

Dinners:

Shrimp and Corn Risotto: (makes 4 servings)
2 tablespoons olive oil

3 cloves garlic, finely chopped

1½ cup bulgur wheat

½–1 teaspoon salt

16 ounces (1lb) fresh or frozen (thawed) raw shrimp, shelled and deveined

2 cups fresh or frozen corn kernels

1 medium red bell pepper, cored, seeded and chopped

2 limes (1 juiced, 1 cut into wedges)

½ teaspoon red pepper flakes

½ cup cilantro, chopped

Heat oil in a large pot over medium heat. Cook garlic, stirring, for 30 seconds; add bulgur and salt; stir 1 minute more. Gradually stir in 2 cups boiling water, 1/2 cup at a time (waiting until bulgur absorbs it to add more), until bulgur is slightly soupy, 8 to 10 minutes. (You might not use all the water.) Add shrimp.

Cook, stirring constantly, until it turns pink, 2 to 3 minutes. Add corn, bell pepper, juice from 1 lime and red pepper flakes; stir, adding water to keep mixture creamy. Cook, stirring, until corn and pepper are warmed through, 1 to 2 minutes. Add cilantro; serve with lime wedges.

Quinoa Cilantro-Lime Salad

Ingredients

1 cup quinoa

2 cups water

1 tsp Kosher salt

— —-

½ cup goat cheese crumbled

½ cup pumpkin seeds

2 whole tomatoes (cubed)

— —-

1 cup packed cilantro

1/2 cup extra-virgin olive oil

1/4 cup lime juice

1/4 cup orange juice

1/2 teaspoon salt

1/2 teaspoon pepper

Pinch of minced garlic

Bring quinoa, water, and salt to a boil in a saucepan. Reduce heat to medium-low, cover, and simmer until the quinoa is tender, 20 to 25 minutes. When the quinoa is done, cool in refrigerator until cold, about 2 hours

When the quinoa is cold, fluff with a spoon, and gently fold in the cilantro dressing, avocados, pumpkin seeds, goat cheese, and tomatoes

Dressing:

Puree cilantro, olive oil, lime juice, orange juice, salt, pepper, and garlic in a blender or food processor until smooth.

Balsamic Chicken: (makes 4 servings)
    2 tsp olive oil
    3 tbsp balsamic vinegar
    2 tsp Dijon mustard
    1 garlic clove, chopped
    4 pieces of boneless skinless chicken breast (about 4 oz serving each)
    2 cups mushrooms, halved
    1/3 cup chicken broth (can use bullion cube in boiling water or
            canned broth)
    ¼ tsp dried thyme
    ¼ tsp dried rosemary

In a nonstick skillet, heat 1 tsp of the olive oil. While heating, mix 2 tbsp of the vinegar, the mustard and garlic. Add the chicken to coat it. Transfer the chicken into the heated oil in the skillet. Sauté until cooked through (about 3 mins on each side). Place chicken on a platter and keep it warm. Heat the rest of oil in the skillet, sauté the mushrooms for about a minute in there. Add the broth, herbs and remaining vinegar. Cook until mushrooms are brown and soft (about 2 minutes). Serve chicken with mushroom sauce on top

Spicy Turkey Meatloaf (serves 4)
    1¼ lbs ground turkey breast (no skin)
    ½ cup old fashioned oats
    1 8-oz can tomato sauce
    ½ cup vegetable juice
    1 egg white

1 tsp red wine vinegar
1 tsp chili powder
½ tsp salt
1 clove garlic, pressed
1 tbsp safflower oil
½ cup finely chopped onion
½ cup finely chopped celery

Combine 1ˢᵗ 8 ingredients and mix well. Sauté onions, celery, and garlic in oil until onions are transparent. Add turkey to the mixture and mix well. Shape into meatloaf and press in 8" x 4" loaf pan. Bake at 350⁰ for 1 hour.

Snack Ideas:
Apple and walnuts
Mixed nuts and Flaxseed chips/crackers
Celery and almond butter
Trail mix made with Brazil nuts, walnuts, chia, flaxseed, toasted oats, etc.

Energy Balls (no bake bites)
Ingredients:
1½ C whey protein powder
1 tsp. honey
¾ c almond butter
1 tsp vanilla extract
¼ c cocoa powder
1/3 c unsweetened shredded coconut

Mix the protein powder, honey, almond extract together to form stiff dough. Chill dough for at least 1 hour. Make round balls from the dough at about 1 ½ tsp each. Roll each in the cocoa powder and coconut. Chill and serve. Can keep in air tight container in fridge for week or so.

Smoothie Ideas:

Spicy Carrot Cooler
The carrot juice in this savory, low-calorie smoothie is rich in vitamin A, which helps regulate the immune system. Fresh ginger adds a sweet, peppery flavor that may help reduce post-exercise muscle pain. Avocado adds a silky texture and heart-healthy monounsaturated fats. Studies show that capsaicin in cayenne pepper briefly boosts metabolism, helping you burn a few extra calories.
Makes 1 serving
¾ cup carrot juice
¼ cup water
¼ avocado, pitted and peeled
1 tablespoon fresh lemon juice
1 tablespoon freshly grated ginger
Pinch cayenne pepper
½ cup ice cubes

In a blender, combine the carrot juice, water, avocado, lemon juice, ginger, pepper, and ice. Blend until smooth.

Green Monster Shake
Scoop vanilla whey
¼ c Greek yogurt
1 banana
½ cup pineapple chunks (or peaches or mangoes or green apple)
1 – 2 Cups spinach/kale
1 Tbsp flaxseed meal
(Truvia optional)
3 – 4 ice cubes
1 cup water
Blend all together

Green Tea Berry Smoothie

¼ cup water (+ more if needed)
1 green tea bag
1 Tbsp milled flaxseeds
¾ cup frozen mixed berries
4 oz low-fat vanilla yogurt
¼ cup cranberry juice
Honey to taste (optional)
Boil water, add teabag, let seep for 3 mins.
Meanwhile, blend until smooth: flaxseed, berries, yogurt, and juice.

Squeeze and remove teabag. Add tea to berry mix, and blend again until smooth. Adjust consistency with additional water, and add honey to taste, if desired.

Power Breakfast

Also a great recovery meal replacement after a hard workout
(Makes a 16 oz serving)
½ cup oatmeal nuked in 1 cup water
1 Tbsp low fat peanut butter
¼ cup (or 1 scoop, or 110 cals) vanilla whey protein powder
1 tsp honey
1 tsp ground flaxseed
6 – 8 ice cubes

Baked Apple Dessert

Great breakfast or an after-dinner dessert
(makes a 16 oz serving)
½ cup oatmeal
1 medium apple cored and cut up
1 Tbsp vanilla whey protein powder
1 tsp honey
1 tsp ground flaxseed
1/8 tsp cinnamon
6-8 ice cubes

Appendix 3

PTSD

**Post-Traumatic Stress Disorder (PTSD) DSM-IV-TR
Criteria for PTSD**

**The person has been exposed to a traumatic event in which both
of the following were present:**
1. Experienced, witnessed, or was confronted with an event or
   events that involved actual or threatened death or serious injury,
   or a threat to the physical integrity of self or others
2. The person's response involved intense fear, helplessness, or horror

**The traumatic event is persistently re-experienced in one (or more)
of the following ways:**
a. Recurrent and intrusive distressing recollections of the event,
   including images, thoughts, or perceptions
b. Recurrent distressing dreams of the event
c. Acting or feeling as if the traumatic event were recurring
   (includes a sense of reliving the experience, illusions, halluci-
   nations, and dissociative flashback episodes, including those
   that occur on awakening or when intoxicated)
d. Intense psychological distress at exposure to internal or external
   cues that symbolize or resemble an aspect of the traumatic event
e. Physiologic reactivity on exposure to internal or external cues
   that symbolize or resemble an aspect of the traumatic event

Persistent avoidance of stimuli associated with the trauma and numbing of general responsiveness (not present before the trauma), as indicated by three (or more) of the following:
1. Efforts to avoid thoughts, feelings, or conversations associated with the trauma
2. Efforts to avoid activities, places, or people that arouse recollections of the trauma
3. Inability to recall an important aspect of the trauma
4. Markedly diminished interest or participation in significant activities
5. Feeling of detachment or estrangement from others
6. Restricted range of affect (e.g., unable to have loving feelings)
7. Sense of foreshortened future (e.g., does not expect to have a normal life)

Persistent symptoms of increased arousal (not present before the trauma), indicated by at least two of the following:
1. Difficulty falling or staying asleep
2. Irritability or outbursts of anger
3. Difficulty concentrating
4. Hyper-vigilance
5. Exaggerated startle response

Duration of the disturbance is one month.
The disturbance causes clinically significant distress or impairment in functioning

Appendix 4

Speak Life Sections

Empower Your Ground Zero: I will not lie down in the Desert of Grief. That is not my destiny. I am on a quest. Though the grasses have browned, the ground has cracked, and the night is full of the unknown, I sense a presence. I ask God to show me the way to the flood lands of the soul. I rise, taking one step and then another, moving forward into the night, pressing on toward the waters of renewal and the light of day.

Forge Your Team: As I press into this journey, I will join others who understand my loss around the campfire, so we may strengthen one another for this quest. We will come together in trust and confidence, for protection, friendship, and renewal. We will speak hope, speak purpose and speak life to one another. Though the plains are arid, we take refreshment at a watering hole, encouraging one another, content to know we are not alone.

Train Your Mind: I have met the constrictor, which stealthily coiled around me while I grieved, almost imperceptible, threatening to constrict my movements and even my very breath. With courage, asking for God's help, I will take conscious steps to firmly unwrap its coils from my life, minimizing chaos and creating healthy boundaries, as I purpose to create calm and peace in my home and my mind.

Train Your Body: Even when the sands were hot, I have purposed to strengthen my body through conscious, healthy choices in what I eat and drink. I commit to an exercise schedule in a supportive, accountable Team, with a definite finish line, in order to accomplish my health goals. I will be open to asking God to be my coach.

Train Your Spirit: I have continued to press into the heart of grief when it felt most dry. I have chosen gratitude, forgiveness, prayer, kindness, and generosity of soul in the most parched of circumstances. Even when the grasses around me were flaming hot with the heat of loss, I have purposed to press on, seeking God in prayer, worship, and Bible reading as an act of will. By the grace of God, I will not run from the desert, but instead will make positive choices in the midst of my tragedy, practicing spiritual discipline, which will yield a mighty harvest in due time. I will follow the ancient paths back to God, trusting and believing that the mighty floodwaters of the Spirit will come, the refreshment from the hand of God.

Cross Your Finish Line: I have arrived at the Okavango at just the right time. I celebrate my Victory and the Victory of my Teammates! We have come a long way! We drink deeply of the fresh water, now spilling into the tremendous basin, shaped like a giant hand, reminding us of God's provision. The floodwaters are rising, and the basin steadily fills. We rest and refresh ourselves, because this is just the beginning. The light of dawn is peeking over the horizon. It is the start of a New Day. I have come far, but my journey isn't over yet.

Live Your Legacy: The Okavango Basin has filled to overflowing and I am being refreshed. Now the fresh waters spill their borders and begin to fill the dry, ancient riverbeds. The water is streaming into the desert, rising with volume, heading to pools and watering holes to revive life all around it. Like those refreshing waters, my heart overflows with streams of kindness that surge forward to help and refresh others in their loss. I will look for these opportunities of service, as they will become a spring of life within me. This is part of my Living Legacy. The sun is rising, and the landscape of my life is transforming right before my eyes.

Unveil Your Triumph: My heart has changed and is better able to handle life's challenges. I am committed to the quest of a renewed life. I will leverage my loss to help lead others, knowing I am a warrior of the spirit, trained to defend, mentor, and protect those who are still hurting. I will be clothed with dignity and strength. I will laugh without fear of the future. I will work industriously, opening my hands to the poor, and promote honor and kindness over the fleeting activity of charm and vanity. May this legacy of strength cause those I love, mentor, and influence to rise up and call me blessed.

Disclaimer

Amystery is a phenomenon that you cannot fully understand because you were not there. So it is with Jason's passing. My best friend and husband died of carbon monoxide poisoning in his car. His death was first deemed a suicide, and, violently disbelieving that conclusion while I was pregnant and grieving, I called a coroner's inquest as soon as possible after my husband passed away. I presented information to the coroner for months and ultimately presented enough doubt that Jason's death was later deemed an accident on his death certificate. But the police investigator who first deemed his death a suicide in his police report would never change his conclusion from suicide to accidental. When Jason died, I was surprised to discover there was a two-year suicide clause in our life insurance policy. We'd had the policy for 3.5 years. Therefore, my husband's cause of death didn't affect what our insurance policy provided for our family, but the determination of his cause of death mattered to me greatly. That is why I fought so hard for Jason's death to be deemed an accident, because that is what I wanted to believe. Then, three years after my husband's death, better able to handle this grief, I went back to the place where Jason died. I had never been there before. I investigated the facts of his passing like a journalist would. I spoke at length with the first responder, a park ranger. I investigated the campsite where he died. I spoke for hours with the police investigator who was at the scene of his death. I even reviewed all the photos that were taken. That's when I finally understood and believed that the police investigator was correct about Jason's cause of death, and I started to process my late husband's passing as a suicide. I was heartsick when I started to accept this conclusion, though it made logical sense to me. Ultimately, I decided it was best to give my daughters the opportunity to heal in truth throughout their childhood with access to skilled grief professionals. Our choice was not to hide from exploring the truth as a family. My daughters and I now process Jason's death, with extreme love and compassion, as a suicide, and so that is why this book reflects that journey.

Author Bios:

Mishael Porembski: Southeastern Emmy Award winning documentarian and a twenty-year network news veteran Mishael Porembski was catapulted into intense grief by her husband's untimely death in 2007. To help her overcome the resulting depression, anger, and despair, Mishael turned to her faith in God and, over time, discovered a healthy, empowered path to a new life. She also founded a non-profit, Team Lady 180, an active health and wellness support group for widows and bereaved women. Now a triathlete, speaker, and author, Mishael helps grieving families mindfully move through their grief journey more efficiently and so leave a lasting legacy of hope.

Bethany Rutledge:

Bethany Rutledge heads up the Atlanta Triathlon Club's racing team and is the acting coaching director for the Atlanta Triathlon Club. She also is a freelance writer, contributing regularly to the training section of *Triathlete Magazine*. Her certifications include USAT&F Level I Clinic, USA Triathlon Level 1 Coaching, American Council of Exercise Certified Personal Trainer, and CPR Certification, and she serves on the board of the USA Triathlon Southeast Council.

A two-time IRONMAN World Champs and 70.3 World Champs Qualifier, her personal focus is the Ironman distance. In the 2013 USAT Rankings she was ranked 3rd in 30-34 in the SE, and 1st in the state. She was also ranked 3rd in the country and the world for 30-34 in the IRONMAN Age Group Rankings for 2013. Her favorite mode of exercise is running with her two vizslas, Sadie and Bailey.

Bethany is passionate about coaching other athletes towards their potential in triathlon and running. She enjoys working with all levels of motivated athletes.

Ilana Katz, MS, RD, CSSD:

Ilana Katz is a licensed dietitian in Atlanta, specializing in sports nutrition and body composition. She participates in many endurance and team events and can relate personally to her client's training and weight management needs.

Ilana is in private practice as well as consulting to coaches, doctors and corporations. She works with many local celebrities, elite athletes, recreational athletes and those ready to look good at the beach.

Whether your goal is to be a leaner, thus faster athlete, or to work on body composition and weight management, or just find your optimal energy, Ilana Katz's Metabolic Boost program can see you to your goal.

The personalized meal planning of the Metabolic Boost program takes into consideration all areas of your life, including training, social, family, and work schedules. You can connect with Ilana through our website at 180YourLife.com.

Bridget Heneghan, PhD:

Bridget Heneghan, PhD, is an editor, teacher, and sometime triathlete in Marietta, Georgia. She earned her doctorate in English and began her career as a writing instructor at Vanderbilt University, later moving to Atlanta and teaching at Georgia Institute of Technology. Bridget has authored articles and reviews, as well as an interdisciplinary literary and archaeological study,

Whitewashing America: Material Culture and Race in Antebellum America. Behind the scenes, she edits and reviews professional, academic, and popular manuscripts and instructs students in the beauty of a well-placed comma and a well-turned phrase.

Consultant Bio:

Larry Keefauver. D.D.:

Dr. Keefauver is married to Judi Keefauver and together he and his wife have been in ministry for over 40 years. Both have extensive experience in counseling and mentoring. Their three adult children are married, are actively living for the Lord and are parenting seven grandchildren. Judi and Larry have traveled internationally leading seminars and conferences on family, marriage, parenting, church leadership and spiritual growth. They have an international  TV program, Family Forum, seen throughout Taiwan, China, Korea and on the Internet through GoodTV.

Dr. Larry Keefauver with degrees from the University of Pennsylvania and Texas Christian University is professionally and educationally trained in pastoral counseling and Judi is a registered nurse. Best-selling family books include: *Lord I Wish My Family Would Get Saved, The 77 Irrefutable Truths of Parenting* (with Judi), *Proactive Parenting—The Early Years, The 77 Irrefutable Truths of Marriage* (with Judi), *Lord I Wish My Teenager Would Talk With Me,* and *Lord I Wish My Husband Would Pray with Me.* Judi's devotional book for women is *Be.*

With over 2.5 million books worldwide in 12 languages, Dr. Keefauver is the noted author of *Inviting God's Presence, When God Doesn't Heal Now, Experiencing the Holy Spirit, The 77 Irrefutable*

Truths of Ministry, Hugs for Grandparents, Hugs for Heroes, Commanding Angels—Invoking the Standing Orders, From the Oval Office: Prayers of the Presidents, The 77 Irrefutable Truths of Prayer and *Friend to Friend.* He edited the bestselling through the Bible in one-year curriculum—*What the Bible Is All About* (Gospel Light). Other adult curricula include *Making Love Last Forever* (with Gary Smalley), *Truth Matters* (with Josh McDowell), and *The Seasons of a Man's Life* (Patrick Morley), all with Lifeway Press.

Dr. Keefauver was ordained by The Christian Church (Disciples of Christ, 1973) and credentialed by the Open Bible Faith Fellowship of Canada (since 2000). He has served 31 years in the local church as associate, executive and senior pastor. He founded Your Ministry Counseling Services in 2000 and has served as President and Executive Director for over twenty-five years. He has written extensively for CfaN, Charisma Media, HarperCollins/Nelson, Simon and Schuster, Gospel Light, Bridge Logos, and numerous other publishers.

Dr. Keefauver has written extensively for Christian magazines and is a contributing editor and writer for *Ministry Today, Kairos* and *Harvest Times.* Dr. Keefauver serves as Senior Editor and Author Coach for Xulon Press and has edited and ghostwritten hundreds of books and curricula over the past decade for Christian leaders in the Church, business, arts and media, and medical/nutrition fields. A partial list is as follows:

Josh McDowell, *The Father Connection* and *Truth Matters*
Dr. Gary Smalley, *Making Love Last Forever* and *How to Win Your Husband Back*
Rod Parsley, *No More Crumbs, No Dry Season, The Day Before Eternity*
Daniel Kolenda, *This Is That*
CfaN, *Harvest Joy*
Editor, *The Holy Spirit Encounter Bible* (Creation House)
Dr. Leeland Jones, *Wholeness*
Bishop David Evans, *Dare to be a Man*
Dr. Keith Johnson, *The Confidence Solution, The LQ Solution*
Winston Nunes, *Driven by the Spirit*
And many more.

Endnotes

—⟡—

1   Jerry Sittser, *A Grace Disguised: How the Soul Grows through Loss* (Grand Rapids, MI: Zondervan, 2004) 42. Print.

2   There are also corresponding companion videos available at 180YourLife.com.

3   "The Great Flood." *Nature's Great Events.* BBC, 31 May 2015. Television.

4   C. S. Lewis, *That Hideous Strength* (NY: Macmillan, 1946) 299. Print.

5   Maurice Lamm, "'Sitting' Shiva," Chabad.org. N.d. Web.

6   C. S. Lewis, *A Grief Observed* (NY: Bantam Books, 1961)1.

7   V. Ajdacic-Gross; M. Ring; E. Gadola; C. Lauber; M. Bopp; F. Gutzwiller; W. Rössler, "Suicide after Bereavement: An Overlooked Problem," *Psychological Medicine*, 38.5 (2008): 673. Web.

8   Roxanne Dryden-Edwards, MD. "Grief, Loss, and Bereavement," Medicinenet.com. 9/12/2014. Web.

9   Tip #37 "Laughter is contagious good health," Karen Salmansohn, *The Bounce Back Book: How to Thrive in the Face of Adversity, Setbacks, and Losses* (NY: Workman Publishing, 2007). Print.

10 "Stress Relief from Laughter," Mayoclinic.org. July 23, 2013.Web.

11 Yagana Shah, "New Study Proves that Laughter Really Is the Best Medicine," Huffingtonpost.com. April 22, 2014. Web.

12 Melinda Smith, M.A. and Jeanne Segal, PhD., "Laughter Is the Best Medicine," Helpguide.org. August 2015. Web.

13 Carrie Romm, "Understanding How Grief Weakens the Body," *The Atlantic*. Sept. 11, 2014. Web.

14 Joan Mathews Larson, *Depression-Free, Naturally: 7 Weeks to Eliminating Anxiety, Despair, Fatigue, and Anger from Your Life* (NY: Ballantine, 1999). Kindle Edition. (Kindle Locations 171-172).

15 Gina Stepp, "Give Sorrow More than Words: The Neuroscience of Grieving," Vision.org (Winter 2007). Web. 12/10/2015.

16 Larson (Kindle Locations 2464-2468).

17 Larson (Kindle Locations 264-266).

18 Dina Aronson, "Cortisol — Its Role in Stress, Inflammation, and Indications for Diet Therapy." *Today's Dietitian* 11.1 (Nov. 2009): 38. Web.

19 "Pyruvate is the key metabolite that extracts the stored energy in glucose, and is involved in the biochemistry of our energy metabolism." Larson (Kindle Locations 2352-2353; 2448-2449).

20 Shaheen E. Lakhan and Karen F. Vieira, "Nutritional Therapies for Mental Disorders," Nutritional Journal 7.2 (2008). January 21, 2008. Web.

21 Emma Young, "Gut Instincts: The Secrets of Your Second Brain," NewScientist.com. December 12, 2012. Web.

22 You can find more Grief Gift ideas on my website at 180YourLife.com.

23 "Ship of Gold" *History's Mysteries*. The History Channel. Season 9, Episode 2, 2006. Television.

24 David B. Feldman and Lee Daniel Kravetz, *Supersurvivors: The Surprising Link Between Suffering and Success* (NY: HarperCollins, 2014) 96. Print.

25 Check out 180YourLife.com for more helpful links.

26 Check out 180YourLife.com for additional resource ideas.

27 Johann Hari, *Chasing the Scream: The First and Last Days of the War on Drugs* (NY: Bloomsbury, 2015) 293. Print.

28 Marie Kondō, *The Life-Changing Magic of Tidying Up: The Japanese Art of Decluttering and Organizing* (Berkeley: Ten Speed Press, 2014) 42. Print.

29 Kondō 182.

30 Kondō 181; 64.

31 Be wise using a public site like this, and take necessary precautions. Other great sites to use are Ebay.com and Amazon.com.

32 You can find that booklet as a free download at 180YourLife.com.

33 To watch a video about their transformations, go to the video page on 180YourLife.com, or simply go to the front page of TeamLady180.com.

34 You can find these plans as a free download on my website at 180YourLife.com.

35 Lizette Borreli. "The Science of Breaking Up: How Heartbreak Hurts Your Physical and Mental Health," Medicaldaily.com. Oct. 6, 2014. Web.

36 Larson (Kindle Locations 2418-2422).

37 Larson (Kindle Locations 4426-4432).

38 Larson (Kindle Locations 3226-3231).

39 Larson (Kindle Locations 1275-1286).

40 Larson (Kindle Locations 2418-2422).

41 M. Katherine Shear, M.D. and Krissa Smith-Caroff, B.S. "Traumatic Loss and the Syndrome of Complicated Grief," *The National Center for Post-Traumatic Stress Disorder* 13:1 (Winter 2002): 1-4. Web.

42 "'Working Out' PTSD—Exercise Is a Vital Part of Treatment," Theconversation.com. December 12, 2014. Web.

43 MJL Staff, "Text of the Mourner's Kaddish." Myjewishlearning.com. N.d. Web.

44 Alan D. Wolfelt, Ph.D. and Kirby J. Duvall, M.D., *Healing your Grief about Aging* (Fort Collins, CO: Companion Press, 2012). Print.

45 Lucy Animus, "The Coolest Thing about Gratitude," Elephantjournal. com. Nov. 27, 2014. Web.

46 Lucy Animus, "The Coolest Thing about Gratitude," Elephantjournal. com. Nov. 27, 2014. Web.

47   Oprah Winfrey. Interview with Amy Grant and Vince Gil. *The Oprah Winfrey Show*. CBS. Nov. 30, 2007. Television.

48   *Best Self* (June 2015): 41.

49   I have made *Burning Questions* available on my website if you are interested. You can see a clip of it at 180YourLife.com.

50   "What Is PTG?" Posttraumatic Growth Research Group, UNC Charlotte. Ptgi.uncc.edu. N.d. Web.

51   Jim Rendon, *Upside: The New Science of Post-Traumatic Growth* (NY: Touchstone, 2015) 74. Print.

52   Graves, Ginny, "Is There an Upside to Tragedy?" *Oprah Magazine* (July 2015): 74-75. Web. Omagcircle.com, 74.

53   Graves 75.

54   Noam Shpancer, Ph.D., "Laws of Attraction: How Do We Select a Life Partner?" Psychologytoday.com. Dec. 02, 2014. Web.

55   To see the Shands Arts in Medicine video clip, visit 180YourLife.com.

56   "Improve Your Health by Helping Others," The University of Texas MD Anderson Cancer Center (2007. Revised 07/13/10). Web.

57   In order, the references come from these versions of the Bible: ERV, ESV, CEV, CJB, CEB, AMP, KJV, OJB.

58   "Valor," Google.com. N.d.; "Valor," Miriam-webster.com. 2015. Web.

59   Chaviva Gordon-Bennett "What Is Aishes Chayel?" Judaism.about.com. 2015. Web.

60   John J. Parsons, "Eschet Chayil—Praising a Woman of Valor," Hebrew4christians.com. N.d. Web.

Other books in this series:

180 Your Life from Tragedy to Triumph: A Woman's Grief Guide

180 Your Life from Tragedy to Triumph: A Facilitator's Guide

180 Your Life from Tragedy to Triumph: A Personal Study Guide & Journal

Learn more at 180YourLife.com

CPSIA information can be obtained
at www.ICGtesting.com
Printed in the USA
LVHW080249150720
660698LV00024B/496